P9-CKX-135

BEN JONSON

BEN JONSON

(Three Plays)

VOLUME 2

A MERMAID DRAMABOOK

 HILL AND WANG · NEW YORK

Library of Congress catalog card number 61-14475

FIRST DRAMABOOK PRINTING AUGUST 1961

Published by special arrangement with Ernest Benn, Ltd.
Manufactured in the United States of America
by The Colonial Press Inc.

CONTENTS

Every Man in His Humour   1

Sejanus   99

Bartholomew Fair   211

BEN JONSON

EVERY MAN IN HIS HUMOUR

AFTER the publication of the quarto edition of *Every Man out of His Humour* in 1601, Jonson took heart of grace and published in 1601—it being entered in the Stationers' Registers on the 14th August, 1600—his *Every Man in His Humour,* his first unaided play, and one which proved a success, though its success, it being a satire on a foible of the day, was mingled with much criticism. It was first produced, as he himself tells us, in 1598 by the Lord Chamberlain's servants at the Globe, that is by Shakespeare's company, the principal comedians according to the folio being, Will. Shakespeare, Aug. Philips, Hen. Condell, Will. Slye, Will. Kempe, Ric. Burbage, Joh. Hemings, Tho. Pope, Chr. Beeston, and Joh. Duke.

This first version of the play, however, was Italian-scened, and Italian-charactered so far as names went. But our present version was first published in the folio of 1616, and as shown by internal evidence was written about or in 1606. Not improbably it was then rewritten that it might be produced before the King of Denmark, who in that year paid a visit to his daughter, Queen Anne, when dramas were among the chief in the entertainments lavishly set before him. Mr. F. G. Fleay indeed has ingeniously argued that this folio version was first produced in 1607, since in that year St. Mark's Day—as stated in Bobadill's speech in III. 1—fell on a Saturday. Unfortunately, however, the same data are found also in the quarto version, and do not allow of its being performed first in 1598, as it undoubtedly was.[1] In this second version, besides that the scene is changed to England, and the characters are English-named, many of the speeches are altered, some omitted, and some added, the acts and scenes re-arranged, and some of the latter transposed.

Hence, while the quarto version has been read, and as far as possible collated, the originals for our text have—on account of the many variations, and the lateness of the date at which the revision by the author was made—only been the two folios.

[1] For proofs fuller than those given in this volume that the play was first produced in 1598, and that the folio version was written about or in 1606, see a paper by the present editor [Brinsley Nicholson] in *The Antiquary* for July and September, 1882.

Until comparatively recent times, this play was brought on the stage at frequent intervals with considerable success. After the Restoration (in 1675) it was revived by the Duke of York's company, Lord Dorset supplying the prologue. Garrick brought it out at Drury Lane with a very powerful cast of actors. In the prologue he appealed to the audience to show favour to the work of "immortal Ben," "the rough old bard," and Kitely became one of his most famous parts. In 1800 Cooke appeared as Kitely, which was considered as his best character after Iago; in 1816 Edmund Kean acted Kitely; Charles Young rather later; while the elder Charles Mathews frequently took the part of Master Matthew. *Every Man in His Humour* was the first play selected for performance by Charles Dickens and his company of amateur actors. It was presented at Miss Kelly's Theatre in Dean Street, Soho, in 1845, and on account of its enthusiastic reception it was repeated at St. James's Theatre and later in the provinces. Dickens himself took the part of Bobadill, and other characters were assumed by Mark Lemon, Douglas Jerrold, George Cattermole, John Leech and other well-known men. Forster says that Dickens presented his part "after a richly coloured picture of bombastical extravagance and comic exaltation in the earlier scenes, a contrast in the later of tragical humility and abasement that had a wonderful effect."

"Haud tamen invideas vati, quem pulpita pascunt."
—JUVENAL, vii. *Sat.*, 93.[1]

TO THE MOST LEARNED, AND
MY HONOURED FRIEND,

MASTER CAMDEN

CLARENCIEUX.[2]

Sir,—There are, no doubt, a supercilious race in the
world, who will esteem all office, done you in this kind, an
injury; so solemn a vice it is with them to use the authority
of their ignorance to the crying down of POETRY, or the professors: but my gratitude must not leave[3] to correct their
error since I am none of those that can suffer the benefits
conferred upon my youth to perish with my age. It is a frail
memory that remembers but present things: and, had the
favour of the times so conspired with my disposition, as it
could have brought forth other, or better, you had the same
proportion, and number of the fruits, the first. Now, I pray
you, to accept this; such wherein neither the confession of
my manners shall make you blush; nor of my studies, repent
you to have been the instructor: and for the profession of
my thankfulness, I am sure it will with good men, find
either praise, or excuse. Your true lover,

BEN JONSON

[1] "Yet envy not the poet whom stages feed."
[2] The Dedication and the Prologue first appeared in the folio of 1616.
[3] Omit.

PROLOGUE

Though need make many poets, and some such
As art, and nature have not bettered much;
Yet ours, for want, hath not so loved the stage,
As he dare serve the ill customs of the age,
Or purchase your delight at such a rate,
As, for it, he himself must justly hate.
To make a child, now swaddled, to proceed
Man, and then shoot up, in one beard, and weed,
Past threescore years: or, with three rusty swords.
And help of some few foot-and-half-foot words,
Fight over York, and Lancaster's long jars,
And in the tyring-house brings wounds, to scars.
He rather prays, you will be pleased to see
One such to-day, as other plays should be;
Where neither chorus wafts you o'er the seas;
Nor creaking throne comes down, the boys to please;
Nor nimble squib is seen, to make afeard
The gentlewomen; nor rolled bullet heard
To say, it thunders; nor tempestuous drum
Rumbles, to tell you when the storm doth come;
But deeds, and language, such as men do use:
And persons, such as comedy would choose,
When she would show an image of the times,
And sport with human follies, not with crimes.
Except we make 'hem such, by loving still
Our popular errors, when we know they're ill.
I mean such errors, as you'll all confess,
By laughing at them, they deserve no less:
Which when you heartily do, there's hope left then,
You, that have so graced monsters, may like men.

DRAMATIS PERSONÆ

KNO'WELL, an old Gentleman.
EDWARD KNO'WELL, his Son.
BRAIN-WORM, the Father's Man.
Master STEPHEN, a Country Gull.
GEORGE DOWN-RIGHT, a plain Squire.
WELL-BRED, his Half-Brother.
KITELY, a Merchant, their Brother-in-law.
THOMAS CASH, his Cashier.
Captain BOBADILL, a Paul's Man.[1]
Master MATTHEW, a Town Gull.
OLIVER COB, a Water-bearer.
Justice CLEMENT, an old merry Magistrate.
ROGER FORMAL, his Clerk.

Dame KITELY, Kitely's Wife.
Mistress BRIDGET, his Sister.
TIB, Cob's Wife.

Well-bred's Servant. Other Servants, &c.

SCENE—LONDON

---

[1] A frequenter, as such were, of the aisle of St. Paul's.

EVERY MAN IN HIS HUMOUR

ACT THE FIRST

SCENE I—*A Plot before* KNO'WELL'S *House*

Enter KNO'WELL *from his house.*

KNO'WELL. A goodly day toward! and a fresh morning.—
    Brain-worm,
               Enter BRAIN-WORM.
Call up your young master: bid him rise, sir.
Tell him, I have some business to employ him.
    Brain-worm. I will, sir, presently.[1]
    Kno'well.   But hear you, sirrah,
If he be 't his book disturb him not.
    Brain-worm.   Well, sir.   [*Exit.*
    Kno'well. How happy yet, should I esteem myself,
Could I, by any practice, wean the boy
From one vain course of study he affects.
He is a scholar, if a man may trust
The liberal voice of fame, in her report,
Of good account in both our Universities,[2]
Either of which hath favoured him with graces:
But their indulgence must not spring in me
A fond [3] opinion that he cannot err.
Myself was once a student; and indeed,
Fed with the self-same humour, he is now,
Dreaming on nought but idle poetry,
That fruitless, and unprofitable art,
Good unto none, but least to the professors,
Which then I thought the mistress of all knowledge:
But since, time, and the truth have waked my judgment,
And reason taught me better to distinguish
The vain, from the useful learnings.

---

[1] Immediately.
[2] Jonson was then, by grace, M.A. of both.
[3] Foolish.

Enter STEPHEN.

Cousin Stephen,
What news with you, that you are here so early?

Stephen. Nothing, but e'en come to see how you do, uncle.

Kno'well. That's kindly done; you are welcome, coz.[1]

Stephen. Ay, I know that, sir; I would not ha' come else.
How does my cousin Edward, uncle?

Kno'well. O, well, coz, go in and see; I doubt he be scarce
stirring yet.

Stephen. Uncle, afore I go in, can you tell me, an he have
e'er a book of the sciences of hawking and hunting? I would
fain borrow it.

Kno'well. Why, I hope you will not a hawking now, will
you?

Stephen. No, wusse;[2] but I'll practise against next year,
uncle: I have bought me a hawk, and a hood, and bells, and
all; I lack nothing but a book to keep it by.

Kno'well. O, most ridiculous!

Stephen. Nay, look you now, you are angry, uncle: why you
know, an a man have not skill in the hawking and hunting
languages[3] now-a-days, I'll not give a rush for him. They are
more studied than the Greek, or the Latin. He is for no gallants' company without 'hem. And by gadslid I scorn it, I,
so I do, to be a consort for every humdrum; hang 'hem,
scroyles,[4] there's nothing in 'hem i' the world. What do you
talk on it? Because I dwell at Hogsden,[5] I shall keep company with none but the archers of Finsbury? or the citizens
that come a ducking[6] to Islington ponds? A fine jest, i'
faith! 'Slid, a gentleman mun[7] show himself like a gentleman. Uncle, I pray you be not angry, I know what I have to
do, I trow, I am no novice.

Kno'well. You are a prodigal, absurd coxcomb; go to!
Nay, never look at me, it's I that speak.
Take't as you will sir, I'll not flatter you.
Ha' you not yet found means enow, to waste

---

[1] These two lines are not verse, but rhythmic leading to prose.
[2] I wis not, I do not intend.
[3] The technical terms, and those of the minutiæ of action, were then in-
sisted on.
[4] Scabs.
[5] Hoxton.
[6] Duck hunting by dogs.
[7] Must.

That which your friends have left you, but you must
Go cast away your money on a kite,
And know not how to keep it, when you ha' done?
O, it's comely! this will make you a gentleman!
Well, cousin, well! I see you are e'en past hope
Of all reclaim.—Ay, so, now you're told on it,
You look another way.

 Stephen.   What would you ha' me do?

 Kno'well. What would I have you do? I'll tell you, kinsman,

Learn to be wise, and practise how to thrive,
That would I have you do: and not to spend
Your coin on every bauble, that you fancy,
Or every foolish brain, that humours you.
I would not have you to invade each place,
Nor thrust yourself on all societies,
Till men's affections, or your own desert,
Should worthily invite you to your rank.
He, that is so respectless in his courses,
Oft sells his reputation at cheap market.
Nor would I, you should melt away yourself
In flashing bravery,[1] lest, while you affect
To make a blaze of gentry to the world,
A little puff of scorn extinguish it,
And you be left like an unsav'ry snuff,
Whose property is only to offend.
I'ld ha' you sober, and contain yourself,
Not that your sail be bigger than your boat;
But moderate your expenses now, at first,
As you may keep the same proportion still:
Nor stand so much on your gentility,
Which is an airy, and mere borrowed thing,
From dead men's dust and bones; and none of yours,
Except you make, or hold it.—Who comes here?[2]

Enter a Servant.[3]

 Servant. Save you, gentlemen!

 Stephen. Nay, we don't stand much on our gentility,
friend; yet you are welcome: and I assure you, mine uncle

---

[1] Gaudy apparel.
[2] He sees him before he appears on the stage.
[3] Scene ii. in old eds.

here, is a man of a thousand a year, Middlesex land: he has
but one son in all the world, I am his next heir, at the common law, Master Stephen, as simple as I stand here, if my
cousin die, as there's hope he will: I have a pretty living o'
mine own too, beside, hard by here.

Servant. In good time, sir.

Stephen. "In good time, sir?" why![1] and in very good
time, sir! You do not flout, friend, do you?

Servant. Not I, sir.

Stephen. Not you, sir? you were not best, sir; an you
should, here be them can perceive it, and that quickly too;
go to. And they can give it again soundly too, an need be.

Servant. Why, sir, let this satisfy you; good faith, I had no
such intent.

Stephen. Sir, an I thought you had, I would talk[2] with
you, and that presently.[3]

Servant. Good Master Stephen, so you may, sir, at your
pleasure.

Stephen. And so I would, sir, good my saucy companion!
an you were out o' mine uncle's ground, I can tell you;
though I do "not stand upon my gentility," neither, in't.

Kno'well. Cousin, cousin! will this ne'er be left?

Stephen. Whoreson-base fellow? a mechanical serving-
man! By this cudgel, an 'twere not for shame, I would—

Kno'well. What would you do, you peremptory gull?
If you cannot be quiet, get you hence.
You see the honest man demeans himself
Modestly towards you, giving no reply
To your unseasoned, quarrelling, rude fashion:
And still you huff [4] it, with a kind of carriage
As void of wit, as of humanity.
Go, get you in; 'fore Heaven, I am ashamed
Thou hast a kinsman's interest in me.   [*Exit* STEPHEN.

Servant. I pray you,[5] sir, is this Master Kno'well's house?

Kno'well. Yes, marry[6] is it, sir.

[1] he supposes him to imply that his "living" will come to him in good
time.
[2] He insinuates more than talking.
[3] Immediately.
[4] Quarrellingly swagger.
[5] 2nd F. omits "you."
[6] By Mary (our Lady).

Servant. I should inquire for a gentleman here, one Master Edward Kno'well: do you know any such, sir, I pray you?

Kno'well. I should forget myself else, sir.

Servant. Are you the gentleman? cry you mercy, sir: I was required by a gentleman i' the city, as I rode out at this end o' the town, to deliver you this letter, sir.

Kno'well. To me, sir! What do you mean? pray you remember your court'sy.[1] [*Reads.*] "To his most selected friend, Master Edward Kno'well." What might the gentleman's name be, sir, that sent it? Nay, pray you be covered.

Servant. One Master Well-bred, sir.

Kno'well. Master Well-bred! a young gentleman, is he not?

Servant. The same, sir; Master Kitely married his sister—the rich merchant i' the Old Jewry.

Kno'well. You say very true.—Brain-worm!

Re-enter BRAIN-WORM.

Brain-worm. Sir.

Kno'well. Make this honest friend drink here:—pray you, go in.   [*Exeunt* BRAIN-WORM *and* Servant.

This letter is directed to my son:
Yet I am Edward Kno'well too, and may,
With the safe conscience of good manners, use
The fellow's error to my satisfaction.
Well, I will break it ope (old men are curious)
Be it but for the style's sake, and the phrase;
To see if both do answer my son's praises,
Who is almost grown the idolater
Of this young Well-bred:—what have we here? what's this?
[*Reads.*] Why, Ned, I beseech thee, hast thou forsworn all thy friends i' the Old Jewry? or dost thou think us all Jews that inhabit there, yet? If thou dost, come over and but see our frippery; change an old shirt for a whole smock with us. Do not conceive that antipathy between us, and Hogsden, as was between Jews, and hogs-flesh. Leave thy vigilant father alone, to number over his green apricots, evening, and morning, o' the north-west wall: an I had been his son, I had saved him the labour, long since, if taking in all the

---
[1] Be covered.

young wenches, that pass by at the back-door, and codling[1]
every kernel of the fruit for 'hem, would ha' served. But,
pr'y thee, come over to me quickly, this morning; I have
such a present for thee!—our Turkey company never sent
the like to the Grand Signior. One is a rhymer, sir, o' your
own batch, your own leaven; but doth think him himself
poet-major o' the town,[2] willing to be shown, and worthy to
be seen. The other, I will not venture his description with
you, till you come, because I would ha' you make hither with
an appetite. If the worst of 'hem be not worth your journey,
draw your bill of charges, as unconscionable as any Guild-
hall verdict will give it you, and you shall be allowed your
viaticum.[3]   From the Windmill.[4]

From the Bordello[5] it might come as well,
The Spittle, or Pict-hatch.[6] Is this the man
My son hath sung so, for the happiest wit,
The choicest brain, the times hath sent us forth!
I know not what he may be, in the arts,
Nor what in schools; but, surely, for his manners,
I judge him a profane and dissolute wretch;
Worse, by possession of such great good gifts,
Being the master of so loose a spirit.
Why, what unhollowed ruffian would have writ
In such a scurrilous manner to a friend!
Why should he think I tell [7] my apricots,
Or play the Hesperian dragon with my fruit,
To watch it? Well, my son, I'd thought[8]
Y'd had more judgment t' have made election
Of your companions, than t' have ta'en on trust
Such petulant, jeering gamesters, that can spare
No argument, or subject from their jest.
But I perceive, affection makes a fool
Of any man, too much the father.—Brain-worm!

[1] Taking out.
[2] Probably a Lit at A. Munday.
[3] Expenses of your journey.
[4] Tavern.
[5] House of ill-fame.
[6] The enforced, and the ordinary habitation of disorderly women.
[7] Number.
[8] So Q. and Ff. Gifford reads "had," and takes the "you" from Y' of next
line.

Re-enter BRAIN-WORM.

Brain-worm. Sir.

Kno'well. Is the fellow gone that brought this letter?

Brain-worm. Yes, sir, a pretty while since.

Kno'well. And where's your young master?

Brain-worm. In his chamber, sir.

Kno'well. He spake not with the fellow, did he?

Brain-worm. No, sir, he saw him not.

Kno'well. Take you this letter, and deliver it my son;
But with no notice that I have opened it, on your life.

Brain-worm. O Lord, sir! that were a jest indeed.[1]   [*Exit.*

Kno'well. I am resolved I will not stop his journey;
Nor practise any violent mean to stay
The unbridled course of youth in him; for that,
Restrained, grows more impatient; and in kind,
Like to the eager, but the generous[2] greyhound,
Who ne'er so little from his game withheld,
Turns head, and leaps up at his holder's throat.
There is a way of winning, more by love,
And urging of the modesty, than fear:
Force works on servile natures, not the free.
He that's compelled to goodness, may be good,
But 'tis but for that fit; where others, drawn
By softness, and example, get a habit.
Then, if they stray, but warn 'hem, and the same
They should for virtue've done, they'll do for shame.

[*Exit.*

SCENE II—*A Room in* KNO'WELL'S *House*[3]

Enter EDWARD KNO'WELL, *with a letter in his hand, followed
by* BRAIN-WORM.

Edward Kno'well. Did he open it, say'st thou?

Brain-worm. Yes, o' my word, sir, and read the contents.

E. Kno'well. That scarce contents me.—What countenance, prithee, made he i' the reading of it? was he angry, or
pleased?

---

[1] Another instance of rhythmic prose interposed. Henceforth they will not
be noted.
[2] Well-bred (Lat. *generosus*).
[3] Scene iii. in old eds.

Brain-worm. Nay sir, I saw him not read it, nor open it, I assure your worship.

E. Know'well. No? how know'st thou then, that he did either?

Brain-worm. Marry, sir, because he charged me, on my life, to tell nobody that he opened it; which, unless he had done, he would never fear to have it revealed.

E. Kno'well. That's true: well, I thank thee, Brain-worm.
                              [*Moves to window to read letter.*

Enter STEPHEN.

Stephen. O, Brain-worm, didst thou not see a fellow here in a what-sha-call-him doublet? he brought mine uncle a letter e'en now.

Brain-worm. Yes, Master Stephen, what of him?

Stephen. O, I ha' such a mind to beat him, where is he, canst thou tell?

Brain-worm. Faith, he is not of that mind: he is gone, Master Stephen.

Stephen. Gone! which way? when went he? how long since?

Brain-worm. He is rid hence; he took horse at the street-door.

Stephen. And I staid i' the fields! Whoreson Scanderbag rogue! Oh that I had but a horse to fetch him back again!

Brain-worm. Why, you may ha' my master's gelding, to save your longing, sir.

Stephen. But I ha' no boots, that's the spite on't.

Brain-worm. Why, a fine wisp of hay, rolled hard,[1] Master Stephen.

Stephen. No faith, it's no boot to follow him now: let him e'en go and hang. 'Pray thee, help to truss me a little. He does so vex me—

Brain-worm. You'll be worse vexed when you are trussed,[2] Master Stephen. Best keep unbraced, and walk yourself till you be cold; your choler may founder you else.

Stephen. By my faith, and so I will, now thou tell'st me on't:—how dost thou like my leg, Brain-worm?

[1] An ordinary rustic practice.
[2] To tie the laces that kept up the breeches—also to be beaten.

Brain-worm. A very good leg, Master Stephen! but the woolen stocking does not commend it so well.

Stephen. Foh! the stockings be good enough, now summer is coming on, for the dust: I'll ha' a pair of silk again winter, that I go to dwell i' the town. I think my leg would show in a silk hose.[1]

Brain-worm. Believe me, Master Stephen, rarely well.

Stephen. In sadness,[2] I think it would: I have a reasonable good leg.

Brain-worm. You have an excellent good leg, Master Stephen, but I cannot stay to praise it longer now, and I am very sorry for't.   [*Exit.*

Stephen. Another time will serve, Brain-worm. Gramercy[3] for this.

E. Kno'well. Ha, ha, ha!

Stephen. 'Slid,[4] I hope he laughs not at me; an he do—

E. Kno'well. Here was a letter indeed, to be intercepted by a man's father, and do him good with him! He cannot but think most virtuously, both of me, and the sender, sure, that make the careful costermonger of him in our familiar epistles. Well, if he read this with patience, I'll be gelt, and troll ballads for Master John Trundle[5] yonder, the rest of my mortality. It is true, and likely, my father may have as much patience as another man; for he takes much physic, and oft taking physic makes a man very patient. But would your packet, Master Well-bred, had arrived at him in such a minute of his patience! then we had known the end of it, which now is doubtful, and threatens—[*Sees* STEPHEN.] What, my wise cousin! nay then, I'll furnish our feast with one gull more to'ard the mess.[6] He writes to me of a brace, and here's one, that's three: oh, for a fourth, Fortune! if ever thou'lt use thine eyes, I entreat thee—

Stephen. Oh, now I see who he laughed at: he laughed at somebody in that letter. By this good light, an he had laughed at me—

E. Kno'well. How now, cousin Stephen, melancholy?

---

[1] The same conceit is hit at in *Twelfth Night,* i. 3. 126-8.
[2] Soberness.
[3] Fr. *Grande merci* (great thanks).
[4] God's lid.
[5] A publisher of ballads.
[6] Four at dinner made "a mess."

Stephen. Yes, a little. I thought you had laughed at me, cousin.

E. Kno'well. Why, what an I had, coz? what would you ha' done?

Stephen. By this light I would ha' told mine uncle.

E. Kno'well. Nay, if you would ha' told your uncle, I did laugh at you, coz.

Stephen. Did you, indeed?

E. Kno'well. Yes, indeed.

Stephen. Why, then—

E. Kno'well. What then?

Stephen. I am satisfied; it is sufficient.

E. Kno'well. Why, be so, gentle coz: and, I pray you, let me entreat a courtesy of you. I am sent for, this morning, by a friend i' the Old Jewry, to come to him; it's but crossing over the fields to Moorgate: Will you bear me company? I protest, it is not to draw you into bond, or any plot against the state, coz.

Stephen. Sir, that's all one an 'twere; you shall command me twice so far as Moorgate, to do you good in such a matter. Do you think I would leave you? I protest—

E. Kno'well. No, no, you shall not protest, coz.

Stephen. By my fackins,[1] but I will, by your leave: I'll protest more to my friend, than I'll speak of at this time.

E. Kno'well. You speak very well, coz.

Stephen. Nay, not so neither, you shall pardon me: but I speak to serve my turn.

E. Kno'well. Your turn, coz? do you know what you say? A gentleman of your sort,[2] parts, carriage, and estimation, to talk o' your turn[3] i' this company, and to me alone, like a tankard-bearer at a conduit! fie! A wight that, hitherto, his every step hath left the stamp of a great foot behind him, as every word the savour of a strong spirit; and he! this man! so graced, gilded, or, to use a more fit metaphor, so tin-foiled by nature, as not ten housewives' pewter, again a good time,[4] shows more bright to the world than he! and he! (as I said last, so I say again, and still shall say it) this man! to

---

[1] An oath (by my faith?) made innocent by change of form.
[2] Rank.
[3] See Cob's use of it, p. 19.
[4] Time of display.

conceal such real ornaments as these, and shadow their glory, as a milliner's wife does her wrought stomacher, with a smoky lawn, or a black cypress![1] Oh, coz! it cannot be answered; go not about it: Drake's old ship at Deptford may sooner circle the world again. Come, wrong not the quality of your desert, with looking downward, coz; but hold up your head, so: and let the idea of what you are, be portrayed i' your face that men may read i' your physnomy, "Here within this place is to be seen the true, rare, and accomplished monster, or miracle of nature," which is all one. What think you of this, coz?

Stephen. Why, I do think of it; and I will b emore proud, and melancholy, and gentlemanlike, than I have been, I'll insure you.

E. Kno'well. Why, that's resolute, Master Stephen! [*Aside.*] Now, if I can but hold him up to his height, as it is happily begun, it will do well for a suburb humour: we may hap have a match with the city, and play him for forty pound.— Come, coz.

Stephen. I'll follow you.

E. Kno'well. Follow me! you must go before.

Stephen. Nay, an I must, I will. Pray you, show me, good cousin.   [*Exeunt.*

SCENE III—*The Lane before* COB'S *House*[2]

Enter MATTHEW.

Matthew. I think this be the house:—what, ho?

COB *opening door.*

Cob. Who's there? O Master Matthew! give your worship good morrow.

Matthew. What, Cob? how dost thou, good Cob? dost thou inhabit here, Cob?

Cob. Ay, sir, I and my lineage ha' kept a poor house, here, in our days.

Matthew. Thy lineage, Monsieur Cob! what lineage, what lineage?

[1] Linen crêpe.
[2] Scene iv. in old eds.

Cob. Why, sir, an ancient lineage, and a princely. Mine ance'try came from a king's belly, no worse man: and yet no man neither—by your worship's leave, I did lie in that— but Herring, the king of fish (from his belly, I proceed), one o' the monarchs o' the world, I assure you. The first red herring that was broiled in Adam and Eve's kitchen, do I fetch my pedigree from, by the harrot's[1] book. His cob[2] was my great-great-mighty-great grandfather.

Matthew. Why mighty? why mighty, I pray thee?

Cob. O, it was a mighty while ago, sir, and a mighty great cob.

Matthew. How know'st thou that?

Cob. How know I? why, I smell his ghost, ever and anon.

Matthew. Smell a ghost! O unsavoury jest! and the ghost of a herring cob?

Cob. Ay sir: with favour of your worship's nose, Master Matthew, why not the ghost of a herring-cob, as well as the ghost of rasher-bacon?

Matthew. Roger Bacon, thou would'st say.

Cob. I say, rasher-bacon. They were both broiled o' the coals; and a man may smell broiled meat, I hope? you are a scholar, upsolve me that, now.

Matthew [*aside*]. O raw ignorance!—Cob, canst thou show me of a gentlemen, one Captain Bobadill, where his lodging is?

Cob. O, my guest, sir, you mean.

Matthew. Thy guest, alas! ha, ha!

Cob. Why do you laugh, sir? Do you not mean Captain Bobadill?

Matthew. Cob, 'pray thee advise thyself well: do not wrong the gentleman, and thyself too. I dare be sworn, he scorns thy house; he! He lodge in such a base, obscure place as thy house! Tut, I know his disposition so well, he would not lie in thy bed if thou'dst gi' it him.

Cob. I will not give it him, though, sir. Mass,[3] I thought somewhat was in't, we could not get him to bed, all night! Well, sir; though he lie not o' my bed, he lies o' my bench: an't please you to go up, sir, you shall find him with two

[1] Vulgar for herald's. A hit at their fabricated pedigrees.
[2] His young herring, *i.e.* his son.
[3] Used as an expletive oath.

cushions under his head, and his cloak wrapt about him, as
though he had neither won nor lost, and yet, I warrant, he
ne'er cast[1] better in his life, than he has done to-night.

Matthew. Why, was he drunk?

Cob. Drunk, sir! you hear not me say so: perhaps he
swallowed a tavern-token,[2] or some such device, sir; I have
nothing to do withal. I deal with water and not with wine.
Gi' me my tankard there, ho! [TIB *brings tankard and exit.*]
God b' wi' you, sir. It's six o'clock: I should ha' carried two
turns by this. What ho! my stopple! come.

Re-enter TIB *with stopple, and exit.*

Matthew. Lie in a water-bearer's house! a gentleman of his
havings? Well, I'll tell him my mind.   [*Enters house.*

Cob. What, Tib, show this gentleman up to the captain.
O, an my house were the Brazen-head now! faith it would
e'en speak "Moe fools yet." [3] You should have some now
would take this Master Matthew to be a gentleman, at
the least. His father's an honest man, a worshipful [4] fishmonger, and so forth; and now does he creep and wriggle
into acquaintance with all the brave gallants about the
town, such as my guest is (O, my guest is a fine man!) , and
they flout him invincibly. He useth every day to a merchant's house where I serve water, one Master Kitely's, i'
the Old Jewry; and here's the jest, he is in love with my
master's sister, Mistress Bridget, and calls her "mistress," [5]
and there he will sit you a whole afternoon sometimes, reading o' these same abominable, vile (a pox on 'hem! I cannot abide them,) rascally verses, poyetry, poyetry, and speaking of enterludes, 'twill make a man burst to hear him. And
the wenches, they do so jeer, and ti-he[6] at him—Well,
should they do so much to me, I'ld forswear them all, "by
the foot of Pharaoh!" There's an oath! How many water-
bearers shall you hear swear such an oath? O, I have a
guest—he teaches me—he does swear the legiblest of any

---

[1] To throw dice, and to throw up.
[2] A phrase intimating the same.
[3] A reference to Friar Bacon and his Head of Brass.
[4] "The Worshipful Company of."
[5] *i.e.* His lady-love.
[6] Titter, giggle.

man christened: "By St. George!—the foot of Pharaoh!—
the body of me!—as I am a gentleman and a soldier!" such
dainty oaths! and withal he does take this same filthy roguish tobacco, the finest, and cleanliest! it would do a
man good to see the fume come forth at's tonnels.[1]—Well,
he owes me forty shillings—my wife lent him out of her
purse, by six-pence at a time—besides his lodging: I would
I had it! I shall ha' it, he says, the next action.[2] Helter
skelter, hang sorrow, care'll kill a cat, up-tails[3] all, and a
louse for the hangman.   [*Exit.*

SCENE IV—*A Room in* Cob's *House*[4]

Bobadill *lying on a bench.*

Bobadill. Hostess, hostess!

Enter Tib.

Tib. What say you, sir?

Bobadill. A cup o' thy small beer, sweet hostess.

Tib. Sir, there's a gentleman below, would speak with
you.

Bobadill. A gentleman! 'odso, I am not within.

Tib. My husband told him you were, sir.

Bobadill. What a plague—what meant he?

Matthew [*below*]. Captain Bobadill!

Bobadill. Who's there?—Take away the bason, good hostess;—Come up, sir.

Tib [*goes to the door*]. He would desire you to come
up, sir.—You come into a cleanly house, here!

Enter Matthew.

Matthew. 'Save you, sir; 'save you, captain!

Bobadill. Gentle Master Matthew! Is it you, sir? please you
to sit down.

---

[1] Tunnel, funnels, *i.e.* nostrils.
[2] He understands it "next term time."
[3] Cats pleased turn up their tails: also meaning glasses upside down
and therefore drained.
[4] Scene v. in old eds.

Matthew. Thank you, good captain; you may see, I am somewhat audacious.

Bobadill. Not so, sir. I was requested to supper last night by a sort[1] of gallants, where you were wished for, and drunk to, I assure you.

Matthew. Vouchsafe me, by whom, good captain?

Bobadill. Marry, by young Well-bred, and others:—Why, hostess, a stool here, for this gentleman.

Matthew. No haste, sir, 'tis very well.

Bobadill. Body of me! it was so late ere we parted last night, I can scarce open my eyes yet; I was but new risen, as you came: how passes the day abroad, sir? you can tell.

Matthew. Faith, some half hour to seven: now, trust me, you have an exceeding fine lodging here, very neat, and private.

Bobadill. Ay, sir: sit down, I pray you. Master Matthew, in any case, possess no gentlemen of our acquaintance with notice of my lodging.

Matthew. Who? I, sir? no.

Bobadill. Not that I need to care who know it, for the cabin is convenient! but in regard I would not be too popular, and generally visited, as some are.

Matthew. True, captain, I conceive you.

Bobadill. For, do you see, sir, by the heart of valour in me, except it be to some peculiar and choice spirits, to whom I am extraordinarily engaged, as yourself, or so, I could not extend thus far.

Matthew. O Lord, sir! I resolve so.

Bobadill. I confess I love a cleanly, and quiet privacy, above all the tumult and roar of fortune. What new book ha' you there? What! "Go by, Hieronymo"? [2]

Matthew. Ay: did you ever see it acted? is't not well penned?

Bobadill. Well penned? I would fain see all the poets of these times pen such another play as that was! they'll prate and swagger, and keep a stir of art and devices, when, as I am a gentleman, read 'hem, they are the most shallow, pitiful, barren fellows that live upon the face of the earth, again.

[1] Company, lot.
[2] *Hieronimo is Mad again*—often the butt of later dramatists. The line is in Act iv.

[*While* MATTHEW *reads,* BOBADILL *makes himself ready.*]

Matthew. Indeed, here are a number of fine speeches in this book. "O eyes, no eyes, but fountains fraught with tears!" there's a conceit! "fountains fraught with tears!" O life, no life, but lively form of death!" another—"O world, no world, but mass of public wrongs!" a third— "Confused and filled with murder and misdeeds!" a fourth.[1] O, the Muses! Is't not excellent? Is't not simply the best that you ever heard, captain? Ha! how do you like it?

Bobadill. 'Tis good.

Matthew. "To thee, the purest object to my sense,

    The most refinèd essence Heaven covers,

  Send I these lines, wherein I do commence

    The happy state of turtle-billing lovers.

If they prove rough, unpolished, harsh, and rude,

Haste made the waste: thus, mildly, I conclude."

Bobadill. Nay proceed, proceed. Where's this?

Matthew. This, sir! a toy o' mine own, in my nonage; the infancy of my muses. But when will you come and see my study? good faith, I can show you some very good things, I have done of late—That boot becomes your leg passing well, captain, methinks.[2]

Bobadill. So, so; it's the fashion gentlemen now use.

Matthew. Troth, captain, and now you speak o' the fashion, Master Well-bred's elder brother, and I, are fallen out exceedingly; this other day I happened to enter into some discourse of a hanger,[3] which, I assure you, both for fashion, and workmanship, was most peremptory beautiful and gentlemanlike: yet he condemned, and cried it down, for the most pied and ridiculous that ever he saw.

Bobadill. Squire Downright, the half-brother, was't not?

Matthew. Ay sir, he.

Bobadill. Hang him, rook![4] he! why he has no more judgment than a malt-horse. By St. George, I wonder you'ld lose a thought upon such an animal; the most peremptory absurd clown of Christendom, this day, he is holden.

[1] All in Act iii. "Enter Hieronimo."
[2] With artificial arrangements, creasings, etc.
[3] Meaning here the side-strap or loop, of a sword belt, which held the dagger, or sometimes a short crooked sword. The word was also applied to the sword itself.
[4] Simpleton, prater.

I protest to you, as I am a gentleman and a soldier, I
ne'er changed words with his like. By his discourse, he
should eat nothing but hay: he was born for the manger,
pannier, or pack-saddle. He has not so much as a good
phrase in his belly, but all old iron, and rusty proverbs:
a good commodity for some smith to make hob-nails of.

Matthew. Ay, and he thinks to carry it away with his manhood still, where he comes: he brags he will gi' me the
bastinado, as I hear.

Bobadill. How! he the bastinado! how came he by that
word, trow?

Matthew. Nay, indeed, he said cudgel me; I termed it so,
for my more grace.

Bobadill. That may be! for I was sure, it was none of his
word: but when, when said he so?

Matthew. Faith, yesterday, they say; a young gallant, a
friend of mine, told me so.

Bobadill. By the foot of Pharaoh, an 'twere my case now,
I should send him a chartel presently. The bastinado!
a most proper and sufficient dependence,[1] warranted by
the great Caranza.[2] Come hither, you shall chartel him;
I'll show you a trick or two you shall kill him with, at
pleasure, the first stoccata, if you will, by this air.

Matthew. Indeed, you have absolute knowledge i' the
mystery, I have heard, sir.

Bobadill. Of whom? of whom, ha' you heard it, I beseech
you?

Matthew. Troth, I have heard it spoken of divers, that you
have very rare, and up-in-one-breath-utter-able skill, sir.

Bobadill. By Heaven, no, not I; so skill i' the earth; some
small rudiments i' the science, as to know my time, distance, or so. I have professed it more for noblemen and
gentlemen's use, than mine own practice, I assure you.—
Hostess, accommodate us with another bed-staff [3] here
quickly. [*Enter* Tib *with a puzzled air.*] Lend us another
bed-staff—[*Exit* Tib.] the woman does not understand the
words of action.—Look you, sir: exalt not your point above

---

[1] The cause on which the duel depended.

[2] A writer on the duel, 1569.

[3] Staff or rod used for beating up the mattress, etc.

this state, at any hand, and let your poniard maintain your defence, thus: [*Re-enter* TIB.]—give it the gentleman, and leave us. [*Exit* TIB.] So, sir. Come on: O, twine your body more about, that you may fall to a more sweet, comely, gentleman-like guard. So, indifferent. Hollow your body more, sir, thus. Now, stand fast o' your left leg, note your distance, keep your due proportion of time—Oh, you disorder your point most irregularly.

Matthew. How is the bearing of it now sir?

Bobadill. O, out of measure ill! a well-experienced hand would pass upon you at pleasure.

Matthew. How mean you, sir, pass upon me? [1]

Bobadill. Why, thus, sir,—make a thrust at me—[MATTHEW *pushes at* BOBADILL.] come in upon the answer, control your point, and make a full career at the body.[2] The best-practised gallants of the time name it the passada; a most desperate thrust, believe it.

Matthew. Well, come, sir.

Bobadill. Why, you do not manage your weapon with any facility, or grace to invite me. I have no spirit to play with you: your dearth of judgment renders you tedious.

Matthew. But one venue,[3] sir.

Bobadill. Venue! fie; most gross denomination as ever I heard: O, the "stoccata," while you live, sir; note that. —Come, put on your cloak, and we'll go to some private place where you are acquainted; some tavern, or so— and have a bit. I'll send for one of these fencers, and he shall breathe you, by my direction; and then, I will teach you your trick: you shall kill him with it, at the first, if you please. Why, I will learn you, by the true judgment of the eye, hand, and foot, to control any enemy's point i' the world. Should your adversary confront you with a pistol 'twere nothing, by this hand; you should, by the same rule, control his bullet, in a line,—except it were hail-shot and spread. What money ha' you about you, Master Matthew?

Matthew. Faith, I ha' not past a two shillings or so.

[1] He thinks it means, "cheat him."
[2] As he makes his replies to the thrust, he expounds them in these words.
[3] A bout ending in a thrust; also a thrust.

Bobadill. 'Tis somewhat with the least; but come. We will
have a bunch of radish, and salt, to taste our wine; and a
pipe of tobacco to close the orifice of the stomach: and
then we'll call upon young Well-bred: perhaps we shall
meet the Corydon[1] his brother there, and put him to the
question.   [*Exeunt.*

ACT THE SECOND

SCENE I—*A Hall in* KITELY'S *House*

Enter KITELY, CASH, *and* DOWN-RIGHT.

KITELY. Thomas, come hither.
There lies a note within upon my desk,
Here take my key:—it is no matter neither.
Where is the boy?
   Cash. Within, sir, i'th' warehouse.
   Kitely. Let him tell over, straight, that Spanish gold,
And weigh it, with th' pieces of eight.[2] Do you
See the delivery of those silver stuffs
To Master Lucar. Tell him, if he will,
He shall ha' the grograns,[3] at the rate I told him,
And I will meet him on the Exchange, anon.
   Cash. Good, sir.   [*Exit.*
   Kitely.   Do you see that fellow, brother Downright?
   Down-right. Ay, what of him?
   Kitely.   He is a jewel, brother.
I took him of a child up at my door,
And christened him, gave him mine own name, Thomas;
Since bred him at the Hospital;[4] where proving
A toward imp, I called him home, and taught him
So much, as I have made him my cashier,
And given him, who had none, a surname, Cash:
And find him in his place, so full of faith,
That I durst trust my life into his hands.
   Down-right. So would not I in any bastard's, brother.

[1] The country swain, or bumpkin.
[2] "The peece of eight ryals, value 8s. 6d."
[3] A ribbed and partly silk stuff.
[4] Blue Coat School.

As it is like he is, although I knew
Myself his father. But you said y' had somewhat
To tell me, gentle brother, what is't? what is't?

   Kitely. Faith, I am very loath to utter it,
As fearing it may hurt your patience:
But, that I know, your judgment is of strength,
Against the nearness of affection——

   Down-right. What need this circumstance? [1] pray you, be
direct.

   Kitely. I will not say, how much I do ascribe
Unto your friendship, nor in what regard
I hold your love; but let my past behaviour,
And usage of your sister, but confirm
How well I've been affected to your——

   Down-right. You are too tedious; come to the matter, the
matter.

   Kitely. Then, without further ceremony, thus.
My brother Well-bred, sir, I know not how,
Of late is much declined in what he was,
And greatly altered in his disposition.
When he came first to lodge here in my house,
Ne'er trust me, if I were not proud of him:
Methought he bare himself in such a fashion,
So full of man, and sweetness in his carriage,
And—what was chief—it showed not borrowed in him,
But all he did, became him as his own,
And seemed as perfect, proper, and possessed,
As breath with life, or colour with the blood.
But now, his course is so irregular,
So loose, affected, and deprived of grace,
And he himself withal so far fallen off
From that first place as scarce no note remains,
To tell men's judgments where he lately stood.
He's grown a stranger to all due respect,
Forgetful of his friends; and not content,
To stale himself in all societies,
He makes my house here, common as a mart,
A theatre, a public receptacle
For a giddy humour, and diseasèd riot;

[1] This staying around your matter, this beating about the bush?

And here, as in a tavern or a stews,
He and his wild associates spend their hours,
In repetition of lascivious jests,
Swear, leap, drink, dance, and revel night by night,
Control my servants; and, indeed, what not?

Down-right. 'Sdeins,[1] I know not what I should say to him, i' the whole world! He values me at a cracked three-farthings, for aught I see. It will never out o' the flesh that's bred i' the bone. I have told him enough, one would think, if that would serve; but counsel to him is as good as a shoulder of mutton to a sick horse. Well! he knows what to trust to, for[2] George: let him spend, and spend, and domineer, till his heart ache; an he think to be relieved by me, when he is got into one o' your city-pounds, the Counters,[3] he has the wrong sow by the ear, i' faith; and claps his dish [4] at the wrong man's door: I'll lay my hand o' my halfpenny, ere I part with 't to fetch him out, I'll assure you.

Kitely. Nay, good brother, let it not trouble you thus.

Down-right. 'Sdeath! he mads me, I could eat my very spurleathers for anger! But, why are you so tame? why do not you speak to him, and tell him how he disquiets your house?

Kitely. O, there are divers reasons to dissuade, brother,
But, would yourself vouchsafe to travail in it,
(Though but with plain and easy circumstance,)
It would, both come much better to his sense,
And savour less of stomach,[5] or of passion.
You are his elder brother, and that title
Both gives and warrants you[6] authority,
Which, by your presence seconded, must breed
A kind of duty in him, and regard:
Whereas, if I should intimate the least,
It would but add contempt, to his neglect,
Heap worse on ill, make up a pile of hatred,
That, in the rearing, would come tottering down,

---

[1] God's death, or possibly God's pleasure.
[2] A corruption of " 'fore."
[3] Two London prisons.
[4] Begs.
[5] Ill-humour.
[6] "Your," 2nd F.

And in the ruin, bury all our love.
Nay, more than this, brother; if I should speak,
He would be ready, from his heat of humour,
And overflowing of the vapour in him,
To blow the ears of his familiars
With the false breath, of telling what disgraces,
And low disparagements, I had put upon him.
Whilst they, sir, to relieve him in the fable,
Make their loose comments, upon every word,
Gesture, or look, I use; mock me all over,
From my flat cap, unto my shining shoes;[1]
And, out of their impetuous rioting phant'sies,
Beget some slander, that shall dwell with me.
And what would that be, think you? marry, this:
They would give out—because my wife is fair,
Myself but lately married, and my sister
Here sojourning a virgin in my house—
That I were jealous!—nay, as sure as death,
That they would say: and, how that I had quarrelled
My brother purposely, thereby to find
An apt pretext to banish them my house.
    Down-right. Mass, perhaps so; they're like enough to do it.
    Kitely. Brother, they would, believe it; so should I,
Like one of these penurious quack-salvers,
But set the bills up, to mine own disgrace,
And try experiments upon myself;
Lend scorn and envy, opportunity
To stab my reputation and good name——

Enter MATTHEW *struggling with* BOBADILL.[2]

    Matthew. I will speak to him——
    Bobadill. Speak to him! By the foot of Pharaoh, you
shall not! you shall not do him that grace.—The time
of day to you, gentleman o' the house. Is Master Well-bred
stirring?
    Down-right. How then? what should he do?
    Bobadill [*to* KITELY]. Gentleman of the house, it is to you:
is he within, sir?

[1] Both marks of the citizen-trader as compared with the gallant; the
shoes were blackened.
[2] Scene ii. in old eds.

Kitely. He came not to his lodging to-night, sir, I assure you.

Down-right. Why, do you hear? you!

Bobadill. The gentleman-citizen hath satisfied me; I'll talk to no scavenger.   [*Exeunt* BOBADILL *and* MATTHEW.

Down-right. How! scavenger? stay, sir, stay!

Kitely. Nay, brother Downright.

Down-right. 'Heart! stand you away, an you love me.

Kitely. You shall not follow him now, I pray you, brother, Good faith you shall not; I will overrule you.

Down-right. Ha! scavenger? well, go to, I say little; but, by this good day (God forgive me I should swear), if I put it up so, say I am the rankest cow that ever pist. 'Sdeins, an I swallow this, I'll ne'er draw my sword in the sight of Fleet-street again, while I live; I'll sit in a barn with madge-howlet, and catch mice, first. Scavenger? 'heart! —and I'll go near to fill that huge tumbrel-slop[1] of yours with somewhat, and I have good luck: your Garagantua breech cannot carry it away.

Kitely. Oh, do not fret yourself thus; never think on't.

Down-right. These are my brother's consorts, these! these are his cam'rades, his walking mates! he's a gallant, a cavaliero too, right hangman cut! Let me not live, an I could not find in my heart to swing[2] the whole ging[3] of 'hem one after another, and begin with him first. I am grieved it should be said, he is my brother, and take these courses. Well, as he brews, so shall he drink, for George, again. Yet he shall hear on't, and that tightly too, an I live, i' faith.

Kitely. But, brother, let your reprehension, then,
Run in an easy current, not o'er-high
Carried with rashness, or devouring choler;
But rather use the soft persuading way,
Whose powers will work more gently, and compose
The imperfect thoughts you labour to reclaim;
More winning, than enforcing the consent.

Down-right. Ay, ay, let me alone for that, I warrant you.
                                                  [*Bell rings.*

---

[1] Largely puffed breeches were then the fashion, and Bobadill wore them.
[2] Editors have adopted "swinge," from the Q. and Ff., but the reference to the hangman seems to show that "swing" is preferable.
[3] Sometimes less disparaging than gang; not so here.

Kitely. How now! Oh,[1] the bell rings to breakfast.
Brother, I pray you go in, and bear my wife
Company till I come; I'll but give order
For some despatch of business to my servants.

[*Exit* DOWN-RIGHT.

COB *passes by with his tankard.*[2]

Kitely. What, Cob! our maids will have you by the back,
     i' faith,
For coming so late this morning.

Cob. Perhaps so, sir; take heed somebody have not them
by the belly, for walking so late in the evening.   [*Exit.*

Kitely. Well, yet my troubled spirit's somewhat eased,
Though not reposed in that security,
As I could wish: but I must be content,
Howe'er I set a face on't to the world.
Would I had lost this finger at a venture,
So Well-bred had ne'er lodged within my house.
Why't cannot be, where there is such resort
Of wanton gallants, and young revellers,
That any woman should be honest long.
Is't like, that factious beauty will preserve
The public-weal of chastity, unshaken,
When such strong motives muster, and make head
Against her single peace? No, no: beware,
When mutual appetite doth meet to treat,
And spirits of one kind, and quality
Come once to parley in the pride of blood,
It is no slow conspiracy that follows.
Well, to be plain, if I but thought, the time
Had answered their affections: all the world
Should not persuade me, but I were a cuckold.
Marry, I hope they ha' not got that start;
For opportunity hath balked 'hem yet,
And shall do still, while I have eyes, and ears
To attend the impositions of my heart.
My presence shall be as an iron bar,
'Twixt the conspiring motions of desire:

[1] Seems to be "Oh-h" prolonged into a dissyllable.
[2] Scene iii. in old eds.

Yea, every look, or glance mine eye ejects,
Shall check occasion, as one doth his slave,
When he forgets the limits of prescription.

Enter Dame KITELY *and* BRIDGET.

Dame Kitely. Sister Bridget, pray you fetch down the rose-
water above in the closet. [*Exit* BRIDGET.]—Sweet-heart,
will you come in to breakfast?

Kitely. An she have overheard me now!

Dame Kitely. I pray thee, good muss,[1] we stay for you.

Kitely. By Heaven, I would not for a thousand angels![2]

Dame Kitely. What ail you, sweet-heart? are you not
well? speak, good muss.

Kitely. Troth my head aches extremely on a sudden.

Dame Kitely [*putting her hand to his forehead*]. Oh, the
Lord!

Kitely. How now? What?

Dame Kitely. Alas, how it burns! Muss, keep you warm;
good truth it is this new disease,[3] there's a number are
troubled withal. For love's sake, sweet-heart, come in, out
of the air.

Kitely. How simple, and how subtle are her answers!
A new disease, and many troubled with it?
Why true; she heard me, all the world to nothing.

Dame Kitely. I pray thee, good sweet-heart, come in; the
air will do you harm, in troth.

Kitely. "The air!" she has me i' the wind![4]—Sweet-heart.
I'll come to you presently; 'twill away, I hope.

Dame Kitely. Pray Heaven it do.   [*Exit.*

Kitely. A new disease? I know not, new, or old,
But it may well be called poor mortals' plague;
For, like a pestilence, it doth infect
The houses of the brain. First, it begins
Solely to work upon the phantasy,
Filling her seat with such pestiferous air,
As soon corrupts the judgment: and from thence,

---

[1] An endearing form of "mouse."
[2] The coins are here meant. (The angel varied in value from 6s. 8d.
to 10s.—*Halliwell.*)
[3] So called for long. Prince Henry died of it.
[4] Scents my thoughts.

Sends like contagion to the memory;
Still each to other giving the infection.
Which, as a subtle vapour, spreads itself
Confusedly through every sensitive part,
Till not a thought, or motion in the mind
Be free from the black poison of suspect.
Ah! but what misery is it to know this?
Or, knowing it, to want the mind's erection,
In such extremes? Well, I will once more strive,
In spite of this black cloud, myself to be,
And shake the fever off, that thus shakes me.   [*Exit.*

SCENE II—*Moorfields*[1]

Enter BRAIN-WORM *like a maimed Sub-officer.*

Brain-worm. 'Slid I cannot choose but laugh, to see myself
translated thus, from a poor creature to a creator; for
now must I create an intolerable sore of lies, or my present profession loses the grace: and yet the lie, to a man
of my coat, is as ominous a fruit as the fico.[2] O, sir, it
holds for good polity ever, to have that outwardly in vilest
estimation, that inwardly is most dear to us: so much for
my borrowed shape. Well, the troth is, my old master
intends to follow my young master, dry-foot,[3] over Moor-
fields[4] to London, this morning; now I knowing of this
hunting-match, or rather conspiracy, and to insinuate with
my young master (for so must we that are blue waiters,[5]
and men of hope and service do, or perhaps we may wear
motley at the year's end, and who wears motley, you
know[6]), have got me afore, in this disguise, determining
here to lie in ambuscado, and intercept him in the mid-
way. If I can but get his cloak, his purse, his hat, nay, any
thing to cut him off, that is, to stay his journey, *Veni, vidi,
vici,*[7] I may say with Captain Cæsar I am made for ever,

[1] Scene iv. in old eds.
[2] Our "fig for you," the thumb protruding between the closed fingers.
Also the poisoned fig of Spain.
[3] By his scentless foot-prints—by guess.
[4] Then the resort of vagrants, &c.
[5] Servants then wore blue livery.
[6] Meaning, of course, the fool.
[7] I came, I saw, I conquered.

i' faith. Well, now must I practise to get the true garb of one of these lance-knights,[1] my arm here, and my—young master! and his cousin, Master Stephen, as I am a true counterfeit man of war, and no soldier!   [*Moves away.*

Enter E. KNO'WELL *and* STEPHEN.

E. Kno'well. So sir, and how then, coz?

Stephen. 'Sfoot! I have lost my purse, I think.

E. Kno'well. How! lost your purse? where? when had you it?

Stephen. I cannot tell;—stay.

Brain-worm. 'Slid, I am afeard they will know me, would I could get by them!

E. Kno'well. What? ha' you it?

Stephen. No; I think I was bewitched, I——   [*Cries.*

E. Kno'well. Nay, do not weep the loss; hang it, let it go.

Stephen. Oh, it's here: No, an it had been lost, I had not cared, but for a jet ring Mistress Mary sent me.

E. Kno'well. A jet ring! O the posy, the posy?

Stephen. Fine, i' faith.—

> "Though Fancy sleep,
> My love is deep."

Meaning, that though I did not fancy her, yet she loved me dearly.

E. Kno'well. Most excellent!

Stephen. And then I sent her another, and my posy was,

> "The deeper the sweeter,
> I'll be judged by St. Peter."

E. Kno'well. How, by St. Peter? I do not conceive that.

Stephen. Marry, St. Peter, to make up the metre.

E. Kno'well. Well, there the saint was your good patron, he helped you at your need: thank him, thank him.

Brain-worm [*aside*]. I cannot take leave on 'hem so; I will venture, come what will. [*Comes toward them.*] Gentlemen, please you change a few crowns for a very excellent good

---

[1] The lowest officer among foot-soldiers, commanding ten men.

blade here? I am a poor gentleman, a soldier; on that, in the better state of my fortunes, scorned so mean a refuge; but now it is the humour of necessity, to have it so. You seem to be gentlemen well affected to martial men, else should I rather die with silence, than live with shame: however, vouchsafe to remember, it is my want speaks, not myself; this condition agrees not with my spirit——

E. Kno'well. Where hast thou served?

Brain-worm. May it please you, sir, in all the late wars of Bohemia, Hungaria, Dalmatia, Poland, where not, sir? I have been a poor servitor by sea and land, any time this fourteen years, and followed the fortunes of the best commanders in Christendom. I was twice shot at the taking of Aleppo, once at the relief of Vienna; I have been at Marseilles, Naples, and the Adriatic gulf, a gentleman-slave in the gallies, thrice, where I was most dangerously shot in the head, through both the thighs; and yet, being thus maimed, I am void of maintenance, nothing left me but my scars, the noted marks of my resolution.

Stephen. How will you sell this rapier, friend?

[*Takes it in his hand.*

Brain-worm. Generous sir, I refer it to your own judgment; you are a gentleman, give me what you please.

Stephen. True, I am a gentleman, I know that, friend; but what though? I pray you say, what would you ask?

Brain-worm. I assure you, the blade may become the side or thigh of the best prince, in Europe.

E. Kno'well. Ay, with a velvet scabbard, I think.

Stephen. Nay, an't be mine, it shall have a velvet scabbard, coz, that's flat; I'd not wear it as 'tis, an you would give me an angel.

Brain-worm. At your worship's pleasure, sir: [STEPHEN *examines the blade.*] nay, 'tis a most pure Toledo.

Stephen. I had rather it were a Spaniard: but tell me, what shall I give you for it? An it had a silver hilt—

E. Kno'well. Come, come, you shall not buy it;—hold, there's a shilling, fellow; take thy rapier.

Stephen. Why, but I will buy it now, because you say so, and there's another shilling, fellow, I scorn to be outbidden. What, shall I walk with a cudgel, like Higgin-bottom,[1] and may have a rapier for money!

E. Kno'well. You may buy one in the city.

Stephen. Tut! I'll buy this i' the field, so I will; I have a mind to't, because 'tis a field rapier.—Tell me your lowest price.

E. Kno'well. You shall not buy it, I say.

Stephen. By this money, but I will, though I give more than 'tis worth.

E. Kno'well. Come away, you are a fool.

Stephen. Friend, I am a fool, that's granted: but I'll have it, for that word's sake. Follow me, for your money.

Brain-worm. At your service, sir.   [*Exeunt.*

SCENE III—*Another Part of Moorfields*[2]

Enter KNO'WELL.

Kno'well. I cannot lose the thought, yet, of this letter,
Sent to my son; nor leave t' admire the change
Of manners, and the breeding of our youth
Within the kingdom, since myself was one.
When I was young, he lived not in the stews
Durst have conceived a scorn, and uttered it,
On a gray head; age was authority
Against a buffoon; and a man had then,
A certain reverence paid unto his years,
That had none due unto his life: so much
The sanctity of some prevailed for others.
But now, we all are fallen; youth, from their fear;
And age, from that which bred it, good example.
Nay, would ourselves were not the first, e'en parents,
That did destroy the hopes in our own children;
Or they not learned our vices, in their cradles,
And sucked in our ill customs, with their milk;
Ere all their teeth be born, or they can speak,
We make their palates cunning! the first words

---

[1] Probably the seditious disturber on the Earl of Shrewsbury's estates.
[2] Scene v. in old eds.

We form their tongues with, are licentious jests!
Can it call, whore? cry, bastard? O, then, kiss it!
A witty child! can't swear? the father's darling!
Give it two plums. Nay, rather than't shall learn
No bawdy song, the mother herself will teach it!
But this is in the infancy; the days
Of the long coat: when it puts on the breeches,
It will put off all this. Ay, it is like,
When it is gone into the bone already!
No, no; this dye goes deeper than the coat.
Or shirt, or skin; it stains into the liver,[1]
And heart, in some: and, rather than it should not,
Note, what we fathers do! look, how we live!
What mistresses we keep! at what expense!
In our sons' eyes! where they may handle our gifts,
Hear our lascivious courtships, see our dalliance,
Taste of the same provoking meats with us,
To ruin of our states! Nay, when our own
Portion is fled, to prey on their remainder,
We call them into fellowship of vice!
Bait 'hem with the young chamber-maid, to seal!
And teach 'hem all bad ways to buy affliction.
This is one path, but there are millions more,
In which we spoil our own, with leading them.
Well, I thank Heaven, I never yet was he
That travelled with my son, before sixteen,
To show him—the Venetian courtezans;
Nor read the grammar of cheating I had made,
To my sharp boy, at twelve; repeating still
The rule, "Get money; still, get money, boy;
No matter by what means; money will do
More, boy, than my lord's letter." Neither have I
Dressed snails, or mushrooms curiously before him,
Perfumed my sauces, and taught him to make 'hem;
Preceding still, with my gray gluttony,
At all the ordinaries,[2] and only feared
His palate should degenerate, not his manners.
These are the trade of fathers, now; however,
My son, I hope, hath met within my threshold

[1] The liver, the supposed seat of fleshly love; the heart of knowledge.
[2] Eating-houses.

None of these household precedents, which are strong,
And swift, to rape youth to their precipice.
But, let the house at home be ne'er so clean-
Swept, or kept sweet from filth, nay dust and cobwebs,
If he will live abroad with his companions,
In dung and leystals,[1] it is worth a fear:
Nor is the danger of conversing less
Than all that I have mentioned of example.

Enter BRAIN-WORM, *disguised as before.*

Brain-worm [*aside*]. My master! nay, faith, have at you; I
am fleshed now, I have sped so well.—— Worshipful sir,
I beseech you, respect the estate of a poor soldier; I am
ashamed of this base course of life—God's my comfort—
but extremity provokes me to't; what remedy?

Kno'well. I have not for you, now.

Brain-worm. By the faith I bear unto truth, gentleman, it
is no ordinary custom in me, but only to preserve manhood.
I protest to you, a man I have been; a man I may be, by
your sweet bounty.

Kno'well. 'Pray thee, good friend, be satisfied.

Brain-worm. Good sir, by that hand, you may do the part
of a kind gentleman, in lending a poor soldier the price of
two cans of beer, a matter of small value; the King of
Heaven shall pay you, and I shall rest thankful: sweet
worship.——

Kno'well. Nay, an you be so importunate——

Brain-worm. Oh, tender sir! need will have its course: I
was not made to this vile use! Well, the edge of the enemy
could not have abated me so much: it's hard when a man
hath served in his prince's cause, and be thus—[*Weeps.*]
Honourable worship, let me derive a small piece of silver
from you, it shall not be given in the course of time; by
this good ground, I was fain to pawn my rapier last night
for a poor supper; I had sucked the hilts long before, I
am a pagan else: Sweet honour——

Kno'well. Believe me, I am taken with some wonder,
To think a fellow of thy outward presence,

[1] Filth-heaps.

Should, in the frame and fashion of his mind,
Be so degenerate, and sordid-base!
Art thou a man? and sham'st thou not to beg?
To practise such a servile kind of life?
Why, were thy education ne'er so mean,
Having thy limbs, a thousand fairer courses
Offer themselves to thy election.
Either the wars might still supply thy wants,
Or service of some virtuous gentleman,
Or honest labour: nay, what can I name,
But would become thee better than to beg:
But men of thy condition feed on sloth,
As doth the beetle, on the dung she breeds in;
Not caring how the metal of your minds
Is eaten with the rust of idleness.
Now, afore me, whate'er he be, that should
Relieve a person of thy quality,
While thou insist'st in this loose desperate course,
I would esteem the sin not thine, but his.

 Brain-worm. Faith, sir, I would gladly find some other course, if so——

 Kno'well. Ay,
You'ld gladly find it, but you will not seek it.

 Brain-worm. Alas, sir, where should a man seek? in the wars, there's no ascent by desert in these days; but——and for service, would it were as soon purchased,[1] as wished for! the air's my comfort!—[*Sighs.*]—I know what I would say—

 Kno'well. What's thy name?

 Brain-worm. Please you, Fitz-Sword, sir.

 Kno'well.   Fitz-Sword!
Say that a man should entertain thee now,
Wouldst thou be honest, humble, just, and true?

 Brain-worm. Sir, by the place, and honour of a soldier——

 Kno'well. Nay, nay, I like not those affected oaths;
Speak plainly, man; what think'st thou of my words?

 Brain-worm. Nothing, sir, but wish my fortunes were as happy, as my service should be honest.

---

[1] Obtained.

Kno'well. Well, follow me; I'll prove thee, if thy deeds
Will carry a proportion to thy words.   [*Exit.*

Brain-worm. Yes, sir, straight; I'll but garter my hose. O
that my belly were hooped now, for I am ready to burst with
laughing! never was bottle or bagpipe fuller. 'Slid, was
there ever seen a fox in years to betray himself thus! now
shall I be possessed of all his counsels; and, by that conduit,
my younger master. Well, he is resolved to prove my honesty;
faith, and I'm resolved to prove his patience; oh, I shall
abuse him intolerably. This small piece of service will bring
him clean out of love with the soldier, for ever. He will
never come within the sign of it, the sight of a cassock,[1]
or a musket-rest[2] again. He will hate the musters at Mile-
end [3] for it, to his dying day. It's no matter, let the world
think me a bad counterfeit, if I cannot give him the slip[4]
at an instant: why, this is better than to have staid his
journey! well, I'll follow him. Oh, how I long to be
employed!   [*Exit.*

ACT THE THIRD

SCENE I—*A Room in the Windmill Tavern*

Enter MATTHEW, WELL-BRED, *and* BOBADILL.

MATTHEW. Yes faith, sir, we were at your lodging to seek
you, too.

Well-bred. Oh, I came not there to-night.

Bobadill. Your brother delivered us as much.

Well-bred. Who, my brother Down-right?

Bobadill. He! Master Well-bred; I know not in what kind
you hold me, but let me say to you this: as sure as honour,
I esteem it so much out of the sunshine of reputation, to
throw the least beam of regard, upon such a——

Well-bred. Sir, I must hear no ill words of my brother.

Bobadill. I protest to you, as I have a thing to be saved
about me, I never saw any gentleman-like part——

---

[1] A loose outer-coat.
[2] A staff that the musket rested on when taking aim.
[3] The training ground of the City-bands.
[4] A slip was a counterfeit coin.

Well-bred. Good captain, "faces about" [1] to some other discourse.

Bobadill. With your leave, sir, an there were no more men living upon the face of the earth, I should not fancy him, by St. George!

Matthew. Troth, nor I; he is a rustical cut, I know not how: he doth not carry himself like a gentleman of fashion.

Well-bred. Oh, Master Matthew, that's a grace peculiar but to a few, *quos æquus amavit Jupiter.*[2]

Matthew. I understand you, sir.

Well-bred. No question you do, [*Aside.*] or you do not, sir.

Enter E. KNO'WELL *and* STEPHEN.

Ned Kno'well! by my soul, welcome: how dost thou, sweet spirit, my genius? 'Slid, I shall love Apollo and the mad Thespian girls the better, while I live, for this, my dear Fury; now, I see there's some love in thee. [*Lower.*] Sirrah, these be the two I writ to thee of: nay, what a drowsy humour is this now! why dost thou not speak?

E. Kno'well. Oh, you are a fine gallant, you sent me a rare letter!

Well-bred. Why, was't not rare?

E. Kno'well. Yes, I'll be sworn, I was ne'er guilty of reading the like; match it in all Pliny, or Symmachus' epistles, and I'll have my judgment burned in the ear for a rogue: make much of thy vein, for it is inimitable. But I mar'le[3] what camel it was, that had the carriage of it; for doubtless, he was no ordinary beast that brought it!

Well-bred. Why?

E. Kno'well. "Why," say'st thou? why, dost thou think that any reasonable creature, especially in the morning, the sober time of the day too, could have mista'en my father for me?

Well-bred. 'Slid, you jest, I hope?

E. Kno'well. Indeed, the best use we can turn it to, is to make a jest on't, now; but I'll assure you, my father had the

[1] A then military term.
[2] "Whom impartial Jove has loved."—*Virgil.*
[3] Marvel.

full view o' your flourishing style, some hour before I
saw it.

Well-bred. What a dull slave was this! but, sirrah, what
said he to it, i' faith?

E. Kno'well. Nay, I know not what he said; but I have a
shrewd guess what he thought.

Well-bred. What, what?

E. Kno'well. Marry, that thou art some strange, dissolute
young fellow, and I—a grain or two better—for keeping
thee company.

Well-bred. Tut, that thought is like the moon in her last
quarter, 'twill change shortly: but, sirrah, I pray thee be
acquainted with my two hang-by's here; thou wilt take
exceeding pleasure in 'hem, if thou hear'st 'hem once go;
my wind-instruments; I'll wind 'hem up—— But what
strange piece of silence is this? the sign of the Dumb
Man?

E. Kno'well. Oh, sir, a kinsman of mine, one that may
make your music the fuller, an he please; he has his humour,
sir.

Well-bred. Oh, what is't, what is't?

E. Kno'well. Nay, I'll neither do your judgment, nor his
folly that wrong, as to prepare your apprehension: I'll leave
him to the mercy o' your search; if you can take him, so!

Well-bred. Well, Captain Bobadill, Master Matthew, 'pray
you know this gentleman here; he is a friend of mine,
and one that will deserve your affection.—[*To* STEPHEN.]
I know not your name, sir, but I shall be glad of any
occasion to render me more familiar to you.

Stephen. My name is Master Stephen, sir; I am this gentleman's own cousin, sir; his father is mine uncle, sir: I am
somewhat melancholy, but you shall command me, sir, in
whatsoever is incident to a gentleman.

Bobadill. Sir, I must tell you this, I am no general man;
but for Master Well-bred's sake, (you may embrace it at
what height of favour you please) I do communicate with
you, and conceive you to be a gentleman of some parts;
I love few words.

E. Kno'well. And I fewer, sir; I have scarce enow to thank
you.

Matthew. But are you, indeed, sir, so given to it?

Stephen. Ay, truly, sir, I am mightily given to melancholy.

Matthew. Oh it's your only fine humour, sir! your true melancholy breeds your perfect fine wit, sir. I am melancholy myself, divers times, sir, and then do I no more but take pen and paper presently, and overflow you half a score, or a dozen of sonnets at a sitting.

E. Kno'well [*aside*]. Sure he utters them then by the gross.

Stephen. Truly, sir, and I love such things, out of measure.

E. Kno'well. I'faith, better than in measure, I'll undertake.

Matthew. Why, I pray you, sir, make use of my study, it's at your service.

Stephen. I thank you, sir, I shall be bold, I warrant you; have you a stool there to be melancholy upon?

Matthew. That I have, sir, and some papers there of mine own doing, at idle hours, that you'll say there's some sparks of wit in 'hem, when you see them.

Well-bred [*aside*]. Would the sparks would kindle once and become a fire amongst 'hem! I might see self-love burnt for her heresy.

Stephen. Cousin, is it well? am I melancholy enough?

E. Kno'well. Oh ay, excellent.

Well-bred. Captain Bobadill; why muse you so?

E. Kno'well. He is melancholy too.

Bobadill. Faith, sir, I was thinking of a most honourable piece of service, was performed to-morrow, being St. Mark's day, shall be some ten years now.

E. Kno'well. In what place, captain?

Bobadill. Why at the beleaguering of Strigonium,[1] where, in less than two hours, seven hundred resolute gentlemen, as any were in Europe, lost their lives upon the breach. I'll tell you, gentlemen, it was the first, but the best leaguer that ever I beheld with these eyes, except the taking in of —what do you call it,[2] last year, by the Genoways; but that, of all other, was the most fatal and dangerous exploit that ever I was ranged in, since I first bore arms before the face of the enemy, as I am a gentleman and soldier.

[1] Graan, retaken from Turks, 1596.
[2] Tortosa in Q., but Jonson, not having a last year's siege in 1606, makes Bobadill ridiculously pretend to forget the name.

Stephen. 'So[1]! I had as lief as an angel [2] I could swear as well as that gentleman!

E. Kno'well. Then, you were a servitor at both, it seems; at Strigonium? and "What-do-you-call't"?

Bobadill. O Lord, sir! by St. George, I was the first man that entered the breach; and had I not effected it with resolution, I had been slain, if I had had a million of lives.

E. Kno'well. 'Twas pity you had not ten; [*Aside.*] a cat's and your own i'faith. But, was it possible?

Matthew [*aside to* STEPHEN]. 'Pray you mark this discourse, sir.

Stephen [*to him*]. So I do.

Bobadill. I assure you, upon my reputation, 'tis true, and yourself shall confess.

E. Kno'well [*aside*]. You must bring me to the rack, first.

Bobadill. Observe me, judicially, sweet sir; they had planted me three demi-culverins[3] just in the mouth of the breach; now sir, as we were to give on, their master-gunner (a man of no mean skill and mark, you must think) confronts me with his linstock, ready to give fire; I, spying his intendment, discharged my petronel [4] in his bosom, and with these single arms, my poor rapier, ran violently upon the Moors that guarded the ordnance, and put 'hem pell-mell to the sword.

Well-bred. To the sword! to the rapier, captain.

E. Kno'well. Oh, it was a good figure observed, sir:—but did you all this, captain, without hurting your blade?

Bobadill. Without any impeach o' the earth: you shall perceive, sir. [*Shows his rapier.*] It is the most fortunate weapon that ever rid on poor gentleman's thigh: Shall I tell you sir? You talk of Morglay, Excalibur, Durindana[5] or so; tut! I lend no credit to that is fabled of 'hem: I know the virtue of mine own, and therefore I dare, the boldlier, maintain it.

Stephen. I mar'le whether it be a Toledo or no.

Bobadill. A most perfect Toledo, I assure you, sir.

Stephen. I have a countryman of his, here.

[1] Godso.
[2] The coin. An attempt at a laughably incongruous speech.
[3] Nine-pounder cannon.
[4] A carbine-like gun.
[5] The swords of Bevis, Arthur, and of Orlando.

Matthew. 'Pray you, let's see, sir; yes, faith, it is.

Bobadill. This a Toledo! Pish!

Stephen. Why do you pish, captain?

Bobadill. A Fleming, by Heaven! I'll buy them for a guilder[1] apiece, an I would have a thousand of them.

E. Kno'well. How say you, cousin? I told you thus much.

Well-bred. Where bought you it, Master Stephen?

Stephen. Of a scurvy rogue soldier—a hundred of lice go with him—he swore it was a Toledo.

Bobadill. A poor provant[2] rapier, no better.

E. Kno'well. Nay, the longer you look on't, the worse. Put it up, put it up.

Stephen. Well, I will put it up! but by—[*To himself.*] I have forgot the captain's oath, I thought to have sworn by it—an e'er I meet him——

Well-bred. O, it is past help now, sir; you must have patience.

Stephen. Whoreson, coney-catching[3] rascal! I could eat the very hilts for anger.

E. Kno'well. A sign of good digestion! you have an ostrich-stomach, cousin.

Stephen. A stomach? would I had him here, you should see, an I had a stomach.[4]

Well-bred. It's better as 'tis.—Come, gentlemen, shall we go?

Enter BRAIN-WORM *disguised as before.*

E. Kno'well. A miracle, cousin; look here, look here!

Stephen. Oh—od's lid! By your leave, do you know me, sir?

Brain-worm. Ay, sir, I know you by sight.

Stephen. You sold me a rapier did you not?

Brain-worm. Yes, marry did I, sir.

Stephen. You said it was a Toledo, ha?

Brain-worm. True, I did so.

Stephen. But it is none.

Brain-worm. No, sir, I confess it; it is none.

Stephen. Do you confess it? Gentlemen, bear witness, he

[1] The silver coin was worth 3s. 1od., the gold, 5s. 9d.
[2] A sutler, or commissariat-provided weapon.
[3] Cheating.
[4] A stomach to beat him.

has confessed it:—Od's will, an you had not confessed it——

E. Kno'well. Oh, cousin, forbear, forbear!

Stephen. Nay, I have done, cousin.

Well-bred. Why, you have done like a gentleman; he has confessed it, what would you more?

Stephen. Yet, by his leave, he is a rascal, under his favour, do you see.

E. Kno'well [*aside to* WELL-BRED]. Ay, "by his leave," he is and "under favour": a pretty piece of civility! Sirrah, how dost thou like him?

Well-bred. Oh it's a most precious fool, make much on him: I can compare him to nothing more happily than a drum; for every one may play upon him.

E. Kno'well. No, no, a child's whistle were far the fitter.

Brain-worm. Sir, shall I intreat a word with you?

[*They move apart.*

E. Kno'well. With me, sir? you have not another Toledo to sell, ha' you?

Brain-worm. You are conceited,[1] sir: Your name is Master Kno'well, as I take it?

E. Kno'well. You are i' the right; you mean not to proceed in the catechism, do you?

Brain-worm. No sir; I am none of that coat.

E. Kno'well. Of as bare a coat, though: well, say sir.

Brain-worm. Faith, sir, I am but servant to the drum extraordinary, and indeed, this smoky varnish being washed off, and three or four patches removed, I appear—your worship's in reversion, after the decease of your good father, Brain-worm.

E. Kno'well. Brain-worm! 'Slight, what breath of a conjurer hath blown thee hither in this shape?

Brain-worm. The breath o' your letter, sir, this morning; the same that blew you to the Windmill, and your father after you.

E. Kno'well. My father?

Brain-worm. Nay, never start, 'tis true; he has followed you over the fields by the foot, as you would do a hare i' the snow.

[1] Full of pleasant conceits.

E. Kno'well. Sirrah Well-bred, what shall we do, sirrah? my father is come over, after me.

Well-bred. Thy father! Where is he?

Brain-worm. At Justice Clement's house, in Coleman-street, where he but stays my return; and then——

Well-bred. Who's this? Brain-worm!

Brain-worm. The same, sir.

Well-bred. Why how, in the name of wit, com'st thou transmuted thus?

Brain-worm. Faith, a device, a device;—nay, for the love of reason, gentlemen, and avoiding the danger, stand not here; withdraw, and I'll tell you all.

Well-bred. But, art thou sure, he will stay thy return?

Brain-worm. Do I live, sir? what a question is that!

Well-bred. We'll prorogue his expectation, then, a little: Brain-worm, thou shalt go with us.——Come on, gentlemen.—— Nay, I pray thee, sweet Ned, droop not; 'heart, an our wits be so wretchedly dull, that one old plodding brain can outstrip us all, would we were e'en pressed [1] to make porters of, and serve out the remnant of our days in Thames-street, or at Custom-house key, in a civil war against the carmen!

Brain-worm. Amen, Amen, Amen, say I.   [*Exeunt.*

SCENE II—Kitely's *Warehouse*[2]

Enter Kitely *and* Cash.

Kitely. What says he, Thomas? Did you speak with him?

Cash. He will expect you, sir, within this half-hour.

Kitely. Has he the money ready, can you tell?

Cash. Yes, sir, the money was brought in, last night.

Kitely. O, that is well; fetch me my cloak, my cloak!—
                                        [*Exit* Cash.

Stay, let me see, an hour, to go and come;
Ay, that will be the least; and then 'twill be
An hour, before I can despatch with him,
Or very near: well, I will say two hours.
Two hours? ha! things never dreamt of yet,
May be contrived, ay, and effected too,

[1] Impressed.
[2] Scene iii. in old eds.

In two hours' absence; well I will not go.
Two hours! No, fleering Opportunity,
I will not give your subtilty that scope.
Who will not judge him worthy to be robbed,
That sets his doors wide open to a thief,
And shows the felon, where his treasure lies?
Again, what earthly spirit but will attempt
To taste the fruit of beauty's golden tree,
When leaden sleep seals up the dragon's eyes?
I will not go.

Re-enter CASH *with cloak.*

Business, "go by" for once.
No, beauty, no; you are of too good caract,[1]
To be left so, without a guard, or open!
Your lustre too, 'll inflame, at any distance,
Draw courtship to you, as a Jet doth straws;
Put motion in a stone, strike fire from ice,
Nay, make a porter leap you, with his burden.
You must be then kept up, close, and well watched,
For, give you opportunity, no quick-sand
Devours, or swallows swifter! He that lends
His wife—if she be fair—or time, or place,
Compels her to be false. I will not go.
The dangers are too many.—And then the dressing
Is a most main attractive! Our great heads,
Within the city, never were in safety,
Since our wives wore these little caps: I'll change 'hem;
I'll change 'hem straight, in mine: mine shall no more
Wear three-piled [2] acorns, to make my horns ache.
Nor will I go. I am resolved for that.
Carry in my cloak again.—Yet stay.—Yet do, too:
I will defer going, on all occasions.

    Cash. Sir, Snare, your scrivener, will be there with th'
bonds.

    Kitely. That's true! fool on me! I had clean forgot it;
I must go. What's a-clock?

    Cash.   Exchange-time, sir.

    Kitely. 'Heart, then will Well-bred presently be here, too,
With one or other of his loose consorts.

---

[1] Carat, equivalent to quality, value.
[2] Therefore of best quality velvet.

I am a knave, if I know what to say,
What course to take, or which way to resolve.
My brain, methinks, is like an hour-glass,
Wherein my imaginations run like sands,
Filling up time; but then are turned, and turned:
So that I know not what to stay upon,
And less, to put in act.—It shall be so.
Nay, I dare build upon his secrecy,
He knows not to deceive me.—Thomas!

    Cash.   Sir.

    Kitely. Yet now I have bethought me too, I will not.—
Thomas, is Cob within?

    Cash.   I think he be, sir.

    Kitely. But he'll prate too, there is no speech of him.
No, there were no man o' the earth to Thomas,
If I durst trust him; there is all the doubt.
But, should he have a chink in him, I were gone,
Lost i' my fame for ever, talk for th' Exchange!
The manner he hath stood with, till this present,
Doth promise no such change! what should I fear then?
Well, come what will, I'll tempt my fortune, once.
Thomas—you may deceive me, but, I hope—
Your love to me is more——

    Cash.   Sir, if a servant's
Duty, with faith, may be called love, you are
More than in hope,—you are possessed of it.

    Kitely. I thank you, heartily, Thomas: gi' me your hand:
With all my heart,[1] good Thomas. I have, Thomas,
A secret to impart, unto you——but,
When once you have it, I must seal your lips up:——
So far I tell you, Thomas.

    Cash.   Sir, for that——

    Kitely. Nay, hear me out. Think, I esteem you, Thomas,
When I will let you in, thus, to my private.
It is a thing sits nearer to my crest,
Than thou art 'ware of, Thomas. If thou should'st
Reveal it, but——

    Cash.   How! I reveal it?

    Kitely.   Nay,

---

[1] Said as Kitely gives his own hand.

I do not think thou would'st; but if thou should'st:
'Twere a great weakness.
    Cash.   A great treachery:
Give it no other name.
    Kitely.   Thou wilt not do't, then?
    Cash. Sir, if I do, mankind disclaim me ever!   [tion,
    Kitely [*aside*]. He will not swear, he has some reserva-
Some concealed purpose, and close meaning, sure;
Else, being urged so much, how should he choose
But lend an oath to all this protestation?
He's no precisian, that I am certain of,
Nor rigid Roman Catholic. He'll play
At fayles, and tick-tack;[1] I have heard him swear.
What should I think of it? urge him again,
And by some other way? I will do so.——
Well, Thomas, thou hast sworn not to disclose:—
Yes, you did swear?
    Cash.   Not yet, sir, but I will,
Please you——
    Kitely.   No, Thomas, I dare take thy word,
But; if thou wilt swear, do as thou think'st good;
I am resolved without it;—at thy pleasure.
    Cash. By my soul's safety then, sir, I protest,
My tongue shall ne'er take knowledge of a word
Delivered me in nature of your trust.
    Kitely. It's too much; these ceremonies need not:
I know thy faith to be as firm as rock.
Thomas, come hither, near: we cannot be
Too private in this business. So it is,——
[*Aside.*] Now he has sworn, I dare the safelier venture.——
I have of late, by divers observations—
[*Aside.*] But, whether his oath can bind him, yea, or no,
Being not taken lawfully? ha?—say you?—
[*Aside.*] I will ask counsel, ere I do proceed——
Thomas, it will be now too long to stay,
I'll spy some fitter time soon, or to-morrow.
    Cash. Sir, at your pleasure.
    Kitely.   I will think:—and, Thomas,
I pray you search the books 'gainst my return,

[1] Varieties of backgammon.

For the receipts 'twixt me, and Traps.

 Cash.   I will, sir.

 Kitely. And hear you, if your mistress' brother, Well-bred,
Chance to bring hither any gentlemen,
Ere I come back; let one straight bring me word.

 Cash. Very well, sir.

 Kitely.   To the Exchange, do you[1] hear?
Or here in Coleman-street, to Justice Clement's.
Forget it not, nor be not out of the way.

 Cash. I will not, sir.

 Kitely.   I pray you have a care on't.
Or, whether he come or no, if any other,
Stranger, or else; fail not to send me word.

 Cash. I shall not, sir.

 Kitely.   Be't your special business
Now to remember it.

 Cash.   Sir, I warrant you.

 Kitely. But, Thomas, this is not the secret, Thomas,
I told you of.

 Cash.   No, sir; I do suppose it.

 Kitely. Believe me, it is not.

 Cash.   Sir, I do believe you.

 Kitely. By Heaven it is not, that's enough. But, Thomas,
I would not, you should utter it, do you see,
To any creature living,—yet, I care not.
Well, I must hence. Thomas, conceive thus much;
It was a trial of you, when I meant
So deep a secret to you, I mean not this,
But that I have to tell you; this is nothing, this.
But, Thomas, keep this from my wife, I charge you,
Locked up in silence, midnight, buried here.—

             [Touches his temple.

[*Aside.*] No greater hell than to be slave to fear. [*Exit.*

 Cash. "Locked up in silence, midnight, buried here!"
Whence should this flood of passion, trow, take head? ha?
Best dream no longer of this running humour,
For fear I sink! the violence of the stream
Already hath transported me so far,

---

[1] Should be pronounced "d'ye."

That I can feel no ground at all! but soft—
Oh, 'tis our water-bearer: somewhat has crossed him now.

Enter COB.[1]

Cob. Fasting-days! what tell you me of fasting-days? 'Slid, would they were all on a light fire for me! They say the whole world shall be consumed with fire one day, but would I had these Ember-weeks and villanous Fridays burnt, in the mean time, and then——

Cash. Why, how now, Cob? what moves thee to this choler, ha?

Cob. Collar, Master Thomas! I scorn your collar, I, sir, I am none o' your cart-horse, though I carry and draw water. An you offer to ride me, with your collar, or halter either, I may hap show you a jade's trick, sir.

Cash. O, you'll slip your head out of the collar? why, goodman Cob, you mistake me.

Cob. Nay, I have my rheum,[2] and I can be angry as well as another, sir.

Cash. Thy rheum, Cob? thy humour, thy humour—thou mistak'st.

Cob. Humour! mack,[3] I think it be so indeed; what is that humour? some rare thing, I warrant.

Cash. Marry, I'll tell thee, Cob: it is a gentleman-like monster, bred in the special gallantry of our time, by affectation; and fed by folly.

Cob. How! must it be fed?

Cash. Oh ay, humour is nothing, if it be not fed. Did'st thou never hear that? it's a common phrase, "Feed my humour."

Cob. I'll none on it: humour, avaunt! I know you not, be gone! Let who will make hungry meals for your monstership, it shall not be I. Feed you, quoth he! 'slid, I ha' much ado to feed myself; especially on these lean rascally days, too; an't had been any other day but a fasting-day—a plague on them all for me—by this light, one might have

---

[1] Scene iv. in old eds.

[2] He was not up in the four humours, but may have heard that "some fleame is salt hot and dry through infection of red choler."

[3] The innocent substitute for "mass."

done the commonwealth good service, and have drowned
them all i' the flood, two or three hundred thousand years
ago. O, I do stomach[1] them hugely. I have a maw[2] now, an
'twere for Sir Bevis his horse, against 'hem.

Cash. I pray thee, good Cob, what makes thee so out of
love with fasting-days?

Cob. Marry, that which will make any man out of love
with 'hem, I think: their bad conditions, an you will needs
know. First, they are of a Flemish breed, I am sure on't,
for they ravin up more butter than all the days of the
week beside: next, they stink of fish, and leek-porridge miserably: thirdly, they'll keep a man devoutly hungry, all day,
and at night send him supperless to bed.

Cash. Indeed, these are faults, Cob.

Cob. Nay, an this were all, 'twere something, but they
are the only known enemies to my generation. A fasting-day
no sooner comes, but my lineage goes to wrack; poor cobs!
they smoke for it, they are made martyrs o' the gridiron, they
melt in passion: and your maids too know this, and yet
would have me turn Hannibal,[3] and eat my own fish and
blood. My princely coz, [*Pulls out a red herring.*] fear nothing; I have not the heart to devour you, an I might be made
as rich as King Cophetua. Oh, that I had room for my tears,
I could weep salt-water enough now to preserve the lives
of ten thousand of my kin. But I may curse none but these
filthy almanacs; for an't were not for them, these days of
persecution would ne'er be known. I'll be hanged, an some
fishmonger's son do not make of 'hem, and puts in more
fasting-days than he should do, because he would utter[4] his
father's dried stock-fish and stinking conger.

Cash. 'Slight peace! thou'lt be beaten like a stock-fish[5]
else; here's Master Matthew. [*Aside.*] Now must I look out
for a messenger to my master.   [*Exit with* COB.

Enter WELL-BRED, E. KNO'WELL, BRAIN-WORM, MATTHEW,
          BOBADILL, *and* STEPHEN.[6]

---

[1] Am angry with.
[2] Stomach, *i.e.* appetite.
[3] He should say "cannibal."
[4] Send out, sell.
[5] Stock-fish was so hard salted, &c., that it had to be beaten before
being cooked.
[6] Scene v. in old eds.

Well-bred. Beshrew me, but it was an absolute good jest, and exceedingly well carried!

E. Kno'well. Ay, and our ignorance maintained it as well, did it not?

Well-bred. Yes faith; but was't possible thou shouldst not know him? I forgive Master Stephen, for he is stupidity itself.

E. Kno'well. 'Fore God, not I, an I might have been joined patten[1] with one of the Seven Wise Masters for knowing him. He had so writhen himself into the habit of one of your poor infantry, your decayed, ruinous worm-eaten gentlemen of the round [2]; such as have vowed to sit on the skirts of the city, let your provost and his half-dozen of halberdiers do what they can; and have translated begging, out of the old hackney pace to a fine easy amble, and made it run as smooth off the tongue as a shove-groat shilling.[3] Into the likeness of one of these reformados[4] had he moulded himself so perfectly, observing every trick of their action, as, varying the accent, swearing with an emphasis, indeed, all, with so special and exquisite a grace, that hadst thou seen him, thou wouldst have sworn he might have been sergeant-major,[5] if not lieutenant-colonel to the regiment.

Well-bred. Why, Brain-worm, who would have thought thou hadst been such an artificer?

E. Kno'well. An artificer? an architect! Except a man had studied begging all his life time, and been a weaver of language from his infancy, for the clothing of it, I never saw his rival.

Well-bred. Where got'st thou this coat, I mar'le?

Brain-worm. Of a Hounsditch man, sir, one of the devil's near kinsmen, a broker.

Well-bred. That cannot be, if the proverb hold, for "A crafty knave needs no broker."

Brain-worm. True, sir; but I did "need a broker," ergo—

Well-bred. Well put off;—"no crafty knave," you'll say.

[1] Joined by a patent.
[2] Sub-officers of the guard inspecting sentinels, &c.
[3] A smooth shilling used at shovel-board.
[4] Disbanded officers.
[5] The then major.

E. Kno'well. Tut, he has more of these shifts.

Brain-worm. And yet, where I have one the broker has ten,[1] sir.

Re-enter CASH.

Cash. Francis! Martin! ne'er a one to be found, now? what a spite's this!

Well-bred. How now, Thomas? is my brother Kitely within?

Cash. No sir, my master went forth e'en now; but Master Down-right is within.—Cob! what, Cob! Is he gone too?

Well-bred. Whither went your master? Thomas, canst thou tell?

Cash. I know not; to Justice Clement's, I think, sir— Cob!   [*Exit.*

E. Kno'well. Justice Clement! what's he?

Well-bred. Why, dost thou not know him? He is a city-magistrate, a justice here, an excellent good lawyer, and a great scholar; but the only mad, merry old fellow in Europe. I showed him you, the other day.

E. Kno'well. Oh, is that he? I remember him now. Good faith, and he has a very strange presence, methinks; it shows as if he stood out of the rank from other men: I have heard many of his jests i' the University. They say, he will commit a man for taking the wall of his horse.

Well-bred. Ay, or wearing his cloak of one shoulder, or serving of God; any thing, indeed, if it come in the way of his humour.

CASH *comes in and out, calling.*

Cash. Gasper!—Martin!—Cob! 'Heart, where should they be, trow?

Bobadill. Master Kitely's man, pray thee vouchsafe us the lighting of this match.

Cash [*aside after taking it*]. Fire on your match! no time but now to "vouchsafe"?—Francis!—Cob!   [*Exit.*

Bobadill. Body o' me! here's the remainder of seven

---

[1] A pun: devices, and shifts of apparel.

pound, since yesterday was seven-night. 'Tis your right
Trinidado! did you never take any, Master Stephen?

Stephen. No truly, sir; but I'll learn to take it now, since
you commend it so.

Bobadill. Sir, believe me, upon my relation, for what I tell
you, the world shall not reprove. I have been in the Indies,
where this herb grows, where neither myself, nor a dozen
gentlemen more, of my knowledge, have received the taste
of any other nutriment in the world, for the space of one
and twenty weeks, but the fume of this simple only: therefore, it cannot be, but 'tis most divine! Further, take it in
the nature, in the true kind, so, it makes an antidote, that,
had you taken the most deadly poisonous plant in all Italy,
it should expel it, and clarify you, with as much ease, as I
speak. And for your green wound, your Balsamum and
your St. John's wort, are all mere gulleries, and trash to it,
especially your Trinidado: your Nicotian is good too. I
could say what I know of the virtue of it, for the expulsion
of rheums, raw humours, crudities, obstructions, with a
thousand of this kind; but I profess myself no quacksalver.
Only thus much, by Hercules, I do hold it, and will affirm
it, before any prince in Europe, to be the most sovereign,
and precious weed, that ever the earth tendered to the use
of man.

E. Kno'well. This speech would ha' done decently in a
tobacco-trader's mouth.

Re-enter CASH *with* COB.

Cash. At Justice Clement's he is, in the middle of Coleman-street.

Cob. Oh, oh!

Bobadill. Where's the match I gave thee, Master Kitely's
man?

Cash [*aside*]. Would his match, and he, and pipe, and
all, were at Sancto Domingo! I had forgot it.   [*Exit.*

Cob. By Gods me, I mar'le what pleasure or felicity they
have in taking this roguish tobacco! it's good for nothing
but to choke a man, and fill him full of smoke, and embers:
there were four died out of one house, last week, with taking
of it, and two more the bell went for, yesternight; one of

them, they say, will ne'er scape it: he voided a bushel of
soot yesterday, upward, and downward.[1] By the stocks, an
there were no wiser men than I, I'ld have it present whipping, man, or woman, that should but deal with a tobacco
pipe: why, it will stifle them all in the end, as many as
use it; it's little better than ratsbane,[2] or rosaker.[3]

[*BOBADILL cudgels him.*

All. Oh, good captain, hold, hold!
Bobadill. You base cullion,[4] you!

Re-enter CASH.

Cash. Sir, here's your match.——Come, thou must needs
be talking too, thou'rt well enough served.

Cob. Nay, he will not meddle with his match, I warrant
you: well, it shall be a dear beating, an I live.

Bobadill. Do you prate? do you murmur?

E. Kno'well. Nay, good captain, will you regard the
humour of a fool?——Away, knave.

Well-bred. Thomas, get him away. [*Exit* CASH *with* COB.

Bobadill. A whoreson filthy slave, a dung-worm, an
excrement! Body o' Cæsar, but that I scorn to let forth so
mean a spirit, I'ld ha' stabbed him to the earth.

Well-bred. Marry, the law forbid, sir.

Bobadill. By Pharaoh's foot, I would have done it.

Stephen [*to himself*]. Oh, he swears most admirably! "By
Pharaoh's foot!"—"Body o' Cæsar!" I shall never do it, sure.
"Upon mine honour, and by St. George!"—No, I ha' not the
right grace.

Matthew. Master Stephen, will you any? By this air, the
most divine tobacco that ever I drunk.[5]

Stephen. None, I thank you, sir. [*To himself.*] O, this
gentleman does it rarely too: but nothing like the other.
[*Practising to the post.*] "By this air!"—"As I am a gentleman!" "By——

Brain-worm [*pointing to* STEPHEN]. Master, glance, glance!
—Master Well-bred!   [*Exeunt* BOBADILL *and* MATTHEW.[6]

[1] An exaggerated form of King James's statement.
[2] White arsenic.
[3] The proto-sulphret of the same.
[4] Cowardly stinkard.
[5] The then common phrase.
[6] Here, or during the next two or three speeches.

Stephen. "As I have somewhat to be saved, I protest—"

Well-bred [*aside*]. You are a fool; it needs no affidavit.

E. Kno'well. Cousin, will you any tobacco?

Stephen. I, sir! Upon my reputation——

E. Kno'well. How now, cousin!

Stephen. I protest, as I am a gentleman, but no soldier, indeed——

Well-bred. No, Master Stephen? As I remember, your name is entered in the artillery-garden.

Stephen. Ay, sir, that's true. Cousin, may I swear, "as I am a soldier" by that?

E. Kno'well. O yes, that you may: it's all you have for your money.

Stephen. Then, as I am a gentleman, and a soldier, it is "divine tobacco!"

Well-bred. But soft, where's Master Matthew? Gone?

Brain-worm. No, sir, they went in here.

Well-bred. O, let's follow them: Master Matthew is gone to salute his mistress in verse. We shall have the happiness to hear some of his poetry now. He never comes unfurnished.—Brain-worm!

Stephen. Brain-worm? Where? Is this Brain-worm?

E. Kno'well. Ay, cousin; no words of it, upon your gentility.

Stephen. Not I, body o' me! By this air! St. George! and the foot of Pharaoh!

Well-bred. Rare! your cousin's discourse is simply drawn out with oaths.

E. Kno'well. 'Tis larded with 'hem; a kind of French dressing, if you love it.   [*Exeunt.*

SCENE III—*A Room in* Justice Clement's *House*[1]

Enter Kitely *and* Cob.

Kitely. Ha! how many are there, say'st thou?

Cob. Marry, sir, your brother, Master Well-bred——

Kitely. Tut, beside him: what strangers are there, man?

Cob. Strangers? let me see, one, two;—mass, I know not well, there are so many.

[1] Scene vi. in old eds.

Kitely. How! so many?

Cob. Ay, there's some five or six of them, at the most.

Kitely [*aside*]. A swarm, a swarm!

Spite of the devil, how they sting my head

With forkèd stings, thus wide and large!——But, Cob,

How long hast thou been coming hither, Cob?

Cob. A little while, sir.

Kitely.   Didst thou come running?

Cob.   No, sir,

Kitely [*aside*]. Nay, then I am familiar with thy haste!

Bane to my fortunes; what meant I to marry?

I, that before was ranked in such content,

My mind at rest too, in so soft a peace,

Being free master of mine own free thoughts,

And now become a slave? What? never sigh,

Be of good cheer, man; for thou art a cuckold,

'Tis done, 'tis done! nay, when such flowing store,

Plenty itself, falls in my wife's[1] lap,

The cornucopiæ will be mine, I know.——But, Cob,

What entertainment had they? I am sure

My sister, and my wife would bid them welcome: ha?

Cob. Like enough, sir; yet I heard not a word of it.

Kitely. No; their lips were sealed with kisses, and the voice—

Drowned in a flood of joy, at their arrival—

Had lost her motion, state, and faculty.——

Cob, which of them was't that first kissed my wife?

My sister, I should say; my wife, alas!

I fear not her: ha? who was it, say'st thou?

Cob. By my troth, sir, will you have the troth of it?

Kitely. Oh ay, good Cob, I pray thee, heartily.

Cob. Then I am a vagabond, and fitter for Bridewell than your worship's company, if I saw any body to be kissed, unless they would have kissed the post,[2] in the middle of the warehouse; for there I left them all, at their tobacco, with a pox!

Kitely. How? were they not gone in, then, ere thou cam'st?

Cob. O no, sir.

---

[1] "Wives," Q. and Ff., seems to be used as a dissyllable.

[2] An attempted witticism, for it meant to be shut out from meals.

Kitely. Spite of the devil! what do I stay here then? Cob, follow me.   [*Exit.*

Cob. Nay, soft and fair; I have eggs on the spit[1]; I cannot go yet, sir. Now am I, for some five and fifty reasons, hammering, hammering revenge: oh, for three or four gallons of vinegar, to sharpen my wits! Revenge, vinegar revenge, vinegar and mustard revenge! Nay, an he had not lien in my house, 'twould never have grieved me, but being my guest, one, that I'll be sworn, my wife has lent him her smock off her back, while his one shirt has been at washing; pawned her neck-kerchers for clean bands for him; sold almost all my platters, to buy him tobacco; and he to turn monster of ingratitude, and strike his lawful host! well, I hope to raise up an host of fury for't: here comes Justice Clement.

Enter CLEMENT, KNO'WELL, *and* FORMAL.

Clement. What's Master Kitely gone? Roger?

Formal. Ay, sir.

Clement. 'Heart of me! what made him leave us so abruptly?—How now, sirrah? what make you here? what would you have, ha?

Cob. An't please your worship, I am a poor neighbour of your worship's——

Clement. A poor neighbour of mine! why, speak, poor neighbour.

Cob. I dwell, sir, at the sign of the Water-tankard, hard by the Green Lattice: I have paid scot and lot[2] there, any time this eighteen years.

Clement. To the Green Lattice?

Cob. No, sir, to the parish: marry, I have seldom scaped scot-free at the Lattice.

Clement. O, well! what business has my poor neighbour with me?

Cob. An't like your worship, I am come, to crave the peace of your worship.

Clement. Of me, knave? Peace of me, knave! Did I ever hurt thee? or threaten thee? or wrong thee, ha?

[1] Work to do.
[2] Portion and charge, *i.e.* rates, taxes, &c.

Cob. No, sir, but your worship's warrant for one that has wronged me, sir; his arms are at too much liberty, I would fain have them bound to a treaty of peace, an my credit could compass it with your worship.

Clement. Thou goest far enough about for't, I'm sure.

Kno'well. Why, dost thou go in danger of thy life for him, friend?

Cob. No, sir; but I go in danger of my death every hour, by his means; an I die within a twelve-month and a day, I may swear, by the law of the land, that he killed me.

Clement. How? how, knave? swear he killed thee? and by the law? What pretence? what colour hast thou for that?

Cob. Marry, an't please your worship, both black, and blue; colour enough, I warrant you. I have it here, to show your worship.   [*Bares his arm.*

Clement. What is he, that gave you this, sirrah?

Cob. A gentleman, and a soldier, he says, he is, o' the city here.

Clement. A soldier o' the city! What call you him?

Cob. Captain Bobadill.

Clement. Bobadill! and why did he bob,[1] and beat you, sirrah? How began the quarrel betwixt you, ha? speak truly, knave, I advise you.

Cob. Marry, indeed, an't please your worship, only because I spake against their vagrant tobacco, as I came by 'hem when they were taking on't; for nothing else.

Clement. Ha! you speak against tobacco? Formal, his name.

Formal. What's your name, sirrah?

Cob. Oliver, sir, Oliver Cob, sir.

Clement. Tell Oliver Cob, he shall go to the jail, Formal.

Formal. Oliver Cob, my master, Justice Clement says, you shall go to the jail.

Cob. O, I beseech your worship, for God's sake, dear Master Justice!

Clement. Nay God's precious! an such drunkards, and tankards as you are, come to dispute of tobacco once, I have done: Away with him!

[1] Strike.

Cob. O, good Master Justice! [*To* KNO'WELL.] Sweet old gentleman!

Kno'well. "Sweet Oliver," [1] would I could do thee any good!—Justice Clement, let me intreat you, sir.

Clement. What? a thread-bare rascal! a beggar! a slave that never drunk out of better than piss-pot metal [2] in his life! and he to deprave and abuse the virtue of an herb so generally received in the courts of princes, the chambers of nobles, the bowers of sweet ladies, the cabins of soldiers!— Roger, away with him! By God's precious—[COB *would implore.*]—I say, go to.

Cob. Dear Master Justice, let me be beaten again, have deserved it; but not the prison, I beseech you.

Kno'well. Alas, poor Oliver!

Clement. Roger, make him a warrant:—he shall not go, I but fear[3] the knave.

Formal. Do not stink, sweet Oliver, you shall not go; my master will give you a warrant.

Cob. O, the Lord maintain his worship, his worthy worship!

Clement. Away, dispatch him. [*Exeunt* FORMAL *with* COB.] How now, Master Kno'well, in dumps, in dumps! Come, this becomes not.

Kno'well. Sir, would I could not feel my cares—

Clement. Your cares are nothing: they are like my cap, soon put on, and as soon put off. What! your son is old enough to govern himself; let him run his course, it's the only way to make him a staid [4] man. If he were an unthrift, a ruffian, a drunkard, or a licentious liver, then you had reason; you had reason to take care: but being none of these, mirth's my witness, an I had twice so many cares as you have, I'd drown them all in a cup of sack.[5] Come, come, let's try it [*Takes some.*]: I muse your parcel of a soldier returns not all this while.   [*Exeunt.*

---

[1] A song commenced thus, and the epithet was also applied to the Oliver of the twelve Peers of France.
[2] Pewter.
[3] Make him to fear.
[4] A pun, stayed.
[5] A white wine, generally sherry.

ACT THE FOURTH

SCENE I—*A Room in* KITELY'S *House*

Enter DOWN-RIGHT *and* Dame KITELY.

DOWN-RIGHT. Well, sister, I tell you true; and you'll find it
so in the end.

Dame Kitely. Alas, brother, what would you have me to
do? I cannot help it; you see my brother brings 'hem in
here; they are his friends.

Down-right. His friends? his fiends. 'Slud! they do nothing but haunt him, up and down like a sort of unlucky
sprites, and tempt him to all manner of villainy that can
be thought of. Well, by this light, a little thing would make
me play the devil with some of 'hem: an 'twere not more for
your husband's sake than anything else, I'd make the house
too hot for the best on 'hem: they should say and swear,
hell were broken loose, ere they went hence. But, by God's
will, 'tis nobody's fault but yours; for an you had done, as
you might have done, they should have been perboiled,[1]
and baked too, every mother's son, ere they should ha' come
in, e'er a one of 'hem.

Dame Kitely. God's my life! did you ever hear the like?
what a strange man is this! Could I keep out all them, think
you? I should put myself against half a dozen men, should
I? Good faiths, you'ld mad the patient'st body in the
world, to hear you talk so, without any sense or reason!

Enter Mistress BRIDGET, *with* Master MATTHEW, *and*
BOBADILL; *followed, at a little distance, by* WELL-BRED,
E. KNO'WELL, STEPHEN, *and* BRAIN-WORM[2]

Bridget. Servant, in troth, you are too prodigal
Of your wit's treasure, thus to pour it forth
Upon so mean a subject, as my worth!

Matthew. You say well, mistress; and I mean as well.

Down-right. Hoy-day, here is stuff!

Well-bred. O, now stand close[3]; pray Heaven, she can get

---

[1] Boiled through and through. Not parboiled.
[2] Scene ii. in old eds.
[3] Secret, quietly apart.

him to read! He should do it, of his own natural impudency.

Bridget. Servant, what is this same, I pray you?

Matthew. Marry, an elegy, an elegy, an odd toy——

Down-right [*aside*]. "To mock an ape withal!" [1] O, I could sew up his mouth, now.

Dame Kitely. Sister, I pray you let's hear it.

Down-right. Are you rhyme-given too?

Matthew. Mistress, I'll read it, if you please.

Bridget. Pray you do, servant.

Down-right [*to himself*]. O, here's no foppery! Death! I can endure the stocks better.   [*Exit.*

E. Kno'well. What ails thy brother? can he not hold his water, at reading of a ballad?

Well-bred. O, no; a rhyme to him is worse than cheese, or a bag-pipe. But mark; you lose the protestation.

Matthew. Faith, I did it in a humour; I know not how it is; but—please you come near, sir. This gentleman has judgment, he knows how to censure of a——pray you, sir, you can judge.

Stephen. Not I, sir; upon my reputation, and by the foot of Pharaoh.

Well-bred. O, chide your cousin for swearing.

E. Kno'well. Not I, so long as he does not forswear himself.

Bobadill. Master Matthew, you abuse the expectation of your dear mistress, and her fair sister: fie! while you live, avoid this prolixity.

Matthew. I shall, sir; well, *incipere dulce.*[2]

E. Kno'well. How! *insipere dulce?* [3] a sweet thing to be a fool, indeed!

Well-bred. What, do you take *insipere* in that sense?

E. Kno'well. You do not? you? This was your villainy, to gull him with a *mot.*[4]

Well-bred. O, the benchers' phrase: "*pauca verba, pauca verba!*" [5]

---

[1] Proverbial saying, meaning to deceive a simpleton with.

[2] It is sweet to begin.

[3] Explained in next clause.

[4] French for "motto."

[5] "Few words": I take this to be the exclamation of the benchers of the Inns of Court at the disputations held for exercise sake.

Matthew [*reads*]. "Rare creature, let me speak without
    offence,
Would God my rude words had the influence
To rule thy thoughts, as thy fair looks do mine,
Then shouldst thou be his prisoner, who is thine."

    E. Kno'well. This is in "Hero and Leander." [1]

    Well-bred. O, ay! peace, we shall have more of this.

    Matthew. "Be not unkind and fair: misshapen stuff
Is of behaviour boisterous and rough." [1]

    Well-bred. How like you that, sir?

                             [STEPHEN *nods several times.*

    E. Kno'well. 'Slight, he shakes his head like a bottle, to
feel an there be any brain in it.

    Matthew. But observe "the catastrophe," now:
"And I in duty will exceed all other,
As you in beauty do excel Love's mother." [1]

    E. Kno'well. Well, I'll have him free of the wit-brokers,
for he utters nothing but stolen remnants.

    Well-bred. O, forgive it him.

    E. Kno'well. A filching rogue, hang him!—and from the
dead! it's worse than sacrilege.

    WELL-BRED, E. KNO'WELL, *and* STEPHEN *come forward.*

    Well-bred. Sister, what ha' you here?—verses? 'pray you,
let's see. Who made these verses? they are excellent good.

    Matthew. O, Master Well-bred, 'tis your disposition to say
so, sir. They were good i' the morning; I made 'hem *extempore* this morning.

    Well-bred. How? *extempore?*

    Matthew. Ay, would I might be hanged else; ask Captain
Bobadill: he saw me write them, at the——pox on it!—the
Star, yonder.

    Brain-worm. Can he find in his heart, to curse the stars so?

    E. Kno'well. Faith, his are even with him; they ha' curst
him enough already.

    Stephen. Cousin, how do you like this gentleman's verse?

    E. Kno'well. O, admirable! the best that ever I heard, coz.

[1] Marlowe's poem, book i., ll. 197—202—5, 219—20, with seven verbal
alterations.

Stephen. Body o' Cæsar, they are admirable!
The best that ever I heard, as I'm a soldier!

Re-enter DOWN-RIGHT.

Down-right. I am vext, I can hold ne'er a bone of me
still! 'Heart, I think they mean to build and breed here.

Well-bred. Sister, you have a simple servant here, that
crowns your beauty with such encomiums, and devices: you
may see what it is, to be the mistress of a wit, that can make
your perfections so transparent, that every blear eye may
look through them, and see him drowned, over head and
ears, in the deep well of desire. Sister Kitely, I marvel you
get you not a servant that can rhyme, and do tricks too.

Down-right. Oh monster! impudence itself! tricks!

Dame Kitely. Tricks, brother? what tricks?

Bridget. Nay, speak, I pray you, what tricks?

Dame Kitely. Ay, never spare any body here; but say,
what tricks.

Bridget. Passion of my heart! do tricks!

Well-bred. 'Slight, here's a trick vied and revied! [1]
Why, you monkeys, you? what a cater-wauling do you keep!
has he not given you rhymes, and verses, and tricks?

Down-right. O, the fiend!

Well-bred. Nay, you lamp of virginity, that take it in
snuff [2] so, come, and cherish this tame poetical fury in your
servant, you'll be begged else shortly for a concealment: [3]
go to, reward his muse. You cannot give him less than a
shilling, in conscience, for the book he had it out of, cost
him a teston [4] at least. How now, gallants? Master Matthew?
Captain? What, all sons of silence? no spirit?

Down-right. Come, you might practise your ruffian trick
somewhere else, and not here. I wuss; this is no tavern, nor
drinking-school, to vent your exploits in.

Well-bred. How now! whose cow has calved? [5]

Down-right. Marry, that has mine, sir. Nay, boy, never

---

[1] Seen and re-seen, *i.e.* betted and re-betted on.
[2] In anger.
[3] Monastery lands, &c., unauthorizedly kept.
[4] Sixpence, but it varied in value.
[5] Who is bragging?

look askance at me for the matter; I'll tell you of it, I, sir;
you and your companions mend yourselves when I ha' done.

Well-bred. My companions?

Down-right. Yes sir, your companions, so I say, I am not
afraid of you, nor them neither; your hangbyes here. You
must have your poets, and your potlings,[1] your soldados, and
foolados to follow you up and down the city, and here they
must come to domineer and swagger.—Sirrah, you ballad-
singer, and slops[2] your fellow there, get you out, get you
home; or, by this steel, I'll cut off your ears and that
presently.

Well-bred. 'Slight, stay, let's see what he dare do: cut off
his ears? cut a whetstone! You are an ass, do you see! touch
any man here, and, by this hand, I'll run my rapier to the
hilts in you.

Down-right. Yea, that would I fain see, boy.

                        [They all draw.

Dame Kitely. O Jesu! murder! Thomas! Gasper!

Bridget. Help, help! Thomas!

  Enter CASH *and some of the house to part them. The*
        women continue their cries.

E. Kno'well. Gentlemen, forbear, I pray you.

Bobadill. Well, sirrah, you Holofernes; by my hand, I will
pink your flesh full of holes with my rapier for this; I will,
by this good Heaven!—Nay, let him come, let him come,
gentlemen; by the body of St. George, I'll not kill him.

        [They offer to fight again, and are parted.

Cash. Hold, hold, good gentlemen.

Down-right. You whoreson, bragging coystrill! [3]

            Enter KITELY.[4]

  Kitely. Why, how now? what's the matter, what's the stir
    here?
Whence springs the quarrel? Thomas! where is he?
Put up your weapons, and put off this rage:
My wife and sister, they are cause of this.

---

[1] Little pots—poetasters whose pot is their muse.
[2] Bobadill See p. 29.
[3] Inferior groom, &c.
[4] Scene iii. in old eds.

What, Thomas?—where is this knave?

Cash. Here, Sir.

Well-bred. Come, let's go: this is one of my brother's ancient humours, this.

Stephen. I am glad nobody was hurt by his "ancient humour."   [*Exeunt all but those of the house.*

Kitely. Why, how now, brother, who enforced this brawl?

Down-right. A sort[1] of lewd rake-hells, that care neither for God nor the devil. And they must come here, to read ballads, and roguery, and trash! I'll mar the knot of 'hem ere I sleep, perhaps; especially Bob[2] there, he that's all manner of shapes; and "Songs and Sonnets," his fellow.

Bridget. Brother, indeed you are too violent,
Too sudden, in your humour: and you know
My brother Well-bred's temper will not bear
Any reproof, chiefly in such a presence,
Where every slight disgrace he should receive
Might wound him in opinion, and respect.

Down-right. Respect! what talk you of respect 'mong such,
As ha' no spark of manhood, nor good manners?
'Sdeins, I am ashamed to hear you! respect!   [*Exit.*

Bridget. Yes, there was one a civil gentleman,
And very worthily demeaned himself.

Kitely. O, that was some love of yours, sister.

Bridget. A love of mine? I would it were no worse, brother! You'ld pay my portion, sooner than you think for.

Dame Kitely. Indeed he seemed to be a gentleman of an exceeding fair disposition, and of very excellent good parts.
                    [*Exeunt* Dame KITELY *and* BRIDGET.

Kitely. Here love, by Heaven! my wife's minion!
"Fair disposition!" "excellent good parts!"
Death! these phrases are intolerable.
"Good parts!" how should she know his parts?
His parts! Well, well, well, well, well, well! [3]
It is too plain, too clear:—Thomas, come hither.
What, are they gone?

---

[1] Lot.
[2] Ironically short for Bobadill.
[3] The first and second "Well," or the first and last, probably drawn ou
disyllabically.

Cash.   Ah, sir, they want in.[1]

My mistress, and your sister——

   Kitely. Are any of the gallants within?

   Cash. No, sir, they are all gone.

   Kitely. Art thou sure of it?

   Cash. I can assure you, sir.

   Kitely. What gentleman was that they praised so, Thomas?

   Cash. One, they call him Master Kno'well, a handsome young gentleman, sir.

   Kitely. Ay, I thought so; my mind gave me as much:

I'll die, but they have hid him i' the house,

Somewhere; I'll go and search:—go with me, Thomas:

Be true to me, and thou shalt find me a master! [2] [*Exeunt.*

SCENE II—*The Lane before* Cob's *House*[3]

Enter Cob.

   Cob [*knocking*]. What, Tib! Tib, I say!

   Tib [*within*]. How now, what cuckold is that knocks so hard? [*She opens.*] O, husband! is't you? What's the news?

   Cob. Nay, you have stunned me, i'faith! you ha' given me a knock o' the forehead will stick by me. Cuckold! 'Slid, cuckold!

   Tib. Away, you fool! did I know it was you that knocked? [4] Come, come, you may call me as bad, when you list.

   Cob. May I?—Tib, you are a whore.

   Tib. You lie in your throat, husband.

   Cob. How, the lie? and in my throat too! do you long to be stabbed, ha?

   Tib. Why, you are no soldier, I hope.

   Cob. O, must you be stabbed by a soldier? Mass, that's true! when was Bobadill here, your captain? that rogue, that foist,[5] that fencing Burgullion? [6] I'll tickle him, i'faith.

   Tib. Why, what's the matter, trow?

---

[1] The Ff. gave this in one, the Q. in two lines. "Ay," or "sir," should most likely be prolonged.

[2] His tone implies "who will remember thee."

[3] Scene iv. in old eds.

[4] Being in a more serious flight, these are two quasi-metrical lines.

[5] Pickpocket.

[6] Braggadoccio.

Cob. O, he has basted me rarely, sumptuously! but I have it here in black and white, [*Touches it in his girdle.*] for his black, and blue, shall pay him. O, the Justice! the honestest old brave Trojan in London! I do honour the very flea of his dog. A plague on him though, he put me once in a villanous filthy fear; marry, it vanished away like the smoke of tobacco; but I was smoked [1] soundly first. I thank the devil, and his good angel, my guest. Well, wife, or Tib, which you will, get you in, and lock the door; I charge you, let nobody in to you, wife, nobody in, to you; those are my words. Not Captain Bob himself, nor the fiend, in his likeness; you are a woman, you have flesh and blood enough in you, to be tempted; therefore, keep the door, shut, upon all comers.

Tib. I warrant you, there shall nobody enter here, without my consent.

Cob. Nor with your consent, sweet Tib, and so I leave you.

Tib. It's more than you know, whether you leave me so.

Cob. How?

Tib. Why, "sweet."

Cob. Tut, sweet or sour, thou art a flower. [*Kissing her.* Keep close thy door, I ask no more.   [*Exeunt.*

SCENE III—*A Room in the Windmill Tavern*[2]

Enter E. KNO'WELL, WELL-BRED, STEPHEN, *and* BRAIN-WORM, *disguised as before.*

E. Kno'well. Well, Brain-worm, perform this business happily, and thou makest a purchase of my love for ever.

Well-bred. I'faith, now let thy spirits use their best faculties. But, at any hand, remember the message to my brother; for there's no other means to start him.

Brain-worm. I warrant you, sir, fear nothing: I have a nimble soul has waked all forces of my phant'sie by this time, and put 'hem in true motion. What you have possessed me withal, I'll discharge it amply, sir. Make it no question.
          [*Exit.*

---

[1] Abused, *i.e.* taken in. *Devon.*
[2] Scene v. in old eds.

Well-bred. Forth, and prosper, Brain-worm.—Faith, Ned, how dost thou approve of my abilities in this device?

E. Kno'well. Troth, well, howsoever; but it will come excellent, if it take.

Well-bred. Take, man? why it cannot choose but take, if the circumstances miscarry not: but tell me, ingenuously, dost thou affect my sister Bridget, as thou pretend'st? [1]

E. Kno'well. Friend am I worth belief?

Well-bred. Come, do not protest. In faith, she is a maid of good ornament, and much modesty: and, except I conceived very worthily of her, thou shouldest not have her.

E. Kno'well. Nay, that, I am afraid, will be a question yet, whether I shall have her, or no?

Well-bred. 'Slid, thou shalt have her; by this light thou shalt.

E. Kno'well. Nay, do not swear.

Well-bred. By this hand, thou shalt have her; I'll go fetch her presently. 'Point but where to meet, and as I am an honest man, I'll bring her.

E. Kno'well. Hold, hold, be temperate.

Well-bred. Why, by——what shall I swear by? thou shalt have her, as I am——

E. Kno'well. 'Pray thee, be at peace, I am satisfied; and do believe, thou wilt omit no offered occasion, to make my desires complete.

Well-bred. Thou shalt see, and know, I will not. [*Exeunt.*

SCENE IV—*The Old Jewry*[2]

Enter FORMAL *and* KNO'WELL.

Formal. Was your man a soldier, sir?

Kno'well. Ay, a knave, I took him begging o' the way,
This morning, as I came over Moorfields.

Enter BRAIN-WORM, *disguised as before.*

O, here he is!—You've made fair speed, believe me:
Where, i' the name of sloth, could you be thus?

Brain-worm. Marry, peace be my comfort, where I thought
I should have had little comfort of your worship's service.

Kno'well. How so?

Brain-worm. O, sir! your coming to the city, your entertainment of me, and your sending me to watch——indeed
all the circumstances either of your charge, or my employment, are as open to your son, as to yourself!

Kno'well. How should that be! unless that villain, Brain-
Have told him of the letter, and discovered   [worm,
All that I strictly charged him to conceal? 'Tis so.

Brain-worm. I am, partly, o' the faith 'tis so, indeed.

Kno'well. But, how should he know thee to be my man?

Brain-worm. Nay, sir, I cannot tell; unless it be by the
black art! is not your son a scholar, sir?

Kno'well. Yes, but I hope his soul is not allied
Unto such hellish practice: if it were,
I had just cause to weep my part in him,
And curse the time of his creation.
But, where did'st thou find them, Fitz-Sword?

Brain-worm. You should rather ask, where they found me,
sir; for I'll be sworn, I was going along in the street thinking nothing, when, of a sudden, a voice calls, "Master
Kno'well's man!" another cries "Soldier!" and thus half a
dozen of them, till they had called me within a house, where
I no sooner came, but they seemed men,[1] and out flew all
their rapiers at my bosom, with some three or fourscore oaths
to accompany 'hem; and all to tell me, I was but a dead
man, if I did not confess where you were, and how I was
employed, and about what; which when they could not get
out of me, (as, I protest, they must ha' dissected, and made
an anatomy o' me first, and so I told 'hem,) they locked me
up into a room i' the top of a high house, whence, by great
miracle (having a light heart) I slid down by a bottom[2]
of packthread into the street, and so 'scaped. But, sir, thus
much I can assure you, for I heard it while I was locked
up, there was a great many rich merchants, and brave[3]
citizens' wives with 'hem at a feast, and your son, Master

---

[1] Possibly a pun, men, mad or angry, Greek μηνη, &c.
[2] Ball or skein.
[3] Richly dressed.

Edward, withdrew with one of 'hem, and has 'pointed to meet her anon, at one Cob's house, a water-bearer, that dwells by the Wall. Now, there your worship shall be sure to take him, for there he preys, and fail he will not.

Kno'well. Nor, will I fail to break his match, I doubt not. Go thou, along with Justice Clement's man, And stay there for me. At one Cob's house, say'st thou?

Brain-worm. Ay, sir, there you shall have him. [*Exit* KNO' WELL.] Yes!—invisible? Much wench, or much son! 'Slight, when he has staid there, three or four hours, travailing with the expectation of wonders, and at length be delivered of air! Oh, the sport that I should then take, to look on him, if I durst! But now, I mean to appear no more afore him, in this shape: I have another trick, to act yet. O, that I were so happy, as to light on a nupson,[1] now, of this justice's novice!——Sir, I make you stay somewhat long.

Formal. Not a whit, sir. 'Pray you what do you mean, sir?

Brain-worm. I was putting up some papers——

Formal. You ha' been lately in the wars, sir, it seems.

Brain-worm. Marry have I, sir, to my loss; and expense of all, almost——

Formal. Troth, sir, I would be glad to bestow a pottle[2] of wine o' you, if it please you to accept it——

Brain-worm. O, sir——

Formal. But, to hear the manner of your services, and your devices in the wars, they say they be very strange, and not like those a man reads in the Roman histories, or sees at Mile-end.[3]

Brain-worm. No, I assure you, sir; why, at any time when it please you, I shall be ready to discourse to you all I know: [*Aside.*] and more too somewhat.

Formal. No better time than now, sir; we'll go to the Windmill: there we shall have a cup of neat grist, we call it. I pray you, sir, let me request you, to the Windmill.

Brain-worm. I'll follow you, sir; [*Aside.*] and make grist o' you, if I have good luck.   [*Exeunt.*

---

[1] Simpleton.
[2] Two quarts.
[3] Exercise ground of the City bands.

SCENE V—*Moorfields*[1]

Enter MATTHEW, E. KNO'WELL, BOBADILL, *and* STEPHEN.

Matthew. Sir, did your eyes ever taste the like clown of him, where we were to-day, Master Well-bred's half-brother? I think the whole earth cannot show his parallel, by this daylight.

E. Kno'well. We were now speaking of him: Captain Bobadill tell me, he is fallen foul o' you too.

Matthew. O, ay, sir, he threatened me with the bastinado.

Bobadill. Ay, but I think I taught you prevention, this morning, for that:—You shall kill him, beyond question; if you be so generously minded.

Matthew. Indeed, it is a most excellent trick.   [*Fences.*

Bobadill. O, you do not give spirit enough to your motion, you are too tardy, too heavy! O, it must be done like lightning, hay!   [*Practices at a post.*

Matthew. Rare captain!

Bobadill. Tut! 'tis nothing, an't be not done in a—*punto.*[2]

E. Kno'well. Captain, did you ever prove yourself, upon any of our masters of defence here?

Matthew. O, good sir! yes, I hope, he has.

Bobadill. I will tell you, sir. Upon my first coming to the city, after my long travail [3] for knowledge (in that mystery only) there came three or four of 'hem to me, at a gentleman's house, where it was my chance to be resident at that time, to intreat my presence at their schools, and withal so much importuned me, that—I protest to you, as I am a gentleman—I was ashamed of their rude demeanour, out of all measure: well, I told 'hem, that to come to a public school, they should pardon me, it was opposite (in diameter) to my humour; but, if so be they would give their attendance at my lodging, I protested to do them what right or favour I could, as I was a gentleman, and so forth.

E. Kno'well. So, sir, then you tried their skill?

[1] Scene vii. in old eds.
[2] Instant.
[3] Used in sense also of travel.

Bobadill. Alas, soon tried! you shall hear, sir. Within two or three days after, they came; and, by honesty, fair sir, believe me, I graced them exceedingly, showed them some two or three tricks of prevention, have purchased 'hem since, a credit to admiration! they cannot deny this: and yet now, they hate me, and why? because I am excellent! and for no other vile reason on the earth.

E. Kno'well. This is strange, and barbarous! as ever I heard!

Bobadill. Nay, for a more instance of their preposterous natures, but note, sir. They have assaulted me some three, four, five, six of them together, as I have walked alone, in divers skirts i' the town, as Turnbull, White-chapel, Shore-ditch,[1] which were then my quarters; and since, upon the Exchange, at my lodging, and at my Ordinary:[2] where I have driven them afore me, the whole length of a street, in the open view of all our gallants, pitying to hurt them, believe me. Yet all this lenity will not o'ercome their spleen; they will be doing with the pismire, raising a hill, a man may spurn abroad with his foot, at pleasure. By myself, I could have slain them all, but I delight not in murder. I am loth to bear any other than this bastinado for 'hem: yet I hold it good polity not to go disarmed, for though I be skillful, I may be oppressed with multitudes.

E. Kno'well. Ay, believe me, may you, sir: and, in my conceit, our whole nation should sustain the loss by it, if it were so.

Bobadill. Alas, no! what's a peculiar man to a nation? not seen.

E. Kno'well. O, but your skill, sir.

Bobadill. Indeed, that might be some loss; but who respects it? I will tell you, sir, by the way of private, and under seal; I am a gentleman, and live here obscure, and to myself. But, were I known to her Majesty and the Lords, —observe me,—I would undertake—upon this poor head, and life—for the public benefit of the state, not only to spare the entire lives of her subjects in general, but to save the one half, nay, three parts of her yearly charge in

[1] Suburbs of ill repute.
[2] Public dining-room.

holding war, and against what enemy soever. And how would I do it, think you?

E. Kno'well. Nay, I know not, nor can I conceive.

Bobadill. Why thus, sir. I would select nineteen more, to myself, throughout the land; gentlemen they should be, of good spirit, strong, and able constitution; I would choose them by an instinct, a character that I have: and I would teach these nineteen, the special rules, as your punto, your reverso, your stoccata, your imbroccata, your passada, your montanto;[1] till they could all play very near or altogether as well as myself. This done, say the enemy were forty thousand strong, we twenty would come into the field, the tenth of March, or therebouts; and we would challenge twenty of the enemy; they could not, in their honour, refuse us, well, we would kill them; challenge twenty more, kill them; twenty more, kill them; twenty more, kill them too; and thus, would we kill, every man, his twenty a day, that's twenty score; twenty score, that's two hundred; two hundred a day, five days a thousand; forty thousand; forty times five, five times forty, two hundred days kills them all up, by computation. And this, will I venture my poor gentleman-like carcase to perform (provided there be no treason practised upon us) by fair, and discreet manhood, that is, civilly by the sword.

E. Kno'well. Why, are you so sure of your hand, captain, at all times?

Bobadill. Tut! never miss thrust, upon my reputation with you.

E. Kno'well. I would not stand in Down-right's state then, an you meet him, for the wealth of any one street in London.

Bobadill. Why, sir, you mistake me! if he were here now, by this welkin, I would not draw my weapon on him! let this gentleman do his mind; but, I will bastinado him, by the bright sun, where-ever I meet him.

Matthew. Faith, and I'll have a fling at him, at my distance.

E. Kno'well. Gods so, look where he is! yonder he goes.
                                    [DOWN-RIGHT *walks over the stage.*

---

[1] Rapier play then included cuts as well as thrusts, and, as shown by "imbroccata," the parrying use of the dagger.

Down-right. What peevish luck have I, I cannot meet with these bragging rascals?

Bobadill. It's not he, is it?

E. Kno'well.   Yes, faith, it is he.[1]

Matthew. I'll be hanged then, if that were he.

E. Kno'well. Sir, keep your hanging good for some greater matter, for I assure you that was he.

Stephen. Upon my reputation, it was he.

Bobadill. Had I thought it had been he, he must not have gone so: but I can hardly be induced to believe it was he, yet.

E. Kno'well. That I think, sir.   [*Re-enter* DOWN-RIGHT.
                                    But see, he is come again.

Down-right. O, "Pharaoh's foot," have I found you? Come, draw, to your tools[2]: draw, gipsy, or I'll thrash you.

Bobadill. Gentleman of valour, I do believe in thee, hear me—

Down-right. Draw your weapon then.

Bobadill. Tall man, I never thought on it, till now, body of me, I had a warrant of the peace served on me, even now, as I came along, by a water-bearer; this gentleman saw it, Master Matthew.

Down-right. 'Sdeath! you will not draw then?

          [*Cudgels him, disarms him, and throws him down.*
                    MATTHEW *runs away.*

Bobadill. Hold, hold, under thy favour, forbear!

Down-right. Prate again, as you like this, you whoreson foist[3] you! You'll "control the point," you! [*Looking about.*] Your consort is gone? had he stayed he had shared with you, sir.   [*Exit.*

Bobadill. Well, gentlemen, bear witness, I was bound to the peace, by this good day.

E. Know'ell. No faith, it's an ill day, captain, never reckon it other: but, say you were bound to the peace, the law allows you to defend yourself: that'll prove but a poor excuse.

Bobadill. I cannot tell, sir. I desire good construction, in fair sort. I never sustained the like disgrace, by Heaven!

---

[1] One line, F. 2.
[2] His rapier and dagger.
[3] Pickpocket.

sure I was struck with a planet thence, for I had no power
to touch my weapon.

E. Kno'well. Ay, like enough; I have heard of many that
have been beaten under a planet: go, get you to a surgeon.
[*Exit* BOBADILL.] 'Slid! an these be your tricks, your
passadas, and your montantos, I'll none of them. O, manners! that this age should bring forth such creatures! that
nature should be at leisure to make 'hem! Come, coz.

Stephen. Mass, I'll ha' this cloak.

E. Kno'well. Gods will, 'tis Down-right's.

Stephen. Nay, it's mine now, another might have ta'en't
up as well as I: I'll wear it, so I will.   [yourself.

E. Kno'well. How, an he see it? he'll challenge it, assure

Stephen. Ah, but he shall not ha' it; I'll say I bought it.

E. Kno'well. Take heed, you buy it not too dear, coz.
                                                        [*Exeunt.*

SCENE VI—*A Room in* KITELY'S *House*[1]

Enter KITELY, WELL-BRED, Dame KITELY, *and* BRIDGET.

Kitely. Now, trust me, brother, you were much to blame,
T'incense his anger, and disturb the peace
Of my poor house, where there are sentinels,
That every minute watch, to give alarms
Of civil war, without adjection[2]
Of your assistance, or occasion.

Well-bred. No harm done, brother, I warrant you, since
there is no harm done. Anger costs a man nothing; and a
tall man is never his own man, till he be angry. To keep his
valour in obscurity, is to keep himself, as it were, in a
cloak-bag. What's a musician, unless he play? What's a
tall man, unless he fight? For indeed, all this, my wise
brother stands upon, absolutely; and that made me fall
in with him, so resolutely.

Dame Kitely. Ay, but what harm might have come of it,
brother?

Well-bred. Might, sister? so might the good warm clothes
your husband wears, be poisoned, for any thing he knows: or

[1] Scene viii. in old eds.
[2] The casting in, addition.

the wholesome wine he drunk, even now, at the table——

Kitely [*aside*]. Now, God forbid! O me! now I remember,
My wife drunk to me last; and changed the cup;
And bade me wear this cursèd suit to-day.
See, if Heaven suffer murder undiscovered!—
I feel me ill; give me some mithridate,[1]
Some mithridate and oil, good sister, fetch me;
O, I am sick at heart! I burn, I burn.
If you will save my life, go fetch it me.

Well-bred. O strange humour! my very breath has poisoned him.

Bridget. Good brother, be content, what do you mean?
The strength of these extreme conceits will kill you.

Dame Kitely. Beshrew your heart-blood, brother Wellbred, now,
For putting such a toy into his head!

Well-bred. Is a fit simile a toy? will he be poisoned with a simile? Brother Kitely, what a strange, and idle imagination is this! For shame, be wiser. O' my soul, there's no such matter.

Kitely. Am I not sick? how am I, then, not poisoned?
Am I not poisoned? how am I, then, so sick?

Dame Kitely. If you be sick, your own thoughts make you sick.

Well-bred. His jealousy, is the poison he has taken.

Enter BRAIN-WORM, *in* FORMAL's *clothes.*

Brain-worm. Master Kitely, my master, Justice Clement, salutes you; and desires to speak with you, with all possible speed.

Kitely. No time but now? when, I think, I am sick? very sick! well, I will wait upon his worship.—Thomas? Cob? [*Aside.*] I must seek them out, and set 'hem sentinels till I return.—Thomas? Cob? Thomas?   [*Exit.*

Well-bred [*takes him aside*]. This is perfectly rare, Brainworm! but how got'st thou this apparel of the justice's man?

Brain-worm. Marry, sir, my proper fine pen-man would needs bestow the grist o' me, at the Windmill, to hear some

---

[1] Supposed general antidote.

martial discourse; where so I marshalled him, that I made
him drunk, with admiration! and, because too much heat
was the cause of his distemper, I stripped him stark naked,
as he lay along asleep, and borrowed his suit, to deliver
this counterfeit message in, leaving a rusty armour, and
an old brown bill [1] to watch him, till my return; which
shall be, when I ha' pawned his apparel, and spent the
better part o' the money, perhaps.

Well-bred. Well, thou art a successful merry knave, Brain-
worm; his absence will be a good subject for more mirth.
I pray thee, return to thy young master, and will him to
meet me, and my sister Bridget, at the Tower instantly;
for, here, tell him, the house is so stored with jealousy,
there is no room for love to stand upright in. We must
get our fortunes committed to some larger prison, say;
and, than the Tower, I know no better air; nor where
the liberty of the house may do us more present service.[2]
Away.   [*Exit* BRAIN-WORM.

Re-enter KITELY, CASH *following.*

Kitely. Come hither, Thomas. Now, my secret's ripe,
And thou shalt have it: lay to both thine ears.
Hark, what I say to thee. I must go forth, Thomas:
Be careful of thy promise, keep good watch,
Note every gallant, and observe him well,
That enters in my absence, to thy mistress:
If she would show him rooms, the jest is stale,
Follow 'hem, Thomas, or else hang on him,
And let him not go after; mark their looks;
Note, if she offer but to see his band,
Or any other amorous toy about him;
But praise his leg; or foot; or if she say,
The day is hot, and bid him feel her hand,
How hot it is; oh, that's a monstrous thing!
Note me all this, good Thomas, mark their sighs,
And, if they do but whisper, break 'hem off:
I'll bear thee out in it. Wilt thou do this?
Wilt thou be true, my Thomas?

[1] Between a halbert and a pike.
[2] They could be immediately married about its precincts.

Cash. As truth's self, sir.

Kitely. Why, I believe thee:—where is Cob, now? Cob?
                                                    [*Exit.*

Dame Kitely. He's ever calling for Cob! I wonder how he
employs Cob so!

Well-bred. Indeed, sister, to ask how he employs Cob, is a
necessary question for you, that are his wife, and a thing
not very easy for you to be satisfied in: but this, I'll assure
you, Cob's wife is an excellent bawd, sister, and oftentimes,
your husband haunts her house; marry, to what end? I
cannot altogether accuse him; imagine you what you
think convenient. But I have known fair hides have foul
hearts ere now, sister.

Dame Kitely. Never said you truer than that, brother, so
much I can tell you for your learning.—Thomas, fetch your
cloak, and go with me. [*Exit* CASH.] I'll after him presently: I would to fortune, I could take him there, i'faith,
I'ld return him his own, I warrant him!   [*Exit.*

Well-bred. So, let 'hem go; this may make sport anon.
Now, my fair sister-in-law, that you knew but how happy a
thing it were, to be fair and beautiful.

Bridget. That touches not me, brother.

Well-bred. That's true; that's even the fault of it: for indeed, beauty stands a woman in no stead, unless it procure
her touching. But sister, whether it touch you or no, it
touches your beauties; and I am sure they will abide the
touch; an they do not, a plague of all ceruse,[1] say I! and it
touches me too in part, though not in the—— Well, there's
a dear and respected friend of mine, sister, stands very
strongly, and worthily affected toward you, and hath
vowed to inflame whole bonfires of zeal at his heart, in
honour of your perfections. I have already engaged my
promise to bring you, where you shall hear him confirm
much more. Ned Kno'well is the man, sister. There's no
exception against the party. You are ripe for a husband;
and a minute's loss to such an occasion, is a great trespass
in a wise beauty. What say you, sister? On my soul, he
loves you. Will you give him the meeting?

Bridget. Faith, I had very little confidence in mine own

---

[1] White lead, a cosmetic.

constancy, brother, if I durst not meet a man: but this
motion of yours savours of an old knight adventurer's
servant, a little too much, methinks.

Well-bred. What's that, sister?

Bridget. Marry, of the squire.[1]

Well-bred. No matter if it did, I would be such an one
for my friend. But see, who is returned to hinder us!

Re-enter KITELY.

Kitely. What villany is this? called out a false message?
This was some plot! I was not sent for.—Bridget,
Where's your sister?

Bridget.   I think she be gone forth, sir.

Kitely. How! is my wife gone forth? whither, for God's
sake?

Bridget. She's gone abroad with Thomas.

Kitely. Abroad with Thomas! oh, that villain dors[2] me:
He hath discovered all unto my wife!
Beast that I was, to trust him! whither, I pray you,
Went she?

Bridget. I know not, sir,

Well-bred.   I'll tell you, brother,
Whither I suspect she's gone.[3]

Kitely.   Whither, good brother?

Well-bred. To Cob's house, I believe: but, keep my coun-
      sel.

Kitely. I will, I will: to Cob's house? doth she haunt Cob's?
She's gone a purpose now, to cuckold me,
With that lewd rascal, who, to win her favour,
Hath told her all.   [*Exit.*

Well-bred.   Come, he is once more gone,
Sister, let's lose no time; the affair is worth it.   [*Exeunt.*

---

[1] *i.e.* The apple-squire, the attendant and pander.
[2] Fools, deceives as does the dor, or cockchafer.
[3] Ff. give Well-bred's speech as a verse line, but also misplace "went
she," at end of previous line.

SCENE VII—*A Street*[1]

Enter MATTHEW *and* BOBADILL.

Matthew. I wonder, captain, what they will say of my going away? ha?

Bobadill. Why, what should they say? but as of a discreet gentleman! quick, wary, respectful of nature's fair lineaments: and that's all.

Matthew. Why, so! but what can they say of your beating?

Bobadill. A rude part, a touch with soft wood, a kind of gross battery used, laid on strongly, borne most patiently; and that's all.

Matthew. Ay, but would any man have offered it in Venice? as you say?

Bobadill. Tut! I assure you, no: you shall have there your *Nobilis,* your *Gentilezza,*[2] come in bravely upon your "reverse," stand you close, stand you firm, stand you fair, save your "retricato" with his left leg, come to the "assalto" with the right, thrust with brave steel, defy your base wood! But, wherefore do I awake this remembrance? I was fascinated, by Jupiter, fascinated: but I will be un-witched, and revenged, by law.

Matthew. Do you hear? is't not best to get a warrant, and have him arrested, and brought before Justice Clement?

Bobadill. It were not amiss, would we had it!

Enter BRAIN-WORM *still as* FORMAL.

Matthew. Why, here comes his man, let's speak to him.

Bobadill. Agreed, do you speak.

Matthew. 'Save you, sir!

Brain-worm. With all my heart, sir.

Matthew. Sir, there is one Down-right hath abused this gentleman, and myself, and we determine to make our amends by law; now, if you would do us the favour to procure a warrant, to bring him afore your master, you shall be well considered, I assure you, sir.

---

[1] Scene ix. in old eds.
[2] Lat. and Ital. meaning the same, "gentry of blood."

Brain-worm. Sir, you know my service is my living; such favours, as these, gotten of my master is his only prefer-ment,[1] and therefore, you must consider me, as I may make benefit of my place.

Matthew. How is that, sir?

Brain-worm. Faith sir, the thing is extraordinary, and the gentleman may be of great account; yet, be what he will, if you will lay me down a brace of angels, in my hand, you shall have it, otherwise not.

Matthew. How shall we do, captain? he asks a brace of angels, you have no money?

Bobadill. Not a cross,[2] by fortune.

Matthew. Nor I, as I am a gentleman, but twopence, left of my two shillings in the morning for wine, and radish: let's find him some pawn.

Bobadill. Pawn? we have none to the value of his demand.

Matthew. O, yes. I'll pawn this jewel in my ear, and you may pawn your silk-stockings, and pull up your boots, they will ne'er be missed: it must be done, now.

Bobadill. Well, an there be no remedy: I'll step aside and pull 'hem off.   [*Withdraws.*

Matthew. Do you hear, sir? we have no store of money at this time, but you shall have good pawns; look you, sir, this jewel, and that gentleman's silk-stockings; because we would have it dispatched, ere we went to our chambers.

Brain-worm. I am content, sir; I will get you the warrant presently,[3] what's his name, say you? Down-right?

Matthew. Ay, ay, George Down-right.

Brain-worm. What manner of man is he?

Matthew. A tall big man, sir; he goes in a cloak most commonly, of silk-russet, laid about with russet lace.

Brain-worm. 'Tis very good, sir.

Matthew. Here, sir, here's my jewel.

Bobadill [*returning*]. And here—are stockings.

Brain-worm. Well, gentlemen, I'll procure you this war-rant presently; but, who will you have to serve it?

Matthew. That's true, captain: that must be considered.

Bobadill. Body o' me, I know not! 'tis service of danger!

---

[1] The only preferment he gives me.
[2] The penny and halfpenny were so marked.
[3] Immediately.

Brain-worm. Why, you were best get one o' the varlets o'
the city, a serjeant; I'll appoint you one, if you please.

Matthew. Will you, sir? why, we can wish no better.

Bobadill. We'll leave it to you, sir.

[*Exeunt* BOBADILL *and* MATTHEW.

Brain-worm. This is rare! Now will I go pawn this cloak
of the justice's man's at the broker's, for a varlet's suit, and
be the varlet myself; and get either more pawns, or more
money of Down-right, for[1] the arrest.   [*Exit.*

SCENE VIII—*The Lane before* COB'S *House* [2]

Enter KNO'WELL.

Kno'well. Oh, here it is; I am glad I have found it now.
Ho! who is within here?   [*Knocking.*

Tib [*within*]. I am within, sir; what's your pleasure?

Kno'well. To know, who is within, besides yourself.

Tib. Why, sir, you are no constable, I hope?

Kno'well. O! fear you the constable? then I doubt not,
You have some guests within, deserve that fear,
I'll fetch him straight.   [TIB *opens.*

Tib.   O' God's name, sir!

Kno'well. Go to. Come, tell me, is not young Kno'well
here?

Tib. Young Kno'well? I know none such, sir, o'mine
honesty.

Kno'well. Your honesty? dame, it flies too lightly from
you: There is no way but, fetch the constable.

Tib. The constable? the man is mad, I think.

[*Claps to the door.*

Enter Dame KITELY *and* CASH.

Cash. Ho! who keeps house, here?

Kno'well. O, this's the female copesmate[3] of my son:
Now shall I meet him straight.

Dame Kitely.   Knock, Thomas, hard.

---

[1] Instead of.
[2] Scene x. in old eds.
[3] Companion.

Cash. Ho, goodwife?   [T<small>IB</small> *slightly re-opens door.*

Tib.   Why, what's the matter with you?

Dame Kitely. Why, woman, grieves it you to ope your door?

Belike, you get something, to keep it shut.

  Tib. What mean these questions, 'pray ye?

  Dame Kitely. So strange you make it! Is not my husband here?

  Kno'well. Her husband!

  Dame Kitely.   My tried husband, Master Kitely?

  Tib. I hope, he needs not to be tried, here.

  Dame Kitely. No dame; he does it not for need, but pleasure.

  Tib. Neither for need, nor pleasure, is he here.

  Kno'well. This is but a device to baulk me withal.

Enter K<small>ITELY</small>, *muffled in his cloak.*

Soft, who is this? 'Tis not my son disguised?

  Dame Kitely [*spies her husband, and runs to him*]. O, sir, have I forestalled your honest market?

Found your close walks? you stand amazed now, do you?

I'faith, I'm glad I have smoked you yet at last.

What is your jewel, trow? In: come, let's see her;—

Fetch forth your housewife, dame;—if she be fairer,

In any honest judgment, than myself,

I'll be content with it: but, she is change,

She feeds you fat, she soothes your appetite,

And you are well! your wife, an honest woman,

Is meat twice sod to you, sir! O, you treacher!

  Kno'well. She cannot counterfeit thus palpably.

  Kitely. Out on thy more than strumpet's[1] impudence!

Steal'st thou thus to thy haunts? and have I taken

Thy bawd, and thee, and thy companion,

This hoary-headed letcher, this old goat,

Close[2] at your villainy, and wouldst thou 'scuse it

With this stale harlot's jest, accusing me?——

O, old incontinent, [*To* K<small>NO'WELL</small>.] dost not thou shame,

When all thy powers in chastity is[3] spent,

[1] So Q. F.; strumpet F.2.
[2] Secretly; but a pun.
[3] Singular, through "chastity." Q. Ff.

To have a mind so hot? and to entice,

And feed the enticements of a lustful woman?

Dame Kitely. Out, I defy thee, I, dissembling wretch!

Kitely. Defy me, strumpet? Ask thy pander here,

Can he deny it? or that wicked elder?

Kno'well. Why, hear you, sir.

Kitely.   Tut, tut, tut; never speak.

Thy guilty conscience will discover thee.

Kno'well. What lunacy is this, that haunts this man?

Kitely. Well, good wife B A 'D,[1] Cob's wife, and you,

That make your husband such a hoddy-doddy[2];—

And you, young apple-squire,—and old cuckold-maker;

I'll ha' you every one before a justice:

Nay, you shall answer it, I charge you go.

Kno'well. Marry, with all my heart, sir: I go willingly;

Though I do taste this as a trick, put on me,

To punish my impertinent search; and justly:

And half forgive my son, for the device.

Kitely. Come, will you go?

Dame Kitely.   Go? to thy shame believe it.

Enter COB.

Cob. Why, what's the matter here, what's here to do?

Kitely. O, Cob, art thou come? I have been abused,

And i' thy house: never was man so wronged!

Cob. 'Slid, in my house? My Master Kitely? Who wrongs

you in my house?

Kitely. Marry, young lust in old, and old in young, here:

Thy wife's their bawd, here have I taken 'hem.

Cob. How? bawd? is my house come to that? Am I pre-

ferred thither? [*Beats his wife.*] Did I charge you to keep

your doors shut, Isbel? and do you let 'hem lie open for

all comers?

Kno'well. Friend, know some cause, before thou beat'st
     thy wife,

This's madness in thee.

Cob.   Why? is there no cause?

---

[1] He spells this word, and, as shown by the 'D, makes a pun or an
attempt at one, as calling Cob's wife "bad" and "bawd."

[2] Generally a simpleton, but perhaps implying here that he is horned.

Kitely. Yes, I'll show cause before the justice, Cob:
Come, let her go with me.

Cob.   Nay, she shall go.

Tib. Nay, I will go. I'll see an you may be allowed to
make a bundle o' hemp[1] o' your right and lawful wife
thus, at every cuckoldy knave's pleasure. Why do you not
go?

Kitely. A bitter quean! Come, we'll ha' you tamed.

                                    [Exeunt.

SCENE IX—*A Street*[2]

Enter Brain-worm *as a City Serjeant.*

Brain-worm. Well, of all my disguises yet, now am I most
like myself; being in this serjeant's gown. A man, of my
present profession, never counterfeits, till he lays hold upon
a debtor, and says, he 'rests him; for then he brings him to
all manner of unrest. A kind of little kings we are, bearing
the diminutive of a mace, made like a young artichoke,
that always carries pepper and salt, in itself. Well, I know
not what danger I undergo by this exploit, 'pray Heaven
I come well off!

Enter Matthew *and* Bobadill.

Matthew. See, I think, yonder is the varlet, by his gown.

Bobadill. Let's go in quest of him.

Matthew. 'Save you, friend! are not you here, by appoint-
ment of Justice Clement's man?

Brain-worm. Yes, an't please you, sir; he told me, two
gentlemen had willed him to procure a warrant from his
master (which I have about me) to be served on one Down-
right.

Matthew. It is honestly done of you both; and see, where
the party comes you must arrest; serve it upon him,
quickly, afore he be aware.

Bobadill. Bear back, Master Matthew.

---

[1] Hemp is prepared by beating.
[2] Scene xi. in old eds.

Enter STEPHEN *in* DOWN-RIGHT'S *cloak.*

Brain-worm. Master Down-right, I arrest you i' the queen's name, and must carry you afore a justice, by virtue of this warrant.

Stephen. Me, friend? I am no Down-right, I. I am Master Stephen, you do not well to arrest me, I tell you truly: I am in nobody's bonds, nor books, I, would you should know it. A plague on you heartily, for making me thus afraid afore my time!

Brain-worm. Why, now are you deceived, gentlemen!

Bobadill. He wears such a cloak, and that deceived us: but see, here a' comes indeed! this is he, officer.

Enter DOWN-RIGHT.

Down-right. Why, how now, Signior gull! are you turned filcher of late? come, deliver my cloak.

Stephen. Your cloak, sir? I bought it, even now, in open market.

Brain-worm. Master Down-right, I have a warrant I must serve upon you, procured by these two gentlemen.

Down-right. These gentlemen? these rascals!

                                        [*Raises his cudgel.*

Brain-worm. Keep the peace, I charge you, in her majesty's name.

Down-right. I obey thee. What must I do, officer?

Brain-worm. Go before Master Justice Clement, to answer what they can object against you, sir, I will use you kindly, sir.

Matthew. Come, let's before, and make[1] the justice, captain.

Bobadill. The varlet's a tall man,[2] afore Heaven!

                              [*Exeunt* BOBADILL *and* MATTHEW.

Down-right. Gull, you'll gi' me my cloak.

Stephen. Sir, I bought it, and I'll keep it.

Down-right. You will.

Stephen. Ay, that I will.

Down-right. Officer, there's thy fee, arrest him.

[1] Prepare or prepossess.
[2] Valiant.

Brain-worm. Master Stephen, I must arrest you.

Stephen. Arrest me! I scorn it. There take your cloak, I'll none on't.

Down-right. Nay, that shall not serve your turn now, sir. Officer, I'll go with thee to the justice's: bring him along.

Stephen. Why, is not here your cloak? what would you have?

Down-right. I'll ha' you answer it, sir.

Brain-worm. Sir, I'll take your word;[1] and this gentleman's too, for his appearance.

Down-right. I'll ha' no words taken: bring him along.

Brain-worm. Sir. I may choose to do that: I may take bail.

Down-right. 'Tis true, you may take bail, and choose, at another time. But you shall not, now, varlet. Bring him along or I'll swindge you.   [*Raises cudgel.*

Brain-worm. Sir, I pity the gentleman's case. Here's your money again.

Down-right. 'Sdeins, tell not me of my money; bring him away, I say.

Brain-worm. I warrant you he will go with you, of himself, sir.

Down-right. Yet more ado.

Brain-worm [*aside*]. I have made a fair mash on't.

Stephen. Must I go?

Brain-worm. I know no remedy, Master Stephen.

Down-right. Come along, afore me, here: I do not love your hanging look behind.

Stephen. Why, sir: I hope you cannot hang me for it.— Can he, fellow?

Brain-worm. I think not, sir: it is but a whipping matter, sure.

Stephen. Why, then, let him do his worst, I am resolute.
                                                    [*Exeunt.*

---

[1] "For your appearance" understood.

ACT THE FIFTH

SCENE I—*A Hall in* Justice CLEMENT's *House*

Enter CLEMENT, KNO'WELL, KITELY, Dame KITELY,
TIB, CASH, COB, *and Servants.*

CLEMENT. Nay, but stay, stay, give me leave:—my chair,
sirrah.—You, Master Kno'well, say you went thither to
meet your son?

Kno'well. Ay, sir.

Clement. But who directed you, thither?

Kno'well. That did mine own man, sir.

Clement. Where is he?

Kno'well. Nay, I know not, now; I left him with your
clerk: and appointed him to stay here for me.[1]

Clement. My clerk? about what time was this?

Kno'well. Marry, between one and two, as I take it.

Clement. And what time came my man with the false
message to you, Master Kitely?

Kitely. After two, sir.

Clement. Very good: but, Mistress Kitely, how chance
that you were at Cob's? ha?

Dame Kitely. An please you, sir, I'll tell you; my brother
Well-bred told me, that Cob's house, was a suspected
place——

Clement. So it appears, methinks; but on.

Dame Kitely. And that my husband used thither, daily.

Clement. No matter, so he used himself well, mistress.

Dame Kitely. True sir, but you know what grows, by
such haunts, oftentimes.

Clement. I see, rank fruits of a jealous brain, Mistress
Kitely: but did you find your husband there, in that case, as
you suspected?

Kitely. I found her there, sir.

Clement. Did you so? that alters the case. Who gave you
knowledge of your wife's being there?

Kitely. Marry, that did my brother Well-bred.

---

[1] Two verse lines in F., but not so in Q. nor in F2.

Clement. How? Well-bred first tell her? then tell you, after? Where is Well-bred?

Kitely. Gone with my sister, sir, I know not whither.

Clement. Why, this is a mere trick, a device; you are gulled in this most grossly, all!—alas, poor wench, wert thou beaten for this?

Tib. Yes, most pitifully, an't please you.

Cob. And worthily, I hope: if it shall prove so.

Clement. Ay, that's like, and a piece of a sentence.—

Enter a Servant.

How now, sir? what's the matter?

Servant. Sir, there's a gentleman i' the court without, desires to speak with your worship.

Clement. A gentleman! what's he?

Servant. A soldier, sir, he says.

Clement. A soldier? take down my armour, my sword, quickly. A soldier speak with me! why when,[1] knaves? come on, come on, hold my cap there, so; give me my gorget,[2] my sword:——stand by, I will end your matters anon.—Let the soldier enter: [*Exit* Servant.

Enter BOBADILL *and* MATTHEW.[3]

now sir, what ha' you to say to me?

Bobadill. By your worship's favour——

                              [*Approaches him.*[4]

Clement. Nay, keep out, sir; I know not your pretence, you send me word, sir, you are a soldier: why, sir, you shall be answered, here, here be them have been amongst soldiers. Sir, your pleasure.

Bobadill. Faith, sir, so it is, this gentleman, and myself have been most uncivilly wronged, and beaten by one Down-right, a coarse fellow, about the town here, and for mine own part, I protest, being a man, in no sort, given to this filthy humour of quarrelling he hath assaulted me in the way of my peace; despoiled me of mine honour; disarmed me of my weapons; and rudely laid me along in the

[1] How long are you going to be?
[2] Neck armour piece.
[3] Scene ii. in old eds.
[4] Intent.

open streets: when I not so much as once offered to resist
him.

Clement. O God's precious! is this the soldier? here, take
my armour off quickly, 'twill make him swoon, I fear;
he is not fit to look on't, that will put up a blow.

Matthew. An't please your worship, he was bound to the
peace.

Clement. Why, an he were, sir, his hands were not bound,
were they?

Re-enter Servant.

Servant. There's one of the varlets of the city, sir, has
brought two gentlemen here; one, upon your worship's
warrant.

Clement. My warrant?

Servant. Yes, sir. The officer says, procured by these two.

Clement. Bid him come in. [*Exit Servant.*] Set by this picture.[1]

Enter DOWN-RIGHT, STEPHEN, *with* BRAIN-WORM *as before.*[2]

What, Master Down-right! are you brought at Master
Freshwater's[3] suit here?   [suit.

Down-right. I'faith, sir. And here's another brought at my

Clement. What are you, sir?

Stephen. A gentleman, sir.—Oh, uncle!

Clement. Uncle? who? Master Kno'well?

Kno'well. Ay, sir! this is a wise kinsman of mine .

Stephen. God's my witness, uncle, I am wronged here,
monstrously, he charges me with stealing his cloak, and
would I might never stir, if I did not find it in the street,
by chance.

Down-right. O, did you "find it," now? You said, "you
bought it," ere-while.

Stephen. And you said, I stole it; nay, now my uncle is
here, I'll do well enough with you.

Clement. Well, let this breathe awhile.—You that have

---

[1] This mere picture of a soldier.

[2] Scene iii. in old eds.

[3] A gibing term, because soldiers who had not crossed the sea had
seen no service. In Greene's *Never too Late*, 1590, Infida says—"Are
you such a freshwater soldier, that you faint at the first skirmish?"

cause to complain there, stand forth:—had you my warrant for this gentleman's apprehension?

Bobadill. Ay, an't please your worship.

Clement. Nay, do not speak in passion[1] so: where had
you it?

Bobadill. Of your clerk, sir.

Clement. That's well! an my clerk can make warrants and
my hand not at 'hem! Where is the warrant?—Officer, have
you it?

Brain-worm. No sir, your worship's man, Master Formal,
bid me do it for these gentlemen, and he would be my discharge.

Clement. Why, Master Down-right, are you such a novice,
to be served, and never see the warrant?

Down-right.[2] He did not serve it on me.

Clement. No? how then?

Down-right. Marry, sir, he came to me, and said, he must
serve it, and he would use me kindly, and so———

Clement. O, God's pity was it so, sir? "He must serve it!"
Give me my long sword there, and help me off: so. Come
on, sir varlet, I "must" cut off your legs, sirrah; [BRAIN-
WORM *kneels.*] nay, stand up, "I'll use you kindly";—I
"must" cut off your legs, I say.

          [*Flourishes over him with his long sword.*

Brain-worm [*kneeling again*]. O, good sir, I beseech you;
nay, good Master Justice!

Clement. I "must" do it; there is no remedy. I "must" cut
off your legs, sirrah—I "must" cut off your ears, you rascal,
I must do it—I "must" cut off your nose—I "must" cut
off your head.

Brain-worm. O, good your worship!

Clement. Well, rise, how dost thou do now? dost thou
feel thyself well? hast thou no harm?

Brain-worm. No, I thank your good worship, sir.

Clement. Why, so! I said "I must cut off thy legs," and,
"I must cut off thy arms," and, "I must cut off thy head";
but, I did not do it: so you said, "you must serve this
gentleman with my warrant," but, you did not serve him.
You knave, you slave, you rogue, do you say you "must?"

---

[1] Emotion.
[2] Taken aback, he hesitates.

—Sirrah, away with him to the jail; I'll teach you a trick for your "must," sir.

Brain-worm. Good sir, I beseech you, be good to me.

Clement. Tell him he shall to the jail,—away with him, I say.

Brain-worm. Nay, sir, if you will commit me, it shall be for committing more than this: I will not lose, by my travail, any grain of my fame, certain.   [*Takes off his disguises.*

Clement. How is this!

Kno'well. My man Brain-worm!

Stephen. O yes, uncle: Brain-worm has been with my cousin Edward and I, all this day.

Clement. I told you all, there was some device.

Brain-worm. Nay, excellent justice, since I have laid myself thus open to you; now, stand strong for me: both with your sword, and your balance.

Clement. Body o' me, a merry knave!—give me a bowl of sack:—if he belong to you, Master Kno'well, I bespeak your patience.

Brain-worm. That is it, I have most need of. Sir, if you'll pardon me only,[1] I'll glory in all the rest of my exploits.

Kno'well. Sir, you know I love not to have my favours come hard from me. You have your pardon; though I suspect you shrewdly, for being of counsel with my son against me.

Brain-worm. Yes, faith, I have, sir, though you retained me doubly this morning for yourself: first, as Brain-worm; after, as Fitz-Sword. I was your reformed [2] soldier, sir. 'Twas I sent you to Cob's, upon the errand without end.

Kno'well. Is it possible! or that thou shouldst disguise thy language so, as I should not know thee?

Brain-worm. O, sir, this has been the day of my metamorphosis. It is not that shape alone, that I have run through to-day. I brought this gentleman, Master Kitely, a message too, in the form of Master Justice's man here, to draw him out o' the way, as well as your worship; while Master Well-bred might make a conveyance of Mistress Bridget to my young master.

Kitely. How! my sister stolen away?

[1] Then a common form for "Only pardon me."
[2] *i.e.* Reformado.

Kno'well. My son is not married, I hope!

Brain-worm. Faith, sir, they are both as sure as love, a priest and three thousand pound—which is her portion—can make 'hem: and by this time are ready to bespeak their wedding-supper at the Windmill, except some friend here prevent[1] 'hem, and invite 'hem home.

Clement. Marry, that will I (I thank thee for putting me in mind on't).—Sirrah, go you and fetch 'hem hither, "upon my warrant." [*Exit* Servant.] Neither's friends have cause to be sorry, if I know the young couple aright.—Here, I drink to thee for thy good news. But, I pray thee, what hast thou done with my man, Formal?

Brain-worm. Faith, sir, after some ceremony past, as making him drunk, first with story, and then with wine,—but all in kindness—and stripping him to his shirt: I left him in that cool vein departed, sold "your worship's warrant" to these two, pawned his livery for that varlet's gown, to serve it in; and thus have brought myself, by my activity, to your worship's consideration.

Clement. And I will consider thee, in another cup of sack. Here's to thee, which having drunk off, this is my sentence:—Pledge me.—Thou hast done, or assisted to nothing, in my judgment, but deserves to be pardoned for the wit o' the offence. If thy master, or any man here, be angry with thee, I shall suspect his ingine[2] while I know him, for't.—How now, what noise is that?

Enter Servant.

Servant. Sir, it is Roger is come home.

Clement. Bring him in, bring him in.

Enter FORMAL *in a suit of armour.*[3]

What! drunk in arms, against me? your reason, your reason for this?

Formal. I beseech your worship to pardon me; I happened into ill company by chance, that cast me into a sleep, and stript me of all my clothes——

Clement. Well, tell him, I am Justice Clement, and do

[1] Anticipate.
[2] Wit, sense.—Lat. *ingenium.*
[3] Scene iv. in old eds.

pardon him:—but what is this to your armour? what may that signify?

Formal. An't please you, sir, it hung up i' the room, where I was stript; and I borrowed it of one o' the drawers[1] to come home in, because I was loth to do penance through the street, i' my shirt.

Clement. Well, stand by a while.

Enter E. KNO'WELL, WELL-BRED, *and* BRIDGET.[2]

Who be these? O, the young company,—welcome, welcome! Gi' you joy. Nay, Mistress Bridget, blush not; you are not so fresh a bride, but the news of it is come hither afore you. Master bridegroom, I ha' made your peace, give me your hand: so will I for all the rest, ere you forsake my roof.

E. Kno'well. We are the more bound to your humanity sir.

Clement. Only these two[3] have so little of man in 'hem, they are no part of my care.

Well-bred. Yes, sir, let me pray you for this gentleman, he belongs to my sister, the bride.

Clement. In what place, sir.

Well-bred. Of her delight, sir; below the stairs, and in public:—her poet, sir.

Clement. A poet? I will challenge him myself presently at extempore.

　　　Mount up thy Phlegon,[4] Muse, and testify,

　　　　How Saturn, sitting in an ebon cloud,

　　　Disrobed his podex, white as ivory,

　　　　And, through the welkin, thundered all aloud.

Well-bred. He is not for extempore, sir. He is all for the pocket-muse; please you command a sight of it.

Clement. Yes, yes, search him for a taste of his vein.

　　　　　　　　　　　　[*They search* MATTHEW's *pockets.*

Well-bred. You must not deny the Queen's Justice, sir, under a writ o' rebellion.

---

[1] Drawers of liquor.
[2] Scene v. in old eds.
[3] Bobadill and Matthew.
[4] One of the horses of the Sun.

Clement. What! all this verse? body o' me, he carries a whole ream,[1] a commonwealth of paper in 's hose; let's see some of his subjects.   [*Reads.*

"Unto the boundless ocean of thy face,
   Runs this poor river, charged with streams of eyes."
How? this is stolen.[2]

E. Kno'well. A parody! a parody! with a kind of miraculous gift, to make it absurder than it was.

Clement. Is all the rest, of this batch?—Bring me a torch; lay it together, and give fire. Cleanse the air.—Here was enough to have infected the whole city, if it had not been taken in time. See, see, how our poet's glory shines! brighter, and brighter! still it increases! Oh, now it's at the highest: and now, it declines as fast. You may see. *Sic transit gloria mundi!* [3]

Kno'well. There's an emblem for you, son, and your studies!

Clement. Nay, no speech, or act of mine be drawn against such, as profess it worthily. They are not born every year, as an alderman. There goes more to the making of a good poet, than a sheriff, Master Kitely. You look upon me! though I live i' the city here, amongst you, I will do more reverence to him, when I meet him, than I will to the mayor—out of his year. But, these paperpedlars! these ink-dabblers! they cannot expect reprehension, or reproach.[4] They have it with the fact.

E. Kno'well. Sir, you have saved me the labour of a defence.

Clement. It shall be discourse for supper, between your father and me, if he dare undertake me. But, to dispatch away these,—you sign o' the soldier, and picture o' the poet, (but both so false, I will not ha' you hanged out at my door till midnight.[5]) while we are at supper, you two shall penitently fast it out in my court, without; and, if you will, you may pray there, that we may be so merry within, as to forgive, or forget you, when we come out.

[1] A quibble on realm.
[2] S. Daniel, sonnet to Delia I., ll. 1-2.
[3] So passes away the glory of this world.
[4] Merely. They are taken in the fact, *i.e.* the act.
[5] When no one can see you.

Here's a third,[1] because we tender your safety, shall watch you, he is provided for the purpose. Look to your charge, sir.

Stephen. And what shall I do?

Clement. O! I had lost a sheep, and he had not bleated! —Why, sir, you shall give Master Down-right his cloak; —and I will intreat him to take it. A trencher and a napkin you shall have, i' the buttery, and keep Cob and his wife company, here;—whom I will intreat first to be reconciled;—and you to endeavour with your wit to keep 'hem so.

Stephen. I'll do my best.

Cob. Why, now I see thou art honest, Tib, I receive thee as my dear, and mortal wife again.

Tib. And I you, as my loving, and obedient husband.

Clement. Good complement! It will be their bridal night too. They are married anew. Come, I conjure the rest, to put off all discontent. You, Master Down-right, your anger; you Master Kno'well, your cares; Master Kitely and his wife, their jealousy.

> For, I must tell you both, while that is fed,
> Horns i' the mind are worse than o' the head.

Kitely. Sir, thus they go from me;—kiss me, sweetheart.

> "See what a drove of horns fly in the air,
> Winged with my cleansed, and my cred'lous breath!
> Watch 'hem, suspicious eyes, watch where they fall.
> See, see! on heads, that think they've none at all!
> O, what a plenteous world, of this will come!
> When air rains horns, all may be sure of some."

I ha' learned so much verse out of a jealous man's part, in a play.

Clement. 'Tis well, 'tis well! This night we'll dedicate to friendship, love, and laughter. Master bridegroom, take your bride, and lead;—every one, a fellow. Here is my mistress,—Brain-worm! to whom all my addresses of courtship shall have their reference. Whose adventures this day, when our grandchildren shall hear to be made a fable, I doubt not, but it shall find both spectators, and applause.   [*Exeunt.*

[1] *i.e.* Formal.

SEJANUS, HIS FALL

THIS "Tragedy" was first acted in 1603, by the company at the Globe; and Shakespeare, Burbage, Lowin, Hemings, Condel, Philips, Cooke, and Sly had parts in it. Though much applauded by the fashionable part of the audience, it proved "caviare to the general," and experienced considerable opposition. *Sejanus* was not published till 1605; when it appeared in quarto, without a dedication, but accompanied by several copies of commendatory verses. Subsequently it seems to have acquired some degree of popularity. Jonson says it had outlived the malice of its enemies, when he republished it in folio, in 1616; and it was one of the first plays revived after the Restoration. *Sejanus* is not divided into scenes in any of the editions; it has neither exits nor entrances; and is, upon the whole, the most involved and puzzling drama, in its internal arrangement, that was ever produced. The motto both to the quarto and folio is the same:—

> *Non hic centauros, non gorgonas, harpyiasque*
> *Invenies: hominem pagina nostra sapit.*

It is taken from Martial, and had already furnished the groundwork for the admirable prologue to *Every Man in His Humour.*

TO THE

NO LESS NOBLE BY VIRTUE THAN BLOOD,

ESME, LORD AUBIGNE.

My Lord,—If ever any ruin were so great as to survive, I think this be one I send you, The Fall of Sejanus. It is a poem, that, if I well remember, in your lordship's sight, suffered no less violence from our people here, than the subject of it did from the rage of the people of Rome; but with a different fate, as, I hope, merit; for this hath out-lived their malice, and begot itself a greater favour than he lost, the love of good men. Amongst whom, if I make your lordship the first it thanks, it is not without a just confession of the bond your benefits have, and ever shall hold upon me,

Your Lordship's most faithful honourer,

BEN. JONSON.

TO THE READERS

THE following and voluntary labours of my friends, prefixed to my book, have relieved me in much whereat, without them, I should necessarily have touched. Now I will only use three or four short and needful notes, and so rest.

First, if it be objected, that what I publish is no true poem, in the strict laws of time, I confess it: as also in the want of a proper chorus; whose habit and moods are such and so difficult, as not any, whom I have seen, since the ancients, no, not they who have most presently affected laws, have yet come in the way of. Nor is it needful, or almost possible in these our times, and to such auditors as commonly things are presented, to observe the old state and splendour of dramatic poems, with preservation of any popular delight. But of this I shall take more seasonable cause to speak, in my observations upon Horace his Art of Poetry, which, with the text translated, I intend shortly to publish. In the meantime, if in truth of argument, dignity of persons, gravity and height of elocution, fulness and frequency of sentence, I have discharged the other offices of a tragic writer, let not the absence of these forms be imputed to me, wherein I shall give you occasion hereafter, and without my boast, to think I could better prescribe, than omit the due use for want of a convenient knowledge.

The next is, lest in some nice nostril the quotations might savour affected, I do let you know, that I abhor nothing more; and I have only done it to show my integrity in the story, and save myself in those common tortures that bring all wit to the rack; whose noses are ever like swine spoiling and rooting up the Muses' gardens; and their whole bodies like moles, as blindly working under earth, to cast any, the least, hills upon virtue.

Whereas they are in Latin, and the work in English, it was presupposed none but the learned would take the pains to confer them; the authors themselves being all in the learned tongues, save one, with whose English side I have had little to do. To which it may be required, since

I have quoted the page, to name what editions I followed: *Tacit. Lips. in quarto, Antwerp, edit.* 1600. *Dio. folio, Hen. Steph.* 1592. For the rest, as *Sueton. Seneca,* &c., the chapter doth sufficiently direct, or the edition is not varied.

Lastly, I would inform you, that this book, in all numbers, is not the same with that which was acted on the public stage; wherein a second pen had good share: in place of which, I have rather chosen to put weaker, and, no doubt, less pleasing, of mine own, than to defraud so happy a genius of his right by my loathed usurpation.

Fare you well and if you read farther of me, and like, I shall not be afraid of it, though you praise me out.

Neque enim mihi cornea fibra est.

But that I should plant my felicity in your general saying, *good,* or *well,* &c., were a weakness which the better sort of you might worthily contemn, if not absolutely hate me for.

BEN. JONSON;
and no such,

Quem
Palma negata macrum, donata reducit optimum.

THE ARGUMENT

AELIUS SEJANUS, son to Seius Strabo, a gentleman of Rome, and born at Vulsinium; after his long service in court, first under Augustus; afterward, Tiberius; grew into that favour with the latter, and won him by those arts, as there wanted nothing but the name to make him a co-partner of the Empire. Which greatness of his, Drusus, the Emperor's son, not brooking; after many smothered dislikes, in one day breaking out, the prince struck him publicly on the face. To revenge which disgrace, Lavia, the wife of Drusus (being before corrupted by him to her dishonour, and the discovery of her husband's counsels) Sejanus practiseth with, together with her physician, called Eudemus, and one Lygdus, an eunuch, to poison Drusus. This their inhuman act having successful and unsuspected passage, it emboldeneth Sejanus to further and more insolent projects, even the ambition of the Empire; where finding the lets he must encounter to be many and hard, in respect of the issue of Germanicus, who were next in hope for the succession, he deviseth to make Tiberius' self his means and instils into his ears many doubts and suspicions, both against the princes, and their mother Agrippina; which Cæsar jealously hearkening to, as covetously consenteth to their ruin, and their friends. In this time, the better to mature and strengthen his design, Sejanus labours to marry Livia, and worketh with all his ingine, to remove Tiberius from the knowledge of public business, with allurements of a quiet and retired life; the latter of which, Tiberius, out of a proneness to lust, and a desire to hide those unnatural pleasures which he could not so publicly practise, embraceth: the former enkindleth his fears, and there gives him first cause of doubt or suspect towards Sejanus: against whom he raiseth in private a new instrument, one Sertorius Macro, and by him underworketh, discovers the other's counsels, his means, his ends, sounds the affections of the senators, divides, distracts them: at last, when Sejanus least looketh, and is most secure; with pretext of doing him an unwonted honour in the senate, he trains him from his guards, and with a long-doubtful letter, in one day hath him suspected, accused, condemned, and torn in pieces by the rage of the people.

DRAMATIS PERSONÆ

TIBERIUS.
DRUSUS SENIOR.
NERO.
DRUSUS JUNIOR.
CALIGULA.
LUCIUS ARRUNTIUS.
CAIUS SILIUS.
TITIUS SABINUS.
MARCUS LEPIDUS.
CREMUTIUS CORDUS.
ASINIUS GALLUS.
REGULUS.
TERENTIUS.
GRACINUS LACO.
EUDEMUS.
RUFUS.
SEJANUS.
LATIARIS.
VARRO.
SERTORIUS MACRO.
COTTA.
DOMITIUS AFER.
HATERIUS.

SANQUINIUS.
POMPONIUS.
JULIUS POSTHUMUS.
FULCINIUS TRIO.
MINUTIUS.
SATRIUS SECUNDUS.
PINNARIUS NATTA.
OPSIUS.

Tribuni.
Præcones.
Flamen.
Tubicines.
Nuntius.
Lictores.
Ministri.
Tibicines.
Servi, &c.

AGRIPPINA.
LIVIA.
SOSIA.

SCENE—Rome

SEJANUS

ACT THE FIRST

SCENE I—*A State Room in the Palace*

Enter SABINUS *and* SILIUS, *followed by* LATIARIS.

SABINUS. Hail, Caius Silius!
  Silius. Titius Sabinus, hail!
You're rarely met in court.
  Sabinus. Therefore, well met.
  Silius. 'Tis true: indeed, this place is not our sphere.
  Sabinus. No, Silius, we are no good inginers.
We want their fine arts, and their thriving use
Should make us graced, or favoured of the times:
We have no shift of faces, no cleft tongues,
No soft and glutinous bodies, that can stick,
Like snails on painted walls; or, on our breasts,
Creep up, to fall from that proud height, to which
We did by slavery, not by service climb.
We are no guilty men, and then no great;
We have no place in court, office in state,
That we can say, we owe unto our crimes:
That burn with no black secrets, which can make
Us dear to the pale authors; or live feared
Of their still waking jealousies, to raise
Ourselves a fortune, by subverting theirs.
We stand not in the lines, that do advance
To that so courted point.

Enter SATRIUS *and* NATTA *at a distance.*

  Silius. But yonder lean
A pair that do.
  Sabinus [*salutes* LATIARIS]. Good cousin Latiaris.
  Silius. Satrius Secundus, and Pinnarius Natta,
The great Sejanus' clients: there be two,
Know more than honest counsels; whose close breasts,
Were they ripped up to light, it would be found
A poor and idle sin, to which their trunks

Had not been made fit organs. These can lie,
Flatter, and swear, forswear, deprave, inform,
Smile, and betray; make guilty men; then beg
The forfeit lives, to get their livings; cut
Men's throats with whisperings; sell to gaping suitors
The empty smoke, that flies about the palace;
Laugh when their patron laughs; sweat when he sweats;
Be hot and cold with him; change every mood,
Habit, and garb, as often as he varies;
Observe him, as his watch observes his clock;
And, true as turquoise in the dear lord's ring,
Look well or ill with him: ready to praise
His lordship, if he spit, or but p— fair,
Have an indifferent stool, or break wind well;
Nothing can scape their catch.

    Sabinus. Alas! these things
Deserve no note, conferred with other vile
And filthier flatteries, that corrupt the times:
When, not alone our gentries chief are fain
To make their safety from such sordid acts;
But all our consuls, and no little part
Of such as have been prætors, yea, the most
Of senators, that else not use their voices,
Start up in public senate, and there strive
Who shall propound most abject things, and base.
So much, as oft Tiberius hath been heard,
Leaving the court, to cry, O race of men,
Prepared for servitude!—which showed that he,
Who least the public liberty could like,
As lothly brooked their flat servility.

    Silius. Well, all is worthy of us, were it more,
Who with our riots, pride, and civil hate,
Have so provoked the justice of the gods:
We, that, within these fourscore years, were born
Free, equal lords of the triumphed world,
And knew no masters but affections;
To which betraying first our liberties,
We since became the slaves to one man's lusts;
And now to many: every minist'ring spy
That will accuse and swear, is lord of you,

Of me, of all our fortunes and our lives.
Our looks are called to question, and our words,
How innocent soever, are made crimes;
We shall not shortly dare to tell our dreams,
Or think, but 'twill be treason.

    Sabinus. Tyrants' arts
Are to give flatterers grace; accusers, power;
That those may seem to kill whom they devour.

          Enter CORDUS *and* ARRUNTIUS.

Now, good Cremutius Cordus.

    Cordus [*salutes* SABINUS]. Hail to your lordship!

    Natta [*whispers* LATIARIS]. Who's that salutes your cousin?

    Latiaris. 'Tis one Cordus,
A gentleman of Rome: one that has writ
Annals of late, they say, and very well.

    Natta. Annals! of what times?

    Latiaris. I think of Pompey's,
And Caius Cæsar's; and so down to these.

    Natta. How stands he affected to the present state?
Is he or Drusian, or Germanican,
Or ours, or neutral?

    Latiaris. I know him not so far.

    Natta. Those times are somewhat queasy to be touched.
Have you or seen, or heard part of his work?

    Latiaris. Not I; he means they shall be public shortly.

    Natta. O, Cordus do you call him?

    Latiaris. Ay.   [*Exeunt* NATTA *and* SATRIUS.

    Sabinus. But these our times
Are not the same, Arruntius.

    Arruntius. Times! the men,
The men are not the same! 'tis we are base,
Poor, and degenerate from the exalted strain
Of our great fathers. Where is now the soul
Of god-like Cato? he, that durst be good,
When Cæsar durst be evil; and had power,
As not to live his slave, to die his master?
Or where's the constant Brutus, that being proof
Against all charm of benefits, did strike
So brave a blow into the monster's heart

That sought unkindly to captive his country?
O, they are fled the light! Those mighty spirits
Lie raked up with their ashes in their urns,
And not a spark of their eternal fire
Glows in a present bosom. All's but blaze,
Flashes and smoke, wherein we labour so,
There's nothing Roman in us; nothing good,
Gallant, or great: 'tis true that Cordus says,
"Brave Cassius was the last of all that race."

> [DRUSUS *passes over the stage, attended by*
> HATERIUS, &c.

   Sabinus. Stand by! Lord Drusus.

   Haterius. The emperor's son! give place.

   Silius. I like the prince well.

   Arruntius. A riotous youth;
There's little hope of him.

   Sabinus. That fault his age
Will, as it grows, correct. Methinks he bears
Himself each day more nobly than other;
And wins no less on men's affections,
Than doth his father lose. Believe me, I love him;
And chiefly for opposing to Sejanus.

   Silius. And I, for gracing his young kinsmen so,
The sons of prince Germanicus: it shows
A gallant clearness in him, a straight mind,
That envies not, in them, their father's name.

   Arruntius. His name was, while he lived, above all envy;
And, being dead, without it. O, that man!
If there were seeds of the old virtue left,
They lived in him.

   Silius. He had the fruits, Arruntius,
More than the seeds: Sabinus, and myself
Had means to know him within; and can report him
We were his followers, he would call us friends;
He was a man most like to virtue; in all,
And every action, nearer to the gods,
Than men, in nature; of a body as fair
As was his mind; and no less reverend
In face than fame: he could so use his states,
Tempering his greatness with his gravity,

As it avoided all self-love in him,
And spite in others. What his funerals lacked
In images and pomp, they had supplied
With honourable sorrow, soldiers' sadness,
A kind of silent mourning, such as men,
Who know no tears but from their captives, use
To show in so great losses.
    Cordus. I thought once,
Considering their forms, age, manner of deaths,
The nearness of the places where they fell,
To have paralleled him with great Alexander:
For both were of best feature, of high race,
Yeared but to thirty, and, in foreign lands,
By their own people alike made away.
    Sabinus. I know not, for his death, how you might wrest
    it:
But, for his life, it did as much disdain
Comparison with that voluptuous, rash,
Giddy, and drunken Macedon's, as mine
Doth with my bondman's. All the good in him,
His valour, and his fortune, he made his;
But he had other touches of late Romans,
That more did speak him: Pompey's dignity,
The innocence of Cato, Cæsar's spirit,
Wise Brutus' temperance: and every virtue,
Which, parted unto others, gave them name,
Flowed mixed in him. He was the soul of goodness;
And all our praises of him are like streams
Drawn from a spring, that still rise full, and leave
The part remaining greatest.
    Arruntius. I am sure
He was too great for us, and that they knew
Who did remove him hence.
    Sabinus. When men grow fast
Honoured and loved, there is a trick in state,
Which jealous princes never fail to use,
How to decline that growth, with fair pretext,
And honourable colours of employment,
Either by embassy, the war, or such,
To shift them forth into another air,

Where they may purge, and lessen; so was he:
And had his seconds there, sent by Tiberius,
And his more subtile dam, to discontent him;
To breed and cherish mutinies; detract
His greatest actions; give audacious check
To his commands; and work to put him out
In open act of treason. All which snares
When his wise cares prevented, a fine poison
Was thought on, to mature their practices.

Enter SEJANUS, *talking to* TERENTIUS; *followed by*
SATRIUS, NATTA, &c.

Cordus. Here comes Sejanus.
    Silius. Now observe the stoops,
The bendings, and the falls.
    Arruntius. Most creeping base!
    Sejanus [*to* NATTA]. I note them well: no more.
Say you?
    Satrius. My lord,
There is a gentleman of Rome would buy——
    Sejanus. How call you him you talked with?
    Satrius. Please your worship,
It is Eudemus, the physician
To Livia, Drusus' wife.
    Sejanus. On with your suit.
Would buy, you said——
    Satrius. A tribune's place, my lord.
    Sejanus. What will he give?
    Satrius. Fifty sestertia.
    Sejanus. Livia's physician, say you, is that fellow?
    Satrius. It is, my lord. Your lordship's answer.
    Sejanus. To what?
    Satrius. The place, my lord. 'Tis for a gentleman
Your lordship will well like of, when you see him,
And one that you may make yours, by the grant.
    Sejanus. Well, let him bring his money, and his name.
    Satrius. 'Thank your lordship. He shall, my lord.
    Sejanus. Come hither.
Know you this same Eudemus? is he learned?
    Satrius. Reputed so, my lord, and of deep practice.

Sejanus. Bring him in to me, in the gallery;
And take you cause to leave us there together:
I would confer with him, about a grief—
On.   [*Exeunt* SEJANUS, SATRIUS, TERENTIUS, *&c.*

    Arruntius. So! yet another? yet? O desperate state
Of grovelling honour! seest thou this, O sun,
And do we see thee after? Methinks, day
Should lose his light, when men do lose their shames,
And for the empty circumstance of life,
Betray their cause of living.

    Silius. Nothing so.
Sejanus can repair, if Jove should ruin.
He is now the court god; and well applied
With sacrifice of knees, of crooks, and cringes;
He will do more than all the house of heaven
Can for a thousand hecatombs. 'Tis he
Makes us our day, or night; hell and elysium
Are in his look: we talk of Rhadamanth,
Furies, and firebrands; but it is his frown
That is all these; where, on the adverse part,
His smile is more than e'er yet poets feigned
Of bliss, and shades, nectar——

    Arruntius. A serving boy!
I knew him, at Caius' trencher, when for hire
He prostituted his abused body
To that great gormond, fat Apicius:
And was the noted pathic of the time.

    Sabinus. And, now, the second face of the whole world!
The partner of the empire, hath his image
Reared equal with Tiberius, born in ensigns;
Commands, disposes every dignity.
Centurions, tribunes, heads of provinces,
Prætors, and consuls; all that heretofore
Rome's general suffrage gave, is now his sale.
The gain, or rather spoil of all the earth,
One, and his house, receives.

    Silius. He hath of late
Made him a strength too, strangely, by reducing
All the prætorian bands into one camp,
Which he commands: pretending that the soldiers,

By living loose and scattered, fell to riot;
And that if any sudden enterprise
Should be attempted, their united strength
Would be far more than severed; and their life
More strict, if from the city more removed.

   Sabinus. Where now he builds what kind of forts he
    please,
Is heard to court the soldier by his name,
Woos, feasts the chiefest men of action,
Whose wants, nor loves, compel them to be his.
And though he ne'er were liberal by kind,
Yet to his own dark ends, he's most profuse,
Lavish, and letting fly, he cares not what
To his ambition.

   Arruntius. Yet, hath he ambition?
Is there that step in state can make him higher,
Or more, or anything he is, but less?

   Silius. Nothing but emperor.

   Arruntius. The name Tiberius,
I hope, will keep, howe'er he hath foregone
The dignity and power.

   Silius. Sure, while he lives.

   Arruntius. And dead, it comes to Drusus. Should he fail,
To the brave issue of Germanicus;
And they are three: too many—ha? for him
To have a plot upon?

   Silius. I do not know
The heart of his designs; but sure their face
Looks farther than the present.

   Arruntius. By the gods,
If I could guess he had but such a thought,
My sword should cleave him down from head to heart,
But I would find it out: and with my hand
I'd hurl his panting brain about the air
In mites as small as atomi, to undo
The knotted bed——

   Sabinus. You are observed, Arruntius.

   Arruntius [*turns to* NATTA, TERRENTIUS, *&c.*]. Death!
        I dare tell him so; and all his spies:

You, sir, I would, do you look? and you.
  Sabinus. Forbear.

         SCENE II—*The former Scene continued*

    A Gallery discovered opening into the State Room.

            Enter SATRIUS *with* EUDEMUS.

  Satrius. Here he will instant be; let's walk a turn;
You're in a muse, Eudemus?
  Eudemus. Not I, sir.
I wonder he should mark me out so! well,
Jove and Apollo form it for the best.   [*Aside.*
  Satrius. Your fortune's made unto you now, Eudemus,
If you can but lay hold upon the means;
Do but observe his humour, and—believe it—
He is the noblest Roman, where he takes—

                Enter SEJANUS.

Here comes his lordship.
  Sejanus. Now, good Satrius.
  Satrius. This is the gentleman, my lord.
  Sejanus. Is this?
Give me your hand, we must be more acquainted.
Report, sir, hath spoke out your art and learning:
And I am glad I have so needful cause,
However in itself painful and hard,
To make me known to so great virtue—Look,
Who is that, Satrius? [*Exit* SATRIUS] I have a grief, sir,
That will desire your help. Your name's Eudemus?
  Eudemus. Yes.
  Sejanus. Sir?
  Eudemus. It is, my lord.
  Sejanus. I hear you are
Physician to Livia, the princess.
  Eudemus. I minister unto her, my good lord.
  Sejanus. You minister to a royal lady, then.
  Eudemus. She is, my lord, and fair.

Sejanus. That's understood
Of all their sex, who are or would be so;
And those that would be, physic soon can make them:
For those that are, their beauties fear no colours.

Eudemus. Your lordship is conceited.

Sejanus. Sir, you know it,
And can, if need be, read a learned lecture
On this, and other secrets. 'Pray you, tell me,
What more of ladies, besides Livia,
Have you your patients?

Eudemus. Many, my good lord.
The great Augusta, Urgulania,
Mutilia Prisca, and Plancina: divers—

Sejanus. And, all these tell you the particulars
Of every several grief? how first it grew,
And then increased; what action caused that;
What passion that; and answer to each point
That you will put them?

Eudemus. Else, my lord, we know not
How to prescribe the remedies.

Sejanus. Go to,
You are a subtile nation, you physicians!
And grown the only cabinets in court,
To ladies' privacies. Faith, which of these
Is the most pleasant lady in her physic?
Come, you are modest now.

Eudemus. 'Tis fit, my lord.

Sejanus. Why, sir, I do not ask you of their urines,
Whose smell's most violet, or whose siege is best,
Or who makes hardest faces on her stool?
Which lady sleeps with her own face a nights?
Which puts her teeth off, with her clothes, in court?
Or, which her hair, which her complexion,
And, in which box she puts it? These were questions
That might, perhaps, have put your gravity
To some defence of blush. But, I inquired,
Which was the wittiest, merriest, wantonest?
Harmless interrogatories, but conceits.——
Methinks Augusta should be most perverse,
And froward in her fit.

Eudemus. She's so, my lord.

Sejanus. I knew it: and Mutilia the most jocund.

Eudemus. 'Tis very true, my lord.

Sejanus. And why would you
Conceal this from me, now? Come, what is Livia?
I know she's quick and quaintly spirited,
And will have strange thoughts, when she is at leisure:
She tells them all to you.

Eudemus. My noblest lord,
He breathes not in the Empire, or on earth,
Whom I would be ambitious to serve
In any act, that may preserve mine honour,
Before your lordship.

Sejanus. Sir, you can lose no honour,
By trusting aught to me. The coarsest act
Done to my service, I can so requite,
As all the world shall style it honourable:
Your idle, virtuous definitions,
Keep honour poor, and are as scorned as vain:
Those deeds breathe honour that do suck in gain.

Eudemus. But, good my lord, if I should thus betray
The counsels of my patient, and a lady's
Of her high place and worth; what might your lordship,
Who presently are to trust me with your own,
Judge of my faith?

Sejanus. Only the best, I swear.
Say now that I should utter you my grief,
And with it the true cause; that it were love,
And love to Livia, you should tell her this:
Should she suspect your faith? I would you could
Tell me as much from her; see if my brain
Could be turned jealous.

Eudemus. Happily, my lord,
I could in time tell you as much and more;
So I might safely promise but the first
To her from you.

Sejanus. As safely, my Eudemus,
I now dare call thee so, as I have put
The secret into thee.

Eudemus. My lord——

Sejanus. Protest not,
Thy looks are vows to me; use only speed,
And but affect her with Sejanus' love,
Thou art a man, made to make consuls. Go.
   Eudemus. My lord, I'll promise you a private meeting
This day together.
   Sejanus. Canst thou?
   Eudemus. Yes.
   Sejanus. The place?
   Eudemus. My gardens, whither I shall fetch your lordship.
   Sejanus. Let me adore my Æsculapius.
Why, this indeed is physic! and outspeaks
The knowledge of cheap drugs, or any use
Can be made out of it! more comforting
Than all your opiates, juleps, apozems,
Magistral syrups, or——Begone, my friend,
Not barely styled, but created so;
Expect things greater than thy largest hopes,
To overtake thee: Fortune shall be taught
To know how ill she hath deserved thus long,
To come behind thy wishes. Go, and speed.

                                          [*Exit* EUDEMUS.

Ambition makes more trusty slaves than need.
These fellows, by the favour of their art,
Have still the means to tempt; oft-times the power.
If Livia will be now corrupted, then
Thou hast the way, Sejanus, to work out
His secrets, who, thou know'st, endures thee not,
Her husband, Drusus: and to work against them.
Prosper it, Pallas, thou that betterest wit;
For Venus hath the smallest share in it.

                Enter TIBERIUS *and* DRUSUS, *attended.*

   Tiberius [*to* HATERIUS, *who kneels to him*]. We not en-
         dure these flatteries; let him stand;
Our empire, ensigns, axes, rods, and state
Take not away our human nature from us:
Look up on us, and fall before the gods.
   Sejanus. How like a god speaks Cæsar!
   Arruntius. There, observe!

He can endure that second, that's no flattery.
O, what is it, proud slime will not believe
Of his own worth, to hear it equal praised
Thus with the gods!
    Cordus. He did not hear it, sir.
    Arruntius. He did not! Tut, he must not, we think
      meanly.
'Tis your most courtly known confederacy,
To have your private parasite redeem
What he, in public, subtilely will lose,
To making him a name.
    Haterius. Right mighty lord——   [*Gives him letters.*
    Tiberius. We must make up our ears 'gainst these assaults
Of charming tongues; we pray you use no more
These contumelies to us; style not us
Or lord, or mighty, who profess ourself
The servant of the senate, and are proud
T' enjoy them our good, just, and favouring lords.
    Cordus. Rarely dissembled!
    Arruntius. Prince-like to the life.
    Sabinus. When power that may command, so much
      descends,
Their bondage, whom it stoops to, it intends.
    Tiberius. Whence are these letters?
    Haterius. From the senate.
    Tiberius. So.   [LATIARIS *gives him letters.*
Whence these?
    Latiaris. From thence too.
    Tiberius. Are they sitting now?
    Latiaris. They stay thy answer, Cæsar.
    Silius. If this man
Hath but a mind allied unto his words,
How blest a fate were it to us, and Rome!
We could not hink that state for which to change,
Although the aim were our old liberty:
The ghosts of those that fell for that, would grieve
Their bodies lived not, now, again to serve.
Men are deceived, who think there can be thrall
Beneath a virtuous prince. Wished liberty
Ne'er lovelier looks, than under such a crown.

But, when his grace is merely but lip-good,
And that, no longer than he airs himself
Abroad in public, there, to seem to shun
The strokes and stripes of flatterers, which within
Are lechery unto him, and so feed
His brutish sense with their afflicting sound,
As, dead to virtue, he permits himself
Be carried like a pitcher by the ears,
To every act of vice: this is a case
Deserves our fear, and doth presage the nigh
And close approach of blood and tyranny.
Flattery is midwife unto prince's rage:
And nothing sooner doth help forth a tyrant,
Than that and whisperers' grace, who have the time,
The place, the power, to make all men offenders.

   Arruntius. He should be told this; and be bid dissemble
With fools and blind men: we that know the evil,
Should hunt the palace-rats, or give them bane;
Fright hence these worse than ravens, that devour
The quick, where they but prey upon the dead:
He shall be told it.

   Sabinus. Stay, Arruntius.
We must abide our opportunity;
And practise what is fit, as what is needful.
It is not safe t' enforce a sovereign's ear:
Princes hear well, if they at all will hear.

   Arruntius. Ha, say you so? well! In the mean time, Jove,
(Say not but I do call upon thee now,)
Of all wild beasts preserve me from a tyrant;
And of all tame, a flatterer.

   Silius. 'Tis well prayed.

   Tiberius [*having read the letters*]. Return the lords this
     voice, We are their creature,
And it is fit a good and honest prince,
Whom they, out of their bounty, have instructed
With so dilate and absolute a power,
Should owe the office of it to their service,
And good of all and every citizen.
Nor shall it e'er repent us to have wished
The senate just, and favouring lords unto us,

Since their free loves do yield no less defence
To a prince's state, than his own innocence.
Say then, there can be nothing in their thought
Shall want to please us, that hath pleased them;
Our suffrage rather shall prevent, than stay
Behind their wills: 'tis empire to obey,
Where such, so great, so grave, so good determine.
Yet, for the suit of Spain, to erect a temple
In honour of our mother and our self,
We must, with pardon of the senate, not
Assent thereto. Their lordships may object
Our not denying the same late request
Unto the Asian cities: we desire
That our defence for suffering that be known
In these brief reasons, with our after purpose.
Since deified Augustus hindered not
A temple to be built at Pergamum,
In honour of himself and sacred Rome;
We, that have all his deeds and words observed
Ever, in place of laws, the rather followed
That pleasing precedent, because with ours,
The senate's reverence, also, there was joined.
But as, t' have once received it, may deserve
The gain of pardon; so, to be adored
With the continued style, and note of gods,
Through all the provinces, were wild ambition,
And no less pride: yea, even Augustus' name
Would early vanish, should it be profaned
With such promiscuous flatteries. For our part,
We here protest it, and are covetous
Posterity should know it, we are mortal;
And can but deeds of men: 'twere glory enough,
Could we be truly a prince. And, they shall add
Abounding grace unto our memory,
That shall report us worthy our forefathers,
Careful of your affairs, constant in dangers,
And not afraid of any private frown
For public good. These things shall be to us
Temples and statues, reared in your minds,
The fairest, and most during imagery:

For those of stone or brass, if they become
Odious in judgment of posterity,
Are more condemned as dying sepulchres,
Than ta'en for living monuments. We then
ake here our suit, alike to gods and men;
he one, until the period of our race,
o inspire us with a free and quiet mind,
Discerning both divine and human laws;
The other, to vouchsafe us after death,
An honourable mention, and fair praise,
To accompany our actions and our name:
The rest of greatness princes may command,
And, therefore, may neglect; only, a long,
A lasting, high, and happy memory
They should, without being satisfied, pursue:
Contempt of fame begets contempt of virtue.
    Natta. Rare!
    Satrius. Most divine!
    Sejanus. The oracles are ceased,
That only Cæsar, with their tongue, might speak.
    Arruntius. Let me be gone: most felt and open this!
    Cordus. Stay.
    Arruntius. What! to hear more cunning and fine words,
With their sound flattered ere their sense be meant?
    Tiberius. Their choice of Antium, there to place the gift
Vowed to the goddess for our mother's health,
We will the senate know, we fairly like;
As also of their grant to Lepidus,
For his repairing the Æmilian place,
And restoration of those monuments:
Their grace too in confining of Silanus
To the other isle Cithera, at the suit
Of his religious sister, much commends
Their policy, so tempered with their mercy.
But for the honours which they have decreed
To our Sejanus, to advance his statue
In Pompey's theatre, (whose ruining fire
His vigilance and labour kept restrained
In that one loss,) they have therein outgone
Their own great wisdoms, by their skilful choice,

And placing of their bounties on a man,
Whose merit more adorns the dignity,
Than that can him; and gives a benefit,
In taking, greater than it can receive.
Blush not, Sejanus, thou great aid of Rome,
Associate of our labours, our chief helper;
Let us not force thy simple modesty
With offering at thy praise, for more we cannot,
Since there's no voice can take it. No man here
Receive our speeches as hyperboles:
For we are far from flattering our friend,
Let envy know, as from the need to flatter.
Nor let them ask the causes of our praise:
Princes have still their grounds reared with themselves,
Above the poor low flats of common men;
And who will search the reasons of their acts,
Must stand on equal bases. Lead, away:
Our loves unto the senate.

> [*Exeunt* TIBERIUS, SEJANUS, NATTA, HATERIUS,
> LATIARIS, *Officers, &c.*

   Arruntius. Cæsar!

   Sabinus. Peace.

   Cordus. Great Pompey's theatre was never ruined
Till now that proud Sejanus hath a statue
Reared on his ashes.

   Arruntius. Place the shame of soldiers
Above the best of generals? crack the world,
And bruise the name of Romans into dust,
Ere we behold it!

   Silius. Check your passion;
Lord Drusus tarries.

   Drusus. Is my father mad,
Weary of life, and rule, lords? thus to heave
An idol up with praise! make him his mate,
His rival in the empire!

   Arruntius. O, good prince.

   Drusus. Allow him statues, titles, honours, such
As he himself refuseth!

   Arruntius. Brave, brave Drusus!

   Drusus. The first ascents to sovereignty are hard;

But, entered once, there never wants or means,
Or ministers, to help the aspirer on.

    Arruntius. True, gallant Drusus.

    Drusus. We must shortly pray

To Modesty, that he will rest contented—

    Arruntius. Ay, where he is, and not write emperor.

    Re-enter SEJANUS, SATRIUS, LATIARIS, Clients, &c.

    Sejanus. There is your bill, and yours; bring you your
       man. [*To* SATRIUS.]

I have moved for you, too, Latiaris.

    Drusus. What!

Is your vast greatness grown so blindly bold,
That you will over us?

    Sejanus. Why then give way.

    Drusus. Give way, Colossus! do you lift? advance you?

Take that!   [*Strikes him.*

    Arruntius. Good! brave! excellent, brave prince!

    Drusus. Nay, come, approach.   [*Draws his sword.*]

       What, stand you off? at gaze?

It looks too full of death for thy cold spirits.

Avoid mine eye, dull camel, or my sword

Shall make thy bravery fitter for a grave,

Than for a triumph. I'll advance a statue

O' your own bulk; but 't shall be on the cross;

Where I will nail your pride at breadth and length,

And crack those sinews, which are yet but stretched

With your swoln fortune's rage.

    Arruntius. A noble prince!

    All. A Castor, a Castor, a Castor, a Castor.

                       [*Exeunt all but* SEJANUS.

    Sejanus. He that, with such wrong moved, can bear it
       through

With patience, and an even mind, knows how

To turn it back. Wrath covered carries fate:

Revenge is lost, if I profess my hate.

What was my practice late, I'll now pursue,

As my fell justice: this hath styled it new.   [*Exit.*

ACT THE SECOND

SCENE I—*The Garden of* EUDEMUS

Enter SEJANUS, LIVIA, *and* EUDEMUS.

SEJANUS. Physician, thou art worthy of a province,
For the great favours done unto our loves;
And, but that greatest Livia bears a part
In the requital of thy services,
I should alone despair of aught, like means,
To give them worthy satisfaction.
    Livia. Eudemus, I will see it, shall receive
A fit and full reward for his large merit.—
But for this potion we intend to Drusus,
No more our husband now, whom shall we choose
As the most apt and abled instrument,
To minister it to him?
    Eudemus. I say, Lygdus.
    Sejanus. Lygdus? what's he?
    Livia. An eunuch Drusus loves.
    Eudemus. Ay, and his cup-bearer.
    Sejanus. Name not a second.
If Drusus love him, and he have that place,
We cannot think a fitter.
    Eudemus. True, my lord.
For free access and trust are two main aids.
    Sejanus. Skilful physician!
    Livia. But he must be wrought
To the undertaking, with some laboured art.
    Sejanus. Is he ambitious?
    Livia. No.
    Sejanus. Or covetous?
    Livia. Neither.
    Eudemus. Yet, gold is a good general charm.
    Sejanus. What is he, then?
    Livia. Faith, only wanton, light.
    Sejanus. How! is he young and fair?

Eudemus. A delicate youth.

Sejanus. Send him to me, I'll work him.—Royal lady,
Though I have loved you long, and with that height
Of zeal and duty, like the fire, which more
It mounts it trembles, thinking nought could add
Unto the fervour which your eye had kindled;
Yet, now I see your wisdom, judgment, strength,
Quickness, and will, to apprehend the means
To your own good and greatness, I protest
Myself through rarified, and turned all flame
In your affection: such a spirit as yours,
Was not created for the idle second
To a poor flash, as Drusus; but to shine
Bright as the moon among the lesser lights,
And share the sov'reignty of all the world.
Then Livia triumphs in her proper sphere,
When she and her Sejanus shall divide
The name of Cæsar, and Augusta's star
Be dimmed with glory of a brighter beam:
When Agrippina's fires are quite extinct,
And the scarce-seen Tiberius borrows all
His little light from us, whose folded arms
Shall make one perfect orb. [*Knocking within.*] Who's that?
    Eudemus,
Look. [*Exit* EUDEMUS.] 'Tis not Drusus, lady, do not fear.
    Livia. Not I, my lord: my fear and love of him
Left me at once.
    Sejanus. Illustrious lady, stay——
    Eudemus [*within*]. I'll tell his lordship.

                Re-enter EUDEMUS.

    Sejanus. Who is it, Eudemus?
    Eudemus. One of your lordship's servants brings you
    word
The emperor hath sent for you.
    Sejanus. O! where is he?
With your fair leave, dear princess, I'll but ask
A question, and return.   [*Exit.*
    Eudemus. Fortunate princess!
How are you blest in the fruition

Of this unequalled man, the soul of Rome,
The Empire's life, and voice of Cæsar's world!
    Livia. So blessed, my Eudemus, as to know
The bliss I have, with what I ought to owe
The means that wrought it. How do I look to-day?
    Eudemus. Excellent clear, believe it. This same focus
Was well laid on.
    Livia. Methinks 'tis here not white.
    Eudemus. Lend me your scarlet, lady. 'Tis the sun,
Hath giv'n some little taint unto the ceruse;
You should have used of the white oil I gave you.
Sejanus, for your love! his very name
Commandeth above Cupid or his shafts——

                                  [Paints her cheek.

    Livia. Nay, now you've made it worse.
    Eudemus. I'll help it straight——
And but pronounced, is a sufficient charm
Against all rumour; and of absolute power
To satisfy for any lady's honour.
    Livia. What do you now, Eudemus?
    Eudemus. Make a light focus,
To touch you o'er withal. Honoured Sejanus!
What act, though ne'er so strange and insolent,
But that addition will at least bear out,
If't do not expiate?
    Livia. Here, good physician.
    Eudemus. I like this study to preserve the love
Of such a man, that comes not every hour
To greet the world.—'Tis now well, lady, you should
Use of the dentifrice I prescribed you too,
To clear your teeth, and the prepared pomatum,
To smooth the skin:—A lady cannot be
Too curious of her form, that still would hold
The heart of such a person, made her captive,
As you have his: who, to endear him more
In your clear eye, hath put away his wife,
The trouble of his bed, and your delights,
Fair Apicata, and made spacious room
To your new pleasures.
    Livia. Have not we returned

That with our hate to Drusus, and discovery
Of all his counsels?

   Eudemus. Yes, and wisely, lady.
The ages that succeed, and stand far off
To gaze at your high prudence, shall admire,
And reckon it an act without your sex:
It hath that rare appearance. Some will think
Your fortune could not yield a deeper sound,
Than mixed with Drusus; but, when they shall hear
That, and the thunder of Sejanus meet,
Sejanus, whose high name doth strike the stars,
And rings about the concave; great Sejanus,
Whose glories, style, and titles are himself,
The often iterating of Sejanus:
They then will lose their thoughts, and be ashamed
To take acquaintance of them.

Re-enter SEJANUS.

   Sejanus. I must make
A rude departure, lady; Cæsar sends
With all his haste both of command and prayer.
Be resolute in our plot; you have my soul,
As certain yours as it is my body's.
And, wise physician, so prepare the poison,
As you may lay the subtile operation
Upon some natural disease of his:
Your eunuch send to me. I kiss your hands,
Glory of ladies, and commend my love
To your best faith and memory.

   Livia. My lord,
I shall but change your words. Farewell. Yet, this
Remember for your heed, he loves you not;
You know what I have told you; his designs
Are full of grudge and danger; we must use
More than a common speed.

   Sejanus. Excellent lady,
How you do fire my blood!

   Livia. Well, you must go?
The thoughts be best, are least set forth to show.

[Exit SEJANUS.

Eudemus. When will you take some physic, lady?

Livia. When
I shall, Eudemus: but let Drusus' drug
Be first prepared.

Eudemus. Were Lygdus made, that's done;
I have it ready. And, to-morrow morning
I'll send you a perfume, first to resolve
And procure sweat, and then prepare a bath
To cleanse and clear the cutis; against when
I'll have an excellent new fucus made,
Resistive 'gainst the sun, the rain, or wind,
Which you shall lay on with a breath, or oil,
As you best like, and last some fourteen hours.
This change came timely, lady, for your health,
And the restoring of your complexion,
Which Drusus' choler had almost burnt up;
Wherein your fortune hath prescribed you better
Than art could do.

Livia. Thanks, good physician,
I'll use my fortune, you shall see, with reverence.
Is my coach ready?

Eudemus. It attends your highness.   [*Exeunt.*

SCENE II—*An Apartment in the Palace*

Enter SEJANUS.

If this be not revenge, when I have done
And made it perfect, let Egyptian slaves,
Parthians, and barefoot Hebrews brand my face,
And print my body full of injuries.
Thou lost thyself, child Drusus, when thou thoughtst
Thou couldst outskip my vengeance, or outstand
The power I had to crush thee into air.
Thy follies now shall taste what kind of man
They have provoked, and this thy father's house
Crack in the flame of my incensed rage,
Whose fury shall admit no shame or mean.—
Adultery! it is the lightest ill
I will commit. A race of wicked acts

Shall flow out of my anger, and o'erspread
The world's wide face, which no posterity
Shall e'er approve, nor yet keep silent: things
That for their cunning, close, and cruel mark,
Thy father would wish his, and shall, perhaps,
Carry the empty name, but we the prize.
On, then, my soul, and start not in thy course;
Though heaven drop sulphur, and hell belch out fire,
Laugh at the idle terrors: tell proud Jove,
Between his power and thine there is no odds:
'Twas only fear first in the world made gods.

Enter TIBERIUS *attended.*

Tiberius. Is yet Sejanus come?
Sejanus. He's here, dread Cæsar.
Tiberius. Let all depart that chamber, and the next.
                                        [*Exeunt* Attendants.
Sit down, my comfort. When the master prince
Of all the world, Sejanus, saith he fears,
Is it not fatal?
Sejanus. Yes, to those are feared.
Tiberius. And not to him?
Sejanus. Not if he wisely turn
That part of fate he holdeth, first on them.
Tiberius. That nature, blood, and laws of kind forbid
Sejanus. Do policy and state forbid it?
Tiberius. No.
Sejanus. The rest of poor respects, then let go by;
State is enough to make the act just, them guilty.
Tiberius. Long hate pursues such acts.
Sejanus. Whom hatred frights,
Let him not dream of sovereignty.
Tiberius. Are rites
Of faith, love, piety, to be trod down,
Forgotten, and made vain?
Sejanus. All for a crown.
The prince who shames a tyrant's name to bear,
Shall never dare do anything but fear;
All the command of sceptres quite doth perish,
If it begin religious thoughts to cherish:

Whole empires fall, swayed by those nice respects;
It is the licence of dark deeds protects
Even states most hated, when no laws resist
The sword, but that it acteth what it list.
   Tiberius. Yet so, we may do all things cruelly,
Not safely.
   Sejanus. Yes, and do them thoroughly.
   Tiberius. Knows yet Sejanus whom we point at?
   Sejanus. Ay,
Or else my thought, my sense, or both do err:
'Tis Agrippina.
   Tiberius. She, and her proud race.
   Sejanus. Proud! dangerous, Cæsar: for in them apace
The father's spirit shoots up. Germanicus
Lives in their looks, their gait, their form, t' upbraid us
With his close death, if not revenge the same.
   Tiberius. The act's not known.
   Sejanus. Not proved; but whispering Fame
Knowledge and proof doth to the jealous give,
Who, than to fail, would their own thought believe.
It is not safe, the children draw long breath,
That are provoked by a parent's death.
   Tiberius. It is as dangerous to make them hence,
If nothing but their birth be their offence.
   Sejanus. Stay, till they strike at Cæsar; then their crime
Will be enough; but late and out of time
For him to punish.
   Tiberius. Do they purpose it?
   Sejanus. You know, sir, thunder speaks not till it hit.
Be not secure; none swiftlier are opprest,
Than they whom confidence betrays to rest.
Let not your daring make your danger such:
All power is to be feared, where 'tis too much.
The youths are of themselves hot, violent,
Full of great thought; and that male-spirited dame,
Their mother, slacks no means to put them on,
By large allowance, popular presentings,
Increase of train and state, suing for titles;
Hath them commended with like prayers, like vows,
To the same gods, with Cæsar: days and nights

She spends in banquets and ambitious feasts
For the nobility; where Caius Silius,
Titius Sabinus, old Arruntius,
Assinius Gallus, Furnius, Regulus,
And others of that discontented list,
Are the prime guests. There, and to these, she tells
Whose niece she was, whose daughter, and whose wife.
And then must they compare her with Augusta,
Ay, and prefer her too; commend her form,
Extol her fruitfulness, at which a shower
Falls for the memory of Germanicus.
Which they blow over straight with windy praise
And puffing hopes of her aspiring sons;
Who, with these hourly ticklings, grow so pleased,
And wantonly conceited of themselves,
As now they stick not to believe they're such
As these do give them out; and would be thought
More than competitors, immediate heirs.
Whilst to their thirst of rule, they win the rout
(That's still the friend of novelty), with hope
Of future freedom, which on every change
That greedily, though emptily expects.
Cæsar, 'tis age in all things breeds neglects,
And princes that will keep old dignity
Must not admit too youthful heirs stand by;
Not their own issue; but so darkly set
As shadows are in picture, to give height
And lustre to themselves.
  Tiberius. We will command
Their rank thoughts down, and with a stricter hand
Than we have yet put forth; their trains must bate,
Their titles, feasts, and factions.
  Sejanus. Or your state.
But how, sir, will you work?
  Tiberius. Confine them.
  Sejanus. No.
They are too great, and that too faint a blow
To give them now; it would have served at first,
When with the weakest touch their knot had burst.
But now, your care must be, not to detect

The smallest cord, or line of your suspect;
For such, who know the weight of princes' fear,
Will, when they find themselves discovered, rear
Their forces, like seen snakes, that else would lie
Rolled in their circles, close: nought is more high,
Daring, or desperate, than offenders found;
Where guilt is, rage and courage both abound.
The course must be, to let them still swell up,
Riot, and surfeit on blind fortune's cup;
Give them more place, more dignities, more style,
Call them to court, to senate; in the while,
Take from their strength some one or twain or more,
Of the main fautors (it will fright the store),
And, by some by-occasion. Thus, with slight
You shall disarm them first; and they, in night
Of their ambition, not perceive the train,
Till in the engine they are caught and slain.

   Tiberius. We would not kill, if we knew how to save;
Yet, than a throne, 'tis cheaper give a grave.
Is there no way to bind them by deserts?

   Sejanus. Sir, wolves do change their hair, but not their
     hearts.
While thus your thought unto a mean is tied,
You neither dare enough, nor do provide.
All modesty is fond, and chiefly where
The subject is no less compelled to bear,
Than praise his sovereign's acts.

   Tiberius. We can no longer
Keep on our mask to thee, our dear Sejanus;
Thy thoughts are ours, in all, and we but proved
Their voice, in our designs, which by assenting
Hath more confirmed us, than if threatening Jove
Had, from his hundred statues, bid us strike,
And at the stroke clicked all his marble thumbs.
But who shall first be struck?

   Sejanus. First, Caius Silius;
He is the most of mark, and most of danger:
In power and reputation equal strong,
Having commanded an imperial army
Seven years together, vanquished Sacrovir

In Germany, and thence obtained to wear
The ornaments triumphal. His steep fall,
By how much it doth give the weightier crack,
Will send more wounding terror to the rest,
Command them stand aloof, and give more way
To our surprising of the principal.

    Tiberius. But what, Sabinus?

    Sejanus. Let him grow awhile,
His fate is not yet ripe: we must not pluck
At all together, lest we catch ourselves.
And there's Arruntius too, he only talks.
But Sosia, Silius' wife, would be wound in
Now, for she hath a fury in her breast,
More than hell ever knew; and would be sent
Thither in time. Then is there one Cremutius
Cordus, a writing fellow, they have got
To gather notes of the precedent times,
And make them into Annals; a most tart
And bitter spirit, I hear: who, under colour
Of praising those, doth tax the present state,
Censures the men, the actions, leaves no trick,
No practice unexamined, parallels
The times, the governments; a profest champion
For the old liberty——

    Tiberius. A perishing wretch!
As if there were that chaos bred in things,
That laws and liberty would not rather choose
To be quite broken, and ta'en hence by us,
Than have the stain to be preserved by such.
Have we the means to make these guilty first?

    Sejanus. Trust that to me: let Cæsar, by his power,
But cause a formal meeting of the senate,
I will have matter and accusers ready.

    Tiberius. But how? let us consult.

    Sejanus. We shall misspend
The time of action. Counsels are unfit
In business, where all rest is more pernicious
Than rashness can be. Acts of this close kind
Thrive more by execution than advice.
There is no lingering in that work begun,

Which cannot praised be, until through done.

   Tiberius. Our edict shall forthwith command a court.

While I can live, I will prevent earth's fury:

Ἐμοῦ θανόντος γαῖα μιχθήτω πυρί.   *[Exit.*

Enter JULIUS POSTHUMUS.

   Posthumus. My lord Sejanus——

   Sejanus. Julius Posthumus!

Come with my wish! What news from Agrippina's?

   Posthumus. Faith, none. They all lock up themselves a'
     late,

Or talk in character; I have not seen

A company so changed. Except that had

Intelligence by augury of our practice.

   Sejanus. When were you there?

   Posthumus. Last night.

   Sejanus. And what guests found you?

   Posthumus. Sabinus, Silius, the old list, Arruntius,

Furnius, and Gallus.

   Sejanus. Would not these talk?

   Posthumus. Little.

And yet we offered choice of argument.

Satrius was with me.

   Sejanus. Well: 'tis guilt enough

Their often meeting. You forgot to extol

The hospitable lady?

   Posthumus. No; that trick

Was well put home, and had succeeded too,

But that Sabinus coughed a caution out;

For she began to swell.

   Sejanus. And may she burst!

Julius, I would have you go instantly

Unto the palace of the great Augusta,

And, by your kindest friend, get swift access;

Acquaint her with these meetings: tell the words

You brought me the other day, of Silius,

Add somewhat to them. Make her understand

The danger of Sabinus, and the times,

Out of his closeness. Give Arruntius' words

Of malice against Cæsar; so, to Gallus:

But, above all, to Agrippina. Say,
As you may truly, that her infinite pride,
Propt with the hopes of her too fruitful womb,
With popular studies gapes for sovereignty,
And threatens Cæsar. Pray Augusta then,
That for her own, great Cæsar's, and the pub-
Lic safety, she be pleased to urge these dangers.
Cæsar is too secure, he must be told,
And best he'll take it from a mother's tongue.
Alas! what is't for us to sound, to explore,
To watch, oppose, plot, practise, or prevent,
If he, for whom it is so strongly laboured,
Shall, out of greatness and free spirit, be
Supinely negligent? our city's now
Divided as in time o' the civil war,
And men forbear not to declare themselves
Of Agrippina's party. Every day
The faction multiplies; and will do more,
If not resisted: you can best enlarge it,
As you find audience. Noble Posthumus,
Commend me to your Prisca: and pray her,
She will solicit this great business,
To earnest and most present execution,
With all her utmost credit with Augusta.
    Posthumus. I shall not fail in my instructions.   [*Exit.*
    Sejanus. This second, from his mother, will well urge
Our late design, and spur on Cæsar's rage;
Which else might grow remiss. The way to put
A prince in blood, is to present the shapes
Of dangers greater than they are, like late
Or early shadows: and, sometimes, to feign
Where there are none, only to make him fear;
His fear will make him cruel: and once entered,
He doth not easily learn to stop, or spare
Where he may doubt. This have I made my rule,
To thrust Tiberius into tyranny,
And make him toil, to turn aside those blocks,
Which I alone could not remove with safety.
Drusus once gone, Germanicus' three sons
Would clog my way; whose guards have too much faith

To be corrupted: and their mother known
Of too too unreproved a chastity,
To be attempted, as light Livia was.
Work then, my art, on Cæsar's fears, as they
On those they fear, till all my lets be cleared,
And he in ruins of his house, and hate
Of all his subjects, bury his own state;
When with my peace, and safety, I will rise,
By making him the public sacrifice.   [*Exit.*

SCENE III—*A Room in* AGRIPPINA'S *House*

Enter SATRIUS *and* NATTA.

Satrius. They're grown exceeding circumspect, and wary.
Natta. They have us in the wind: and yet Arruntius
Cannot contain himself.
Satrius. Tut, he's not yet
Looked after; there are others more desired,
That are more silent.
Natta. Here he comes. Away.   [*Exeunt.*

Enter SABINUS, ARRUNTIUS, *and* CORDUS.

Sabinus. How is it, that these beagles haunt the house
Of Agrippina?
Arruntius. O, they hunt, they hunt!
There is some game here lodged, which they must rouse,
To make the great ones sport.
Cordus. Did you observe
How they inveighed 'gainst Cæsar?
Arruntius. Ay, baits, baits,
For us to bite at: would I have my flesh
Torn by the public hook, these qualified hangmen
Should be my company.
Cordus. Here comes another.
                    [DOMITIUS AFER *passes over the stage.*
Arruntius. Ay, there's a man, Afer the orator!
One that hath phrases, figures, and fine flowers,
To strew his rhetoric with, and doth make haste,
To get him note, or name by any offer

Where blood or gain be objects; steeps his words
When he would kill, in artificial tears:
The crocodile of Tyber! him I love,
That man is mine; he hath my heart and voice
When I would curse! he, he.

 Sabinus. Contemn the slaves,
Their present lives will be their future graves.

[Exeunt.

SCENE IV—*Another Apartment in the same*

Enter SILIUS, AGRIPPINA, NERO, *and* SOSIA.

 Silius. May't please your highness not forget yourself;
I dare not, with my manners, to attempt
Your trouble farther.

 Agrippina. Farewell, noble Silius!

 Silius. Most royal princess.

 Agrippina. Sosia stays with us?

 Silius. She is your servant, and doth owe your grace
An honest, but unprofitable love.

 Agrippina. How can that be, when there's no gain but
  virtue's?

 Silius. You take the moral, not the politic sense.
I meant, as she is bold, and free of speech,
Earnest to utter what her zealous thought
Travails withal, in honour of your house;
Which act, as it is simply born in her,
Partakes of love and honesty; but may,
By the over-often, and unseasoned use,
Turn to your loss and danger: for your state
Is waited on by envies, as by eyes;
And every second guest your tables take
Is a fee'd spy, to observe who goes, who comes;
What conference you have, with whom, where, when,
What the discourse is, what the looks, the thoughts
Of every person there, they do extract,
And make into a substance.

 Agrippina. Hear me, Silius.
Were all Tiberius' body stuck with eyes,

And every wall and hanging in my house
Transparent, as this lawn I wear, or air;
Yea, had Sejanus both his ears as long
As to my inmost closet, I would hate
To whisper any thought, or change an act,
To be made Juno's rival. Virtue's forces
Show ever noblest in conspicuous courses.

    Silius. 'Tis great, and bravely spoken, like the spirit
Of Agrippina: yet, your highness knows,
There is nor loss nor shame in providence;
Few can, what all should do, beware enough.
You may perceive with what officious face,
Satrius, and Natta, Afer, and the rest
Visit your house, of late, to inquire the secrets;
And with what bold and privileged art, they rail
Against Augusta, yea, and at Tiberius;
Tell tricks of Livia, and Sejanus: all
To excite, and call your indignation on,
That they might hear it at more liberty.

    Agrippina. You're too suspicious, Silius.

    Silius. Pray the gods,
I be so, Agrippina; but I fear
Some subtile practice. They that durst to strike
At so exampless, and unblamed a life,
As that of the renowned Germanicus,
Will not sit down with that exploit alone:
He threatens many that hath injured one.

    Nero. 'Twere best rip forth their tongues, sear out their
      eyes,
When next they come.

    Sosia. A fit reward for spies.

Enter DRUSUS JUNIOR.

    Drusus junior. Hear you the rumour?

    Agrippina. What?

    Drusus junior. Drusus is dying.

    Agrippina. Dying!

    Nero. That's strange!

    Agrippina. You were with him yesternight.

    Drusus junior. One met Eudemus the physician,

Sent for, but now; who thinks he cannot live.

    Silius. Thinks! if it be arrived at that, he knows,
Or none.

    Agrippina. 'Tis quick! what should be his disease?

    Silius. Poison, poison——

    Agrippina. How, Silius!

    Nero. What's that?

    Silius. Nay, nothing. There was late a certain blow
Given o' the face.

    Nero. Ay, to Sejanus.

    Silius. True.

    Drusus junior. And what of that?

    Silius. I'm glad I gave it not.

    Nero. But there is somewhat else?

    Silius. Yes, private meetings,
With a great lady—at a physician's,
And a wife turned away.

    Nero. Ha!

    Silius. Toys, mere toys:
What wisdom's now in th' streets, in the common mouth?

    Drusus junior. Fears, whisperings, tumults, noise, I know
      not what:
They say the Senate sit.

    Silius. I'll thither straight;
And see what's in the forge.

    Agrippina. Good Silius, do;
Sosia and I will in.

    Silius. Haste you, my lords,
To visit the sick prince; tender your loves,
And sorrows to the people. This Sejanus,
Trust my divining soul, hath plots on all:
No tree, that stops his prospect, but must fall.

                             [*Exeunt.*

ACT THE THIRD

SCENE I—*The Senate House*

Enter Præcones, Lictores, SEJANUS, VARRO, LATIARIS,
COTTA, *and* AFER.

SEJANUS. 'Tis only you must urge against him, Varro;
Nor I, nor Cæsar may appear therein,
Except in your defence, who are the consul;
And, under colour of late enmity
Between your father and his, may better do it,
As free from all suspicion of a practice.
Here be your notes, what points to touch at; read:
Be cunning in them. Afer has them too.
   Varro. But is he summoned?
   Sejanus. No. It was debated
By Cæsar, and concluded as most fit
To take him unprepared.
   Afer. And prosecute
All under name of treason.
   Varro. I conceive.

Enter SABINUS, GALLUS, LEPIDUS, *and* ARRUNTIUS.

   Sabinus. Drusus being dead, Cæsar will not be here.
   Gallus. What should the business of this senate be?
   Arruntius. That can my subtle whisperers tell you: we
That are the good-dull-noble lookers-on.
Are only called to keep the marble warm.
What should we do with those deep mysteries,
Proper to these fine heads? let them alone.
Our ignorance may, perchance, help us be saved
From whips and furies.
   Gallus. See, see, see their action!
   Arruntius. Ay, now their heads do travail, now they work;
Their faces run like shittles; they are weaving
Some curious cobweb to catch flies.
   Sabinus. Observe,
They take their places.

Arruntius. What, so low!

Gallus. O yes,

They must be seen to flatter Cæsar's grief,

Though but in sitting.

Varro. Bid us silence.

Præcones. Silence!

Varro. "Fathers conscript, may this our present meeting
Turn fair, and fortunate to the commonwealth!"

Enter SILIUS *and other* Senators.

Sejanus. See, Silius enters.

Silius. Hail, grave fathers!

Lictores. Stand.

Silius, forbear thy place.

Senators. How!

Præcones. Silius, stand forth,

The consul hath to charge thee.

Lictores. Room for Cæsar.

Arruntius. Is he come too! nay then expect a trick.

Sabinus. Silius accused! sure he will answer nobly.

Enter TIBERIUS *attended.*

Tiberius. We stand amazed, fathers, to behold
This general dejection. Wherefore sit
Rome's consuls thus dissolved, as they had lost
All the remembrance both of style and place?
It not becomes. No woes are of fit weight,
To make the honour of the Empire stoop:
Though I, in my peculiar self may meet
Just reprehension, that so suddenly,
And, in so fresh a grief, would greet the senate,
When private tongues, of kinsmen and allies,
Inspired with comforts, lothly are endured,
The face of men not seen, and scarce the day,
To thousands that communicate our loss.
Nor can I argue these of weakness; since
They take but natural ways; yet I must seek
For stronger aids, and those fair helps draw out
From warm embraces of the commonwealth.
Our mother, great Augusta, 's struck with time,

Our self imprest with aged characters,
Drusus is gone, his children young and babes;
Our aims must now reflect on those that may
Give timely succour to these present ills,
And are our only glad surviving hopes,
The noble issue of Germanicus,
Nero and Drusus: might it please the consul
Honour them in, they both attend without.
I would present them to the senate's care,
And raise those suns of joy that should drink up
These floods of sorrow in your drowned eyes.
    Arruntius. By Jove, I am not Œdipus enough
To understand this Sphinx.
    Sabinus. The princes come.

Enter NERO *and* DRUSUS JUNIOR.

    Tiberius. Approach you, noble Nero, noble Drusus.
These princes, fathers, when their parent died,
I gave unto their uncle, with this prayer,
That though he had proper issue of his own,
He would no less bring up, and foster these,
Than that self-blood; and by that act confirm
Their worths to him, and to posterity.
Drusus ta'en hence, I turn my prayers to you,
And 'fore our country and our gods, beseech
You take, and rule Augustus' nephew's sons,
Sprung of the noblest ancestors; and so
Accomplish both my duty, and your own.
Nero, and Drusus, these shall be to you
In place of parents, these your fathers, these;
And not unfitly: for you are so born,
As all your good, or ill's the commonwealth's.
Receive them, you strong guardians; and blest gods,
Make all their actions answer to their bloods:
Let their great titles find increase by them,
Not they by titles. Set them as in place,
So in examples, above all the Romans:
And may they know no rivals but themselves.
Let Fortune give them nothing; but attend
Upon their virtue: and that still come forth

Greater than hope, and better than their fame.
Relieve me, fathers, with your general voice.
 Senators. "May all the gods consent to Cæsar's wish,
And add to any honours that may crown
The hopeful issue of Germanicus!"
 Tiberius. We thank you, reverend fathers, in their right.
 Arruntius. If this were true, now! but the space, the space
Between the breast and lips—Tiberius' heart
Lies a thought farther than another man's.   [*Aside.*
 Tiberius. My comforts are so flowing in my joys,
As, in them, all my streams of grief are lost,
No less than are land waters in the sea,
Or showers in rivers; though their cause was such,
As might have sprinkled ev'n the gods with tears:
Yet, since the greater doth embrace the less,
We covetously obey.
 Arruntius. Well acted, Cæsar.   [*Aside.*
 Tiberius. And now I am the happy witness made
Of your so much desired affections
To this great issue, I could wish, the Fates
Would here set peaceful period to my days;
However to my labours, I entreat,
And beg it of this senate, some fit ease.
 Arruntius. Laugh, fathers, laugh: have you no spleens
  about you?   [*Aside.*
 Tiberius. The burden is too heavy I sustain
On my unwilling shoulders; and I pray
It may be taken off, and reconferred
Upon the consuls, or some other Roman,
More able, and more worthy.
 Arruntius. Laugh on still.   [*Aside.*
 Sabinus. Why, this doth render all the rest suspected!
 Gallus. It poisons all.
 Arruntius. O, do you taste it then?
 Sabinus. It takes away my faith to anything
He shall hereafter speak.
 Arruntius. Ay, to pray that,
Which would be to his head as hot as thunder,
'Gainst which he wears that charm, should but the court
Receive him at his word.

    Gallus. Hear!
    Tiberius. For myself
I know my weakness, and so little covet,
Like some gone past, the weight that will oppress me,
As my ambition is the counter-point.
    Arruntius. Finely maintained; good still!
    Sejanus. But Rome, whose blood,
Whose nerves, whose life, whose very frame relies
On Cæsar's strength, no less than heaven on Atlas,
Cannot admit it but with general ruin.
    Arruntius. Ah! are you there to bring him off?   [*Aside.*
    Sejanus. Let Cæsar
No more than urge a point so contrary
To Cæsar's greatness, the grieved senate's vows,
Or Rome's necessity.
    Gallus. He comes about——
    Arruntius. More nimbly than Vertumnus.
    Tiberius. For the public,
I may be drawn to show I can neglect
All private aims, though I affect my rest;
But if the senate still command me serve,
I must be glad to practise my obedience.
    Arruntius. You must and will, sir. We do know it. [*Aside.*
    Senators. "Cæsar,
Live long and happy, great and royal Cæsar;
The gods preserve thee and thy modesty
Thy wisdom and thy innocence!"
    Arruntius. Where is't?
The prayer is made before the subject.   [*Aside.*
    Senators. "Guard
His meekness, Jove, his piety, his care,
His bounty——"
    Arruntius. And his subtilty, I'll put in:
Yet he'll keep that himself, without the gods.
All prayers are vain for him.   [*Aside.*
    Tiberius. We will not hold
Your patience, fathers, with long answer; but
Shall still contend to be what you desire,
And work to satisfy so great a hope.
Proceed to your affairs.

  Arruntius. Now, Silius, guard thee;
The curtain's drawing. Afer advanceth.   *[Aside.*
  Præcones. Silence!
  Afer. Cite Caius Silius.
  Præcones. Caius Silius!
  Silius. Here.
  Afer. The triumph that thou hadst in Germany
For thy late victory on Sacrovir,
Thou hast enjoyed so freely, Caius Silius,
As no man it envied thee; nor would Cæsar,
Or Rome admit, that thou wert then defrauded
Of any honours thy deserts could claim
In the fair service of the commonwealth;
But now, if after all their loves and graces,
(Thy actions, and their courses being discovered)
It shall appear to Cæsar and this senate,
Thou hast defiled those glories with thy crimes——
  Silius. Crimes!
  Afer. Patience, Silius.
  Silius. Tell thy mule of patience;
I am a Roman. What are my crimes? proclaim them.
Am I too rich, too honest for the times?
Have I or treasure, jewels, land, or houses
That some informer gapes for? is my strength
Too much to be admitted, or my knowledge?
These now are crimes.
  Afer. Nay, Silius, if the name
Of crime so touch thee, with what impotence
Wilt thou endure the matter to be searched?
  Silius. I tell thee, Afer, with more scorn than fear:
Employ your mercenary tongue and art.
Where's my accuser?
  Varro. Here.
  Arruntius. Varro, the consul!
Is he thrust in?   *[Aside.*
  Varro. 'Tis I accuse thee, Silius.
Against the majesty of Rome, and Cæsar,
I do pronounce thee here a guilty cause,
First of beginning and occasioning,
Next, drawing out the war in Gallia,

For which thou late triumph'st; dissembling long
That Sacrovir to be an enemy,
Only to make thy entertainment more.
Whilst thou, and thy wife Sosia, polled the province:
Wherein, with sordid, base desire of gain,
Thou hast discredited thy actions' worth,
And been a traitor to the state.

    Silius. Thou liest.

    Arruntius. I thank thee, Silius, speak so still and often.

    Varro. If I not prove it, Cæsar, but unjustly
Have called him into trial; here I bind
Myself to suffer, what I claim against him;
And yield to have what I have spoke, confirmed
By judgment of the court, and all good men.

    Silius. Cæsar, I crave to have my cause deferred,
Till this man's consulship be out.

    Tiberius. We cannot,
Nor may we grant it.

    Silius. Why? shall he design
My day of trial? Is he my accuser,
And must he be my judge?

    Tiberius. It hath been usual,
And is a right that custom hath allowed
The magistrate, to call forth private men;
And to appoint their day: which privilege
We may not in the consul see infringed,
By whose deep watches, and industrious care
It is so laboured, as the commonwealth
Receive no loss, by any oblique course.

    Silius. Cæsar, thy fraud is worse than violence.

    Tiberius. Silius, mistake us not, we dare not use
The credit of the consul to thy wrong;
But only do preserve his place and power,
So far as it concerns the dignity
And honour of the state.

    Arruntius. Believe him, Silius.

    Cotta. Why, so he may, Arruntius.

    Arruntius. I say so.
And he may choose too.

    Tiberius. By the Capitol,

And all our gods, but that the dear republic,
Our sacred laws, and just authority
Are interested therein, I should be silent.

    Afer. 'Please Cæsar to give way unto his trial,
He shall have justice.

    Silius. Nay, I shall have law;
Shall I not, Afer? speak.

    Afer. Would you have more?

    Silius. No, my well-spoken man, I would no more;
Nor less: might I enjoy it natural,
Not taught to speak unto your present ends,
Free from thine, his, and all your unkind handling,
Furious enforcing, most unjust presuming,
Malicious, and manifold applying,
Foul wrestling, and impossible construction.

    Afer. He raves, he raves.

    Silius. Thou durst not tell me so,
Hadst thou not Cæsar's warrant. I can see
Whose power condemns me.

    Varro. This betrays his spirit:
This doth enough declare him what he is.

    Silius. What am I? speak.

    Varro. An enemy to the state.

    Silius. Because I am an enemy to thee,
And such corrupted ministers o' the state,
That here art made a present instrument
To gratify it with thine own disgrace.

    Sejanus. This, to the consul, is most insolent,
And impious!

    Silius. Ay, take part. Reveal yourselves,
Alas! I scent not your confederacies,
Your plots, and combinations! I not know
Minion Sejanus hates me; and that all
This boast of law, and law, is but a form,
A net of Vulcan's filing, a mere ingine,
To take that life by a pretext of justice,
Which you pursue in malice! I want brain,
Or nostril to persuade me, that your ends
And purposes are made to what they are,
Before my answer! O, you equal gods,

Whose justice not a world of wolf-turned men
Shall make me to accuse, howe'er provoked;
Have I for this so oft engaged myself?
Stood in the heat and fervour of a fight,
When Phœbus sooner hath forsook the day
Than I the field, against the blue-eyed Gauls,
And crisped Germans? when our Roman eagles
Have fanned the fire with their labouring wings,
And no blow dealt, that left not death behind it?
When I have charged, alone, into the troops
Of curled Sicambrians, routed them, and came
Not off with backward ensigns of a slave;
But forward marks wounds on my breast and face,
Were meant to thee, O Cæsar, and thy Rome?
And have I this return! did I, for this,
Perform so noble, and so brave defeat,
On Sacrovir! O Jove, let it become me
To boast my deeds, when he, whom they concern,
Shall thus forget them.
    Afer. Silius, Silius,
These are the common customs of thy blood,
When it is high with wine, as now with rage:
This well agrees with that intemperate vaunt,
Thou lately mad'st at Agrippina's table,
That, when all other of the troops were prone
To fall into rebellion, only thine
Remained in their obedience. Thou wert he
That saved the Empire, which had then been lost
Had but thy legions there rebelled, or mutinied;
Thy virtue met, and fronted every peril.
Thou gav'st to Cæsar, and to Rome their surety;
Their name, their strength, their spirit, and their state,
Their being was a donative from thee.
    Arruntius. Well worded, and most like an orator.
    Tiberius. Is this true, Silius?
    Silius. Save thy questions, Cæsar,
Thy spy of famous credit hath affirmed it.
    Arruntius. Excellent Roman!
    Sabinus. He doth answer stoutly.
    Sejanus. If this be so, there needs no farther cause

Of crime against him.

   Varro. What can more impeach
The royal dignity and state of Cæsar,
Than to be urged with a benefit
He cannot pay.

   Cotta. In this, all Cæsar's fortune
Is made unequal to the courtesy.

     Latiaris. His means are clean destroyed that should re-
       quite.

     Gallus. Nothing is great enough for Silius' merit.

     Arruntius. Gallus on that side too!   *[Aside.*

     Silius. Come, do not hunt,
And labour so about for circumstance,
To make him guilty, whom you have foredoomed:
Take shorter ways, I'll meet your purposes.
The words were mine, and more I now will say:
Since I have done thee that great service, Cæsar,
Thou still hast feared me; and, in place of grace,
Returned me hatred: so soon all best turns,
With doubtful princes, turn deep injuries
In estimation, when they greater rise
Than can be answered. Benefits, with you,
Are of no longer pleasure, than you can
With ease restore them; that transcended once,
Your studies are not how to thank, but kill.
It is your nature, to have all men slaves
To you, but you acknowledging to none.
The means that make your greatness, must not come
In mention of it; if it do, it takes
So much away, you think: and that which helped
Shall soonest perish, if it stand in eye,
Where it may front, or but upbraid the high.

   Cotta. Suffer him speak no more.

   Varro. Note but his spirit.

   Afer. This shows him in the rest.

   Latiaris. Let him be censured.

   Sejanus. He hath spoke enough to prove him Cæsar's foe.

   Cotta. His thoughts look through his words.

   Sejanus. A censure.

   Silius. Stay,

Stay, most officious senate, I shall straight
Delude thy fury. Silius hath not placed
His guards within him, against fortune's spite,
So weakly but he can escape your gripe
That are but hands of fortune: she herself,
When virtue doth oppose, must lose her threats.
All that can happen in humanity,
The frown of Cæsar, proud Sejanus' hatred,
Base Varro's spleen, and Afer's bloodying tongue,
The senate's servile flattery, and these
Mustered to kill, I'm fortified against;
And can look down upon: they are beneath me.
It is not life whereof I stand enamoured
Nor shall my end make me accuse my fate.
The coward and the valiant man must fall,
Only the cause, and manner how, discerns them:
Which then are gladdest, when they cost us dearest.
Romans, if any here be in this senate,
Would know to mock Tiberius' tyranny,
Look upon Silius, and so learn to die.   [*Stabs himself.*

    Varro. O desperate act!
    Arruntius. An honourable hand!
    Tiberius. Look, is he dead?
    Sabinus. 'Twas nobly struck, and home.
    Arruntius. My thought did prompt him to it. Farewell,
        Silius.
Be famous ever for thy great example.
    Tiberius. We are not pleased in this sad accident,
That thus hath stalled, and abused our mercy,
Intended to preserve thee, noble Roman,
And to prevent thy hopes.
    Arruntius. Excellent wolf!
Now he is full he howls.   [*Aside.*

    Sejanus. Cæsar doth wrong
His dignity and safety thus to mourn
The deserved end of so profest a traitor
And doth, by this his lenity, instruct
Others as factious to the like offence.
    Tiberius. The confiscation merely of his state
Had been enough.

Arruntius. O, that was gaped for then?   [*Aside.*

Varro. Remove the body.

Sejanus. Let citation

Go out for Sosia.

Gallus. Let her be proscribed:

And for the goods, I think it fit that half

Go to the treasure, half unto the children.

Lepidus. With leave of Cæsar, I would think that fourth,

The which the law doth cast on the informers,

Should be enough; the rest go to the children.

Wherein the prince shall show humanity,

And bounty; not to force them by their want,

Which in their parent's trespass they deserved,

To take ill courses.

Tiberius. It shall please us.

Arruntius. Ay.

Out of necessity. This Lepidus

Is grave and honest, and I have observed

A moderation still in all his censures.

Sabinus. And bending to the better——Stay, who's this?

Enter SATRIUS *and* NATTA, *with* CREMUTIUS CORDUS,
guarded.

Cremutius Cordus! What! is he brought in?

Arruntius. More blood into the banquet! Noble Cordus,

I wish thee good; be as thy writings, free

And honest.

Tiberius. What is he?

Sejanus. For the Annals, Cæsar.

Præcones. Cremutius Cordus!

Cordus. Here.

Præcones. Satrius Secundus,

Pinnarius Natta, you are his accusers.

Arruntius. Two of Sejanus' blood-hounds, whom he
breeds

With human flesh, to bay at citizens.

Afer. Stand forth before the senate, and confront
him.

Satrius. I do accuse thee here, Cremutius Cordus,

To be a man factious and dangerous.

A sower of sedition in the state,
A turbulent and discontented spirit,
Which I will prove from thine own writings, here,
The Annals thou hast published; where thou bit'st
The present age, and with a viper's tooth,
Being a member of it, dar'st that ill
Which never yet degenerous bastard did
Upon his parent.

    Natta. To this I subscribe;
And, forth a world of more particulars,
Instance in only one: comparing men,
And times, thou praisest Brutus, and affirm'st
That Cassius was the last of all the Romans.

    Cotta. How! what are we then?

    Varro. What is Cæsar? nothing?

    Afer. My lords, this strikes at every Roman's private,
In whom reigns gentry, and estate of spirit,
To have a Brutus brought in parallel,
A parricide, an enemy of his country,
Ranked, and preferred to any real worth
That Rome now holds. This is most strangely invective,
Most full of spite, and insolent upbraiding.
Nor is 't the time alone is here disprised,
But the whole man of time, yea, Cæsar's self
Brought in disvalue; and he aimed at most,
By oblique glance of his licentious pen.
Cæsar, if Cassius were the last of Romans,
Thou hast no name.

    Tiberius. Let's hear him answer. Silence!

    Cordus. So innocent I am of fact, my lords,
As but my words are argued: yet those words
Not reaching either prince or prince's parent;
The which your law of treason comprehends.
Brutus and Cassius I am charged to have praised;
Whose deeds, when many more, besides myself,
Have writ, not one hath mentioned without honour.
Great Titus Livius, great for eloquence,
And faith amongst us, in his History,
With so great praises Pompey did extol
As oft Augustus called him a Pompeian:

Yet this not hurt their friendship. In his book
He often names Scipio, Afranius,
Yea, the same Cassius, and this Brutus too,
As worthiest men; not thieves and parricides
Which notes upon their fames are now imposed.
Asinius Pollio's writings quite throughout
Give them a noble memory; so Messala
Renowned his general Cassius: yet both these
Lived with Augustus, full of wealth and honours.
To Cicero's book, where Cato was heaved up
Equal with heaven, what else did Cæsar answer,
Being then dictator, but with a penned oration,
As if before the judges? Do but see
Antonius' letters; read but Brutus' pleadings:
What vile reproach they hold against Augustus,
False, I confess, but with much bitterness.
The epigrams of Bibaculus and Catullus
Are read, full stuft with spite of both the Cæsars;
Yet deified Julius, and no less Augustus,
Both bore them, and contemned them: I not know,
Promptly to speak it, whether done with more
Temper, or wisdom; for such obloquies
If they despised be, they die supprest;
But if with rage acknowledged, they are confest.
The Greeks I slip, whose licence not alone,
But also lust did scape unpunished:
Or where some one, by chance, exception took,
He words with words revenged. But, in my work,
What could be aimed more free or farther off
From the time's scandal, than to write of those,
Whom death from grace or hatred had exempted?
Did I, with Brutus and with Cassius,
Armed, and possessed of the Philippi fields,
Incense the people in the civil cause,
With dangerous speeches? Or do they, being slain
Seventy years since, as by their images,
Which not the conqueror hath defaced, appears,
Retain that guilty memory with writers?
Posterity pays every man his honour:
Nor shall there want, though I condemned am,

That will not only Cassius well approve,
And of great Brutus' honour mindful be,
But that will also mention make of me.

    Arruntius. Freely and nobly spoken!

    Sabinus. With good temper;
I like him, that he is not moved with passion.

    Arruntius. He puts them to their whisper.

    Tiberius. Take him hence;
We shall determine of him at next sitting.

                    [*Exeunt* Officers *with* CORDUS.

    Cotta. Mean time, give order, that his books be burnt,
To the ædiles.

    Sejanus. You have well advised.

    Afer. It fits not such licentious things should live
T' upbraid the age.

    Arruntius. If the age were good, they might.

    Latiaris. Let them be burnt.

    Gallus. All sought, and burnt to-day.

    Præcones. The court is up; lictors, resume the fasces.

             [*Exeunt all but* ARRUNTIUS, SABINUS, *and* LEPIDUS.

    Arruntius. Let them be burnt! O, how ridiculous
Appear the senate's brainless diligence,
Who think they can, with present power, extinguish
The memory of all succeeding times!

    Sabinus. 'Tis true; when, contrary, the punishment
Of wit, doth make the authority increase.
Nor do they aught, that use this cruelty
Of interdiction, and this rage of burning,
But purchase to themselves rebuke and shame,
And to the writers an eternal name.

    Lepidus. It is an argument the times are sore,
When virtue cannot safely be advanced;
Nor vice reproved.

    Arruntius. Ay, noble Lepidus;
Augustus well foresaw what we should suffer
Under Tiberius, when he did pronounce
The Roman race most wretched, that should live
Between so slow jaws, and so long a bruising.

                          [*Exeunt.*

SCENE II—*A Room in the Palace*

Enter TIBERIUS *and* SEJANUS.

Tiberius. This business hath succeeded well, Sejanus;
And quite removed all jealousy of practice
'Gainst Agrippina, and our nephews. Now,
We must bethink us how to plant our ingines
For th'other pair, Sabinus and Arruntius,
And Gallus too; howe'er he flatter us,
His heart we know.
      Sejanus. Give it some respite, Cæsar.
Time shall mature, and bring to perfect crown,
What we, with so good vultures have begun:
Sabinus shall be next.
      Tiberius. Rather Arruntius.
      Sejanus. By any means, preserve him. His frank tongue
Being lent the reins, would take away all thought
Of malice, in your course against the rest:
We must keep him to stalk with.
      Tiberius. Dearest head,
To thy most fortunate design I yield it.
      Sejanus. Sir, I have been so long trained up in grace,
First with your father, great Augustus; since,
With your most happy bounties so familiar;
As I not sooner would commit my hopes
Or wishes to the gods, than to your ears,
Nor have I ever yet been covetous
Of over-bright and dazzling honours; rather
To watch and travail in great Cæsar's safety,
With the most common soldier.
      Tiberius. 'Tis confest.
      Sejanus. The only gain, and which I count most fair
Of all my fortunes, is, that mighty Cæsar
Has thought me worthy his alliance. Hence
Begin my hopes.
      Tiberius. Umph!
      Sejanus. I have heard, Augustus,
In the bestowing of his daughter, thought

But even of gentlemen of Rome: if so—
I know not how to hope so great a favour—
But if a husband should be sought for Livia,
And I be had in mind, as Cæsar's friend,
I would but use the glory of the kindred:
It should not make me slothful, or less caring
For Cæsar's state; it were enough to me
It did confirm, and strengthen my weak house,
Against the now unequal opposition
Of Agrippina; and for dear regard
Unto my children, this I wish: myself
Have no ambition farther than to end
My days in service of so dear a master.
    Tiberius. We cannot but commend thy piety;
Most loved Sejanus, in acknowledging
Those bounties; which we, faintly, such remember—
But to thy suit. The rest of mortal men,
In all their drifts and counsels, pursue profit;
Princes alone are of a different sort,
Directing their main actions still to fame;
We therefore will take time to think and answer.
For Livia she can best, herself, resolve
If she will marry, after Drusus, or
Continue in the family; besides,
She hath a mother, and a grandam yet,
Whose nearer counsels she may guide her by:
But I will simply deal. That enmity
Thou fear'st in Agrippina, would burn more,
If Livia's marriage should, as 'twere in parts,
Divide the imperial house; an emulation
Between the women might break forth; and discord
Ruin the sons and nephews on both hands.
What if it cause some present difference?
Thou art not safe, Sejanus, if thou prove it.
Canst thou believe, that Livia, first the wife
To Caius Cæsar, then my Drusus, now
Will be contented to grow old with thee,
Born but a private gentleman of Rome,
And raise thee with her loss, if not her shame?
Or say that I should wish it, canst thou think

The senate, or the people (who have seen
Her brother, father, and our ancestors,
In highest place of empire) will endure it?
The state thou hold'st already, is in talk;
Men murmur at thy greatness; and the nobles
Stick not, in public, to upbraid thy climbing
Above our father's favours, or thy scale:
And dare accuse me, from their hate to thee.
Be wise, dear friend. We would not hide these things,
For friendship's dear respect: nor will we stand
Adverse to thine, or Livia's designments.
What we have purposed to thee, in our thought,
And with what near degrees of love to bind thee,
And make thee equal to us; for the present,
We will forbear to speak. Only, thus much
Believe, our loved Sejanus, we not know
That height in blood or honour, which thy virtue
And mind to us, may not aspire with merit.
And this we'll publish, on all watched occasion
The senate or the people shall present.

   Sejanus. I am restored, and to my sense again,
Which I had lost in this so blinding suit.
Cæsar hath taught me better to refuse,
Than I knew how to ask. How pleaseth Cæsar
T' embrace my late advice for leaving Rome?

   Tiberius. We are resolved.

   Sejanus. Here are some motives more, [*Gives him a paper.*
Which I have thought on since, may more confirm.

   Tiberius. Careful Sejanus! we will straight peruse them:
Go forward in our main design, and prosper.   [*Exit.*

   Sejanus. If those but take, I shall. Dull, heavy Cæsar!
Wouldst thou tell me, thy favours were made crimes,
And that my fortunes were esteemed thy faults,
That thou for me wert hated, and not think
I would with winged haste prevent that change,
When thou might'st win all to thyself again,
By forfeiture of me? Did those fond words
Fly swifter from thy lips, than this my brain,
This sparkling forge, created me an armour
T' encounter chance and thee? Well, read my charms,

And may they lay that hold upon thy senses,
As thou hadst snuft up hemlock, or ta'en down
The juice of poppy and of mandrakes. Sleep,
Voluptuous Cæsar, and security
Seize on thy stupid powers, and leave them dead
To public cares; awake but to thy lusts,
The strength of which makes thy libidinous soul
Itch to leave Rome! and I have thrust in on;
With blaming of the city business,
The multitude of suits, the confluence
Of suitors: then their importunacies,
The manifold distractions he must suffer,
Besides ill-rumours, envies, and reproaches,
All which a quiet and retired life,
Larded with ease and pleasure, did avoid:
And yet for any weighty and great affair,
The fittest place to give the soundest counsels.
By this I shall remove him both from thought
And knowledge of his own most dear affairs;
Draw all dispatches through my private hands;
Know his designments, and pursue mine own;
Make mine own strengths by giving suits and places,
Conferring dignities and offices;
And these that hate me now, wanting access
To him, will make their envy none, or less:
For when they see me arbiter of all,
They must observe; or else with Cæsar fall.   [*Exit.*

SCENE III—*Another Room in the same*

Enter TIBERIUS.

Tiberius. To marry Livia! will no less, Sejanus,
Content thy aims? no lower object? well!
Thou know'st how thou art wrought into our trust;
Woven in our design; and think'st we must
Now use thee, whatsoe'er thy projects are:
'Tis true. But yet with caution and fit care.
And, now we better think—who's there within?

Enter an Officer.

Officer. Cæsar!

Tiberius. To leave our journey off, were sin
'Gainst our decreed delights; and would appear
Doubt; or, what less becomes a prince, low fear.
Yet doubt hath law, and fears have their excuse,
Where princes' states plead necessary use;
As ours doth now: more in Sejanus' pride,
Than all fell Agrippina's hates beside.
Those are the dreadful enemies, we raise
With favours, and make dangerous with praise;
The injured by us may have will alike,
But 'tis the favourite hath the power to strike;
And fury ever boils more high and strong,
Heat with ambition, than revenge of wrong.
'Tis then a part of supreme skill, to grace
No man too much; but hold a certain space
Between the ascender's rise and thine own flat,
Lest, when all rounds be reached, his aim be that.
'Tis thought [*Aside*]. Is Maco in the palace? see:
If not, go seek him, to come to us. [*Exit* Officer.] *He*
Must be the organ we must work by now;
Though none less apt for trust: need doth allow
What choice would not. I have heard that aconite,
Being timely taken, hath a healing might
Against the scorpion's stroke; the proof we'll give:
That, while two poisons wrestle, we may live.
He hath a spirit too working to be used
But to the encounter of his like; excused
Are wiser sov'reigns then, that raise one ill
Against another, and both safely kill:
The prince that feeds great natures, they will sway him;
Who nourisheth a lion, must obey him.—

Re-enter Officer *with* MACRO.

Macro, we sent for you.
    Macro. I heard so, Cæsar.
    Tiberius. Leave us a while.   [*Exit* Officer.
When you shall know, good Macro,
The causes of our sending, and the ends,
You will then hearken nearer; and be pleased

You stand so high both in our choice and trust.

    Macro. The humblest place in Cæsar's choice or trust,
May make glad Macro proud; without ambition,
Save to do Cæsar service.

    Tiberius. Leave your courtings.
We are in purpose, Macro, to depart
The city for a time, and see Campania;
Not for our pleasures, but to dedicate
A pair of temples, one to Jupiter
At Capua; th' other at Nola, to Augustus:
In which great work, perhaps our stay will be
Beyond our will produced. Now, since we are
Not ignorant what danger may be born
Out of our shortest absence in a state
So subject unto envy, and embroiled
With hate and faction; we have thought on thee,
Amongst a field of Romans, worthiest Macro,
To be our eye and ear: to keep strict watch
On Agrippina, Nero, Drusus; ay,
And on Sejanus: not that we distrust
His loyalty, or do repent one grace,
Of all that heap we have conferred on him;
For that were to disparage our election,
And call that judgment now in doubt, which then
Seemed as unquestioned as an oracle—
But greatness hath his cankers. Worms and moths
Breed out of too much humour, in the things
Which after they consume, transferring quite
The substance of their makers into themselves.
Macro is sharp, and apprehends: besides,
I know him subtile, close, wise, and well read
In man, and his large nature; he hath studied
Affections, passions, knows their springs, their ends,
Which way, and whether they will work: 'tis proof
Enough of his great merit that we trust him.
Then to a point, because our conference
Cannot be long without suspicion—
Here, Marco, we assign thee both to spy,
Inform, and chastise; think, and use thy means,
Thy ministers, what, where, on whom thou wilt;

Explore plot, practise: all thou dost in this
Shall be as if the senate or the laws
Had given it privilege, and thou thence styled
The saviour both of Cæsar and of Rome.
We will not take thy answer but in act:
Whereto, as thou proceed'st, we hope to hear
By trusted messengers. If't be inquired
Wherefore we called you, say you have in charge
To see our chariots ready, and our horse.
Be still our loved and, shortly, honoured Macro.   [*Exit.*

   Macro. I will not ask why Cæsar bids do this;
But joy, that he bids me. It is the bliss
Of courts to be employed, no matter how;
A prince's power makes all his actions virtue.
We, whom he works by, are dumb instruments,
To do, but not inquire: his great intents
Are to be served, not searched. Yet, as that bow
Is most in hand whose owner best doth know
To affect his aims: so let that statesman hope
Most use, most price, can hit his prince's scope.
Nor must he look at what or whom to strike,
But loose at all; each mark must be alike.
Were it to plot against the fame, the life
Of one with whom I twinned; remove a wife
From my warm side, as loved as is the air;
Practise away each parent; draw mine heir
In compass, though but one; work all my kin
To swift perdition; leave no untrained engin,
For friendship, or for innocence; nay, make
The gods all guilty; I would undertake
This, being imposed me, both with gain and ease:
The way to rise is to obey and please.
He that will thrive in state, he must neglect
The trodden paths that truth and right respect;
And prove new, wilder ways: for virtue there
Is not that narrow thing, she is elsewhere;
Men's fortune there is virtue; reason their will;
Their licence, law; and their observance, skill.
Occasion is their foil; conscience, their stain;
Profit their lustre; and what else is, vain.

If then it be the lust of Cæsar's power,
To have raised Sejanus up, and in an hour
O'erturn him, tumbling down, from height of all;
We are his ready engine: and his fall
May be our rise. It is no uncouth thing
To see fresh buildings from old ruins spring.   [*Exit.*

ACT THE FOURTH

SCENE I—*An Apartment in* AGRIPPINA'S *House*

Enter GALLUS *and* AGRIPPINA.

GALLUS. You must have patience, royal Agrippina.

   Agrippina. I must have vengeance first; and that were
     nectar
Unto my famished spirits. O, my fortune,
Let it be sudden thou prepar'st against me;
Strike all my powers of understanding blind,
And ignorant of destiny to come!
Let me not fear, that cannot hope.

   Gallus. Dear princess,
These tyrannies on yourself are worse than Cæsar's.

   Agrippina. Is this the happiness of being born great?
Still to be aimed at? still to be suspected?
To live the subject of all jealousies?
At least the colour made, if not the ground
To every painted danger? who would not
Choose once to fall, than thus to hang for ever?

   Gallus. You might be safe if you would——

   Agrippina. What, my Gallus!
Be lewd Sejanus's trumpet, or the bawd
To Cæsar's lusts, he now is gone to practise?
Not these are safe, where nothing is. Yourself,
While thus you stand but by me, are not safe,
Was Silius safe? or the good Sosia safe?
Or was my niece, dear Claudia Pulchra, safe,
Or innocent Furnius? they that latest have
(By being made guilty) added reputation

To Afer's eloquence? O, foolish friends,
Could not so fresh example warn your loves,
But you must buy my favours with that loss
Unto yourselves; and when you might perceive
That Cæsar's cause of raging must forsake him,
Before his will! Away, good Gallus, leave me.
Here to be seen, is danger; to speak, treason:
To do me least observance, is called faction.
You are unhappy in me, and I in all.
Where are my sons Nero and Drusus? We
Are they be shot at; let us fall apart;
Not in our ruins, sepulchre our friends.
Or shall we do some action like offence,
To mock their studies that would make us faulty,
And frustrate practice by preventing it?
The danger's like: for what they can contrive,
They will make good. No innocence is safe,
When power contests: nor can they trespass more,
Whose only being was all crime before.

Enter NERO, DRUSUS, *and* CALIGULA.

   Nero. You hear Sejanus is come back from Cæsar?
   Gallus. No. How? disgraced?
   Drusus. More graced now than ever.
   Gallus. By what mischance?
   Caligula. A fortune like enough
Once to be had.
   Drusus. But turned too good to both.
   Caligula. What was't?
   Nero. Tiberius sitting at his meat,
In a farm-house they call Spelunca, sited
By the sea-side, among the Fundane hills,
Within a natural cave; part of the grot,
About the entry, fell, and overwhelmed
Some of the waiters; others ran away:
Only Sejanus with his knees, hands, face,
O'erhanging Cæsar, did oppose himself
To the remaining ruins, and was found
In that so labouring posture by the soldiers
That came to succour him. With which adventure,

He hath so fixed himself in Cæsar's trust,
As thunder cannot move him, and is come
With all the height of Cæsar's praise to Rome.
    Agrippina. And power to turn those ruins all on us;
And bury whole posterities beneath them.
Nero, and Drusus, and Caligula,
Your places are the next, and therefore most
In their offence. Think on your birth and blood,
Awake your spirits, meet their violence;
'Tis princely when a tyrant doth oppose,
And is a fortune sent to exercise
Your virtue, as the wind doth try strong trees,
Who by vexation grow more sound and firm.
After your father's fall, and uncle's fate,
What can you hope, but all the change of stroke
That force or sleight can give? then stand upright;
And though you do not act, yet suffer nobly:
Be worthy of my womb, and take strong cheer;
What we do know will come, we should not fear.

                              [Exeunt.

SCENE II—*The Street*

Enter MACRO.

    Macro. Returned so soon! renewed in trust and grace!
Is Cæsar then so weak, or hath the place
But wrought this alteration with the air;
And he, on next remove, will all repair?
Macro, thou art engaged: and what before
Was public; now, must be thy private, more.
The weal of Cæsar, fitness did imply;
But thine own fate confers necessity
On thy employment; and the thoughts born nearest
Unto ourselves, more swiftest still, and dearest.
If he recover, thou art lost; yea, all
The weight of preparation to his fall
Will turn on thee, and crush thee: therefore strike
Before he settle, to prevent the like
Upon thyself. He doth his vantage know,

That makes it home, and gives the foremost blow.

                                       [*Exit.*

SCENE III—*An Upper Room of* AGRIPPINA'S
House

Enter LATIARIS, RUFUS, *and* OPSIUS.

  Latiaris. It is a service Lord Sejanus will
See well requited, and accept of nobly.
Here place yourselves between the roof and ceiling;
And when I bring him to his words of danger,
Reveal yourselves, and take him.
  Rufus. Is he come?
  Latiaris. I'll now go fetch him.   [*Exit.*
  Opsius. With good speed.—I long
To merit from the state in such an action.
  Rufus. I hope it will obtain the consulship
For one of us.
  Opsius. We cannot think of less,
To bring in one so dangerous as Sabinus.
  Rufus. He was a follower of Germanicus,
And still is an observer of his wife
And children, though they be declined in grace;
A daily visitant, keeps them company
In private and in public, and is noted
To be the only client of the house:
Pray Jove, he will be free to Latiaris.
  Opsius. He's allied to him, and doth trust him well.
  Rufus. And he'll requite his trust!
  Opsius. To do an office
So grateful to the state, I know no man
But would strain nearer bands than kindred——
  Rufus. List!
I hear them come.
  Opsius. Shift to our holes with silence.   [*They retire.*

Re-enter LATIARIS *with* SABINUS.

  Latiaris. It is a noble constancy you show
To this afflicted house; that not like others,

The friends of season, you do follow fortune,
And, in the winter of their fate, forsake
The place whose glories warmed you. You are just,
And worthy such a princely patron's love,
As was the world's renowned Germanicus,
Whose ample merit when I call to thought,
And see his wife and issue, objects made
To so much envy, jealousy, and hate;
It makes me ready to accuse the gods
Of negligence, as men of tyranny.
   Sabinus. They must be patient, so must we.
   Latiaris. O Jove,
What will become of us or of the times,
When, to be high or noble, are made crimes,
When land and treasure are most dangerous faults?
   Sabinus. Nay, when our table, yea our bed, assaults
Our peace and safety? when our writings are
By any envious instruments, that dare
Apply them to the guilty, made to speak
What they will have to fit their tyrannous wreak?
When ignorance is scarcely innocence;
And knowledge made a capital offence?
When not so much, but the bare empty shade
Of liberty is reft us; and we made
The prey to greedy vultures and vile spies,
That first transfix us with their murdering eyes?
   Latiaris. Methinks the genius of the Roman race
Should not be so extinct, but that bright flame
Of liberty might be revived again,
(Which no good man but with his life should lose)
And we not sit like spent and patient fools,
Still puffing in the dark at one poor coal,
Held on by hope till the last spark is out.
The cause is public, and the honour, name,
The immortality of every soul,
That is not bastard or a slave in Rome,
Therein concerned: whereto, if men would change
The wearied arm, and for the weighty shield
So long sustained, employ the facile sword,
We might have soon assurance of our vows.

This ass's fortitude doth tire us all:
It must be active valour must redeem
Our loss, or none. The rock and our hard steel
Should meet to enforce those glorious fires again,
Whose splendour cheered the world, and heat gave life,
No less than doth the sun's.

    Sabinus. 'Twere better stay
In lasting darkness, and despair of day.
No ill should force the subject undertake
Against the sovereign, more than hell should make
The gods do wrong. A good man should and must
Sit rather down with loss than rise unjust.
Though, when the Romans first did yield themselves
To one man's power, they did not mean their lives,
Their fortunes and their liberties should be
His absolute spoil, as purchased by the sword.

    Latiaris. Why, we are worse, if to be slaves, and bond
To Cæsar's slave, be such, the proud Sejanus!
He that is all, does all, gives Cæsar leave
To hide his ulcerous and anointed face,
With his bald crown at Rhodes, while he here stalks
Upon the heads of Romans, and their princes,
Familiarly to empire.

    Sabinus. Now you touch
A point indeed, wherein he shows his art,
As well as power.

    Latiaris. And villainy in both.
Do you observe where Livia lodges? how
Drusus came dead? what men have been cut off?

    Sabinus. Yes, those are things removed. I nearer looked
Into his later practice, where he stands
Declared a master in his mystery.
First, ere Tiberius went, he wrought his fear
To think that Agrippina sought his death.
Then put those doubts in her; send her oft word,
Under the show of friendship, to beware
Of Cæsar, for he laid to poison her:
Drave them to frowns, to mutual jealousies,
Which, now, in visible hatred are burst out.
Since, he hath had his hired instruments

To work on Nero, and to heave him up;
To tell him Cæsar's old, that all the people,
Yea, all the army have their eyes on him;
That both do long to have him undertake
Something of worth, to give the world a hope;
Bids him to court their grace: the easy youth
Perhaps gives ear, which straight he writes to Cæsar;
And with this comment: "See yon dangerous boy;
Note but the practice of the mother, there;
She's tying him for purposes at hand,
With men of sword." Here's Cæsar put in fright
'Gainst son and mother. Yet he leaves not thus.
The second brother, Drusus, a fierce nature,
And fitter for his snares, because ambitious
And full of envy, him he clasps and hugs,
Poisons with praise, tells him what hearts he wears,
How bright he stands in popular expectance;
That Rome doth suffer with him in the wrong
His mother does him, by preferring Nero:
Thus sets he them asunder, each 'gainst other,
Protects the course that serves him to condemn,
Keeps in opinion of a friend to all,
And all drives on to ruin.

    Latiaris. Cæsar sleeps,
And nods at this.

    Sabinus. Would he might ever sleep,
Bogged in his filthy lusts!

                    [OPSIUS *and* RUFUS *rush in.*

    Opsius. Treason to Cæsar!

    Rufus. Lay hands upon the traitor, Latiaris,
Or take the name thyself.

    Latiaris. I am for Cæsar.

    Sabinus. Am I then catched?

    Rufus. How think you, sir? you are.

    Sabinus. Spies of this head, so white, so full of years!
Well, my most reverend monsters, you may live
To see yourselves thus snared.

    Opsius. Away with him!

    Latiaris. Hale him away.

    Rufus. To be a spy for traitors,

Is honourable vigilance.

   Sabinus. You do well,
My most officious instruments of state;
Men of all uses: drag me hence, away.
The year is well begun, and I fall fit
To be an offering to Sejanus. Go!

   Opsius. Cover him with his garments, hide his face.

   Sabinus. It shall not need. Forbear your rude assault.
The fault's not shameful, villainy makes a fault.

                            [Exeunt.

SCENE IV—*The Street before* AGRIPPINA'S *House*

Enter MACRO *and* CALIGULA.

   Macro. Sir, but observe how thick your dangers meet
In his clear drifts! your mother and your brothers,
Now cited to the senate; their friend Gallus,
Feasted to-day by Cæsar, since committed!
Sabinus here we meet, hurried to fetters:
The senators all strook with fear and silence,
Save those whose hopes depend not on good means,
But force their private prey from public spoil.
And you must know, if here you stay, your state
Is sure to be the subject of his hate,
As now the object.

   Caligula. What would you advise me?

   Macro. To go for Capreæ presently; and there
Give up yourself entirely to your uncle.
Tell Cæsar (since your mother is accused
To fly for succours to Augustus' statue,
And to the army, with your brethren) you
Have rather chose to place your aids in him,
Than live suspected; or in hourly fear
To be thrust out, by bold Sejanus' plots:
Which you shall confidently urge to be
Most full of peril to the state, and Cæsar,
As being laid to his peculiar ends,
And not to be let run with common safety.
All which, upon the second, I'll make plain,

So both shall love and trust with Cæsar gain.

Caligula. Away then, let's prepare us for our journey.

[*Exeunt.*

SCENE V—*Another Part of the Street*

Enter ARRUNTIUS.

Arruntius. Still dost thou suffer, heaven! will no flame,
No heat of sin, make thy just wrath to boil
In thy distempered bosom, and o'erflow
The pitchy blazes of impiety,
Kindled beneath thy throne! Still canst thou sleep,
Patient, while vice doth make an antick face
At thy dread power, and blow dust and smoke
Into thy nostrils! Jove, will nothing wake thee?
Must vile Sejanus pull thee by the beard,
Ere thou wilt open thy black-lidded eye,
And look him dead? Well! snore on, dreaming gods;
And let this last of that proud giant-race
Heave mountain upon mountain 'gainst your state—
Be good unto me, Fortune and you powers,
Whom I, expostulating, have profaned;
I see, what's equal with a prodigy,
A great, a noble Roman, and an honest,
Live an old man!—

Enter LEPIDUS.

O Marcus Lepidus,
When is our turn to bleed? Thyself and I,
Without our boast, are almost all the few
Left to be honest in these impious times.

Lepidus. What we are left to be, we will be, Lucius;
Though tyranny did stare as wide as death,
To fright us from it.

Arruntius. 'T hath so on Sabinus.

Lepidus. I saw him now drawn from the Gemonies,
And what increased the direness of the fact,
His faithful dog, upbraiding all us Romans,
Never forsook the corpse, but, seeing it thrown

Into the stream, leaped in, and drowned with it.

Arruntius. O act, to be envied him of us men!
We are the next the hook lays hold on, Marcus:
What are thy arts, good patriot, teach them me,
That have preserved thy hair to this white dye,
And kept so reverend and so dear a head
Safe on his comely shoulders?

Lepidus. Arts, Arruntius!
None, but the plain and passive fortitude,
To suffer and be silent; never stretch
These arms against the torrent; live at home,
With my own thoughts and innocence about me,
Not tempting the wolves' jaws: these are my arts.

Arruntius. I would begin to study 'em, if I thought
They would secure me. May I pray to Jove
In secret and be safe? ay, or aloud,
With open wishes, so I do not mention
Tiberius or Sejanus? yes I must,
If I speak out. 'Tis hard that. May I think,
And not be racked? What danger is't to dream,
Talk in one's sleep, or cough? Who knows the law?
May I shake my head without a comment? say
It rains, or it holds up, and not be thrown
Upon the Gemonies? These now are things,
Whereon men's fortune, yea, their fate depends.
Nothing hath privilege 'gainst the violent ear.
No place, no day, no hour, we see, is free,
Not our religious and most sacred times,
From some one kind of cruelty: all matter,
Nay, all occasion pleaseth. Madmen's rage,
The idleness of drunkards, women's nothing,
Jester's simplicity, all, all is good
That can be catcht at. Nor is now the event
Of any person, or for any crime,
To be expected; for 'tis always one:
Death, with some little difference of place,
Or time——What's this? Prince Nero, guarded!

Enter LACO *and* NERO *with* Guards.

Laco. On, lictors, keep your way. My lords, forbear.

On pain of Cæsar's wrath, no man attempt
Speech with the prisoner.
   Nero. Noble friends, be safe;
To lose yourselves for words, were as vain hazard,
As unto me small comfort: fare you well.
Would all Rome's sufferings in my fate did dwell!
   Laco. Lictors, away.
   Lepidus. Where goes he, Laco?
   Laco. Sir,
He's banished into Pontia by the senate.
   Arruntius. Do I see, hear, and feel? May I trust sense,
Or doth my phant'sie form it?
   Lepidus. Where's his brother?
   Laco. Drusus is prisoner in the palace.
   Arruntius. Ha!
I smell it now: 'tis rank. Where's Agrippina?
   Laco. The princess is confined to Pandataria.
   Arruntius. Bolts, Vulcan; bolts for Jove! Phœbus, thy
     bow;
Stern Mars, thy sword; and, blue-eyed maid, thy spear;
Thy club, Alcides: all the armoury
Of heaven is too little!—Ha! to guard
The gods, I meant. Fine, rare dispatch! this same
Was swiftly born! Confined, imprisoned, banished?
Most tripartite! the cause, sir?
   Laco. Treason.
   Arruntius. O!
The complement of all accusings! that
Will hit, when all else fails.
   Lepidus. This turn is strange!
But yesterday the people would not hear,
Far less objected, but cried Cæsar's letters
Were false and forged; that all these plots were malice
And that the ruin of the prince's house
Was practised 'gainst his knowledge. Where are now
Their voices, now that they behold his heirs
Locked up, disgraced, led into exile?
   Arruntius. Hushed,
Drowned in their bellies. Wild Sejanus' breath
Hath, like a whirlwind, scattered that poor dust,

With his rude blast.—We'll talk no treason, sir,

> [*Turns to* LACO *and the rest.*

If that be it you stand for. Fare you well.
We have no need of horse-leeches. Good spy,
Now you are spied, be gone.

> [*Exeunt* LACO, NERO, *and* Guards.

   Lepidus. I fear you wrong him:
He has the voice to be an honest Roman.

   Arruntius. And trusted to this office! Lepidus,
I'd sooner trust Greek Sinon than a man
Our state employs. He's gone: and being gone,
I dare tell you, whom I dare better trust,
That our night-eyed Tiberius doth not see
His minion's drifts; or, if he do, he's not
So arrant subtile, as we fools do take him;
To breed a mongrel up, in his own house,
With his own blood, and, if the good gods please,
At his own throat flesh him to take a leap.
I do not beg it, heaven; but if the fates
Grant it these eyes, they must not wink.

   Lepidus. They must
Not see it, Lucius.

   Arruntius. Who should let them?

   Lepidus. Zeal,
And duty; with the thought he is our prince.

   Arruntius. He is our monster: forfeited to vice
So far, as no racked virtue can redeem him.
His loathed person fouler than all crimes:
An emperor only in his lusts. Retired,
From all regard of his own fame, or Rome's,
Into an obscure island, where he lives
Acting his tragedies with a comic face,
Amidst his rout of Chaldees: spending hours,
Days, weeks, and months, in the unkind abuse
Of grave astrology, to the bane of men,
Casting the scope of men's nativities
And having found aught worthy in their fortune,
Kill, or precipitate them in the sea,
And boast he can mock fate. Nay, muse not: these
Are far from ends of evil, scarce degrees.

He hath his slaughter-house at Capreæ;
Where he doth study murder as an art;
And they are dearest in his grace, that can
Devise the deepest tortures. Thither, too,
He hath his boys, and beauteous girls ta'en up
Out of our noblest houses, the best formed,
Best nurtured, and most modest; what's their good,
Serves to provoke his bad. Some are allured,
Some threatened; others, by their friends detained,
Are ravished hence, like captives, and, in sight
Of their most grieved parents dealt away
Unto his spintries, sellaries, and slaves,
Masters of strange and new commented lusts,
For which wise nature hath not left a name.
To this (what most strikes us, and bleeding Rome)
He is, with all his craft, become the ward
To his own vassal, a stale catamite:
Whom he, upon our low and suffering necks,
Hath raised from excrement to side the gods,
And have his proper sacrifice in Rome:
Which Jove beholds, and yet will sooner rive
A senseless oak with thunder than his trunk!

Re-enter LACO, *with* POMPONIUS *and* MINUTIUS.

Laco. These letters make men doubtful what t' expect,
Whether his coming, or his death.
  Pomponius. Troth, both:
And which comes soonest, thank the gods for.
  Arruntius. List!
Their talk is Cæsar; I would hear all voices.

[ARRUNTIUS *and* LEPIDUS *stand aside.*
  Minutius. One day, he's well; and will return to Rome;
The next day, sick; and knows not when to hope it.
  Laco. True; and to-day, one of Sejanus' friends
Honoured by special writ; and on the morrow
Another punished——
  Pomponius. By more special writ.
  Minutius. This man receives his praises of Sejanus,
A second but slight mention, a third none,
A fourth rebukes: and thus he leaves the senate

Divided and suspended, all uncertain.

Laco. These forked tricks, I understand them not:
Would he would tell us whom he loves or hates,
That we might follow, without fear or doubt.

Arruntius. Good Heliotrope! Is this your honest man?
Let him be yours so still; he is my knave.

Pomponius. I cannot tell, Sejanus still goes on,
And mounts, we see; new statues are advanced,
Fresh leaves of titles, large inscriptions read,
His fortune sworn by, himself new gone out
Cæsar's colleague in the fifth consulship;
More altars smoke to him than all the gods:
What would be more?

Arruntius. That the dear smoke would choke him,
That would I more.

Lepidus. Peace, good Arruntius.

Latiaris. But there are letters come, they say, ev'n now,
Which do forbid that last.

Minutius. Do you hear so?

Laco. Yes.

Pomponius. By Castor that's the worst.

Arruntius. By Pollux, best.

Minutius. I did not like the sign, when Regulus,
Whom all we know no friend unto Sejanus,
Did, by Tiberius' so precise command,
Succeed a fellow in the consulship:
It boded somewhat.

Pomponius. Not a mote. His partner,
Fulcinius Tiro, is his own, and sure.—
Here comes Terentius.

Enter TERENTIUS.

He can give us more.
                    [*They whisper with* TERENTIUS.

Lepidus. I'll ne'er believe but Cæsar hath some scent
Of bold Sejanus' footing. These cross points
Of varying letters, and opposing consuls,
Mingling his honours and his punishments,
Feigning now ill, now well, raising Sejanus,
And then depressing him, as now of late

In all reports we have it, cannot be
Empty of practise: 'tis Tiberius' art.
For having found his favourite grown too great,
And with his greatness strong; that all the soldiers
Are, with their leaders, made at his devotion;
That almost all the senate are his creatures,
Or hold on him their main dependencies,
Either for benefit, or hope, or fear;
And that himself hath lost much of his own,
By parting unto him; and, by th' increase
Of his rank lusts and rages, quite disarmed
Himself of love, or other public means,
To dare an open contestation;
His subtilty hath chose this doubling line,
To hold him even in: not so to fear him,
As wholly put him out, and yet give check
Unto his farther boldness. In mean time,
By his employments, makes him odious
Unto the staggering rout, whose aid in fine
He hopes to use, as sure, who, when they sway,
Bear down o'erturn all objects in their way.
    Arruntius. You may be a Lynceus, Lepidus: yet **I**
See no such cause, but that a politic tyrant,
Who can so well disguise it, should have ta'en
A nearer way: feigned honest, and come home
To cut his throat, by law.
    Lepidus. Ay, but his fear
Would ne'er be masked, allbe his vices were.
    Pomponius. His lordship then is still in grace?
    Terentius. Assure you,
Never in more, either of grace or power.
    Pomponius. The gods are wise and just.
    Arruntius. The fiends they are,
To suffer thee belie 'em.
    Terentius. I have here
His last and present letters, where he writes him,
"The partner of his cares," and "his Sejanus."—
    Laco. But is that true, it is prohibited
To sacrifice unto him?
    Terentius. Some such thing

Cæsar makes scruple of, but forbids it not;
No more than to himself: says he could wish
It were forborn to all.
   Laco. Is it no other?
   Terentius. No other, on my trust. For your more surety,
Here is that letter too.
   Arruntius. How easily
Do wretched men believe what they would have!
Looks this like plot?
   Lepidus. Noble Arruntius, stay.
   Laco. He names him here without his titles.
   Lepidus. Note!
   Arruntius. Yes, and come off your notable fool. I will.
   Laco. No other than Sejanus.
   Pomponius. That's but haste
In him that writes: here he gives large amends.
   Minutius. And with his own hand written?
   Pomponius. Yes.
   Laco. Indeed?
   Terentius. Believe it, gentlemen, Sejanus' breast
Never received more full contentments in,
Than at this present.
   Pomponius. Takes he well the escape
Of young Caligula, with Macro?
   Terentius. Faith,
At the first air it somewhat troubled him.
   Lepidus. Observe you?
   Arrentius. Nothing; riddles. Till I see
Sejanus struck, no sound thereof strikes me.
                    [*Exeunt* ARRENTIUS *and* LEPIDUS.
   Pomponius. I like it not. I muse he would not attempt
Somewhat against him in the consulship,
Seeing the people 'gin to favour him.
   Terentius. He doth repent it now; but he has employed
Pagonianus after him: and he holds
That correspondence there, with all that are
Near about Cæsar, as no thought can pass
Without his knowledge, thence in act to front him.
   Pomponius. I gratulate the news.
   Laco. But how comes Macro

So in trust and favour with Caligula?

    Pomponius. O, sir, he has a wife; and the young prince
An appetite: he can look up and spy
Flies in the roof, when there are fleas i' the bed;
And hath a learned nose to assure his sleeps.
Who to be favoured of the rising sun,
Would not lend little of his waning moon?
It is the saf'st ambition. Noble Terentius!

    Terentius. The night grows fast upon us. At your service.

                                 [*Exeunt.*

ACT THE FIFTH

SCENE I—*An Apartment in* SEJANUS' *House*

Enter SEJANUS.

SEJANUS. Swell, swell, my joys; and faint not to declare
Yourselves as ample as your causes are.
I did not live till now: this my first hour;
Wherein I see my thoughts reached by my power.
But this, and gripe my wishes. Great and high,
The world knows only two, that's Rome and I.
My roof receives me not; 'tis air I tread;
And, at each step, I feel my advanced head
Knock out a star in heaven! reared to this height,
All my desires seem modest, poor, and slight,
That did before sound impudent: 'tis place,
Not blood, discerns the noble and the base.
Is there not something more than to be Cæsar?
Must we rest there? it irks t' have come so far,
To be so near a stay. Caligula,
Would thou stood'st stiff, and many in our way!
Winds lose their strength, when they do empty fly,
Unmet of woods or buildings; great fires die,
That want their matter to withstand them: so,
It is our grief, and will be our loss, to know
Our power shall want opposites; unless
The gods, by mixing in the cause, would bless

Our fortune with their conquest. That were worth
Sejanus' strife; durst fates but bring it forth.

Enter TERENTIUS.

   Terentius. Safety to great Sejanus!
   Sejanus. Now, Terentius?
   Terentius. Hears not my lord the wonder?
   Sejanus. Speak it; no.
   Terentius. I meet it violent in the people's mouth,
Who run in routs to Pompey's theatre,
To view your statue, which, they say, sends forth
A smoke, as from a furnace, black and dreadful.
   Sejanus. Some traitor hath put fire in: you, go see,
And let the head be taken off, to look
What 'tis. [*Exit* TERENTIUS.] Some slave hath practised an
   imposture
To stir the people.—How now! why return you?

Re-enter TERENTIUS, *with* SATRIUS *and* NATTA.

   Satrius. The head, my lord, already is ta'en off,
I saw it; and, at opening, there leapt out
A great and monstrous serpent.
   Sejanus. Monstrous! why?
Had it a beard, and horns? no heart? a tongue
Forked as flattery? looked it of the hue,
To such as live in great men's bosoms? was
The spirit of it Macro's?
   Natta. May it please
The most divine Sejanus, in my days,
(And by his sacred fortune, I affirm it,)
I have not seen a more extended, grown,
Foul, spotted, venomous, ugly——
   Sejanus. O, the fates!
What a wild muster's here of attributes,
T' express a worm, a snake!
   Terentius. But how that should
Come there, my lord!
   Sejanus. What, and you too, Terentius!
I think you mean to make 't a prodigy
In your reporting.

Terentius. Can the wise Sejanus
Think heaven hath meant it less?
   Sejanus. O, superstition!
Why, then the falling of our bed, that brake
This morning, burdened with the populous weight
Of our expecting clients, to salute us;
Or running of the cat betwixt our legs,
As we set forth unto the Capitol,
Were prodigies.
   Terentius. I think them ominous:
And would they had not happened! As, to-day,
The fate of some your servants: who declining [1]
Their way, not able, for the throng, to follow,
Slipt down the Gemonies, and brake their necks!
Besides, in taking your last augury,
No prosperous bird appeared; but croaking ravens
Flagged up and down, and from the sacrifice
Flew to the prison, where they sat all night,
Beating the air with their obstreperous beaks!
I dare not counsel, but I could entreat,
That great Sejanus would attempt the gods
Once more with sacrifice.
   Sejanus. What excellent fools
Religion makes of men! Believes Terentius,
If these were dangers, as I shame to think them,
The gods could change the certain course of fate?
Or, if they could they would, now in a moment,
For a beeve's fat, or less, be bribed to invert
These long decrees? Then think the gods like flies,
Are to be taken with the steam of flesh,
Or blood, diffused about their altars: think
Their power as cheap as I esteem it small.
Of all the throng that fill th' Olympian hall,
And, without pity, lade poor Atlas' back,
I know not that one deity, but Fortune,
To whom I would throw up in begging smoke,
One grain of incense; or whose ear I'd buy
With thus much oil. Her I indeed adore;
And keep her grateful image in my house,

[1] Turning out of the way.

Sometime belonging to a Roman king,
But now called mine, as by the better style:
To her I care not, if, for satisfying
Your scrupulous phant'sies, I go offer. Bid
Our priest prepare us honey, milk, and poppy,
His masculine odours, and night-vestments: say
Our rites are instant; which performed, you'll see
How vain, and worthy laughter, your fears be.

[*Exeunt.*

SCENE II—*Another Room in the same*

Enter COTTA *and* POMPONIUS.

   Cotta. Pomponius, whither in such speed?
   Pomponius. I go
To give my lord Sejanus notice——
   Cotta. What?
   Pomponius. Of Macro.
   Cotta. Is he come?
   Pomponius. Entered but now
The house of Regulus.
   Cotta. The opposite consul!
   Pomponius. Some half hour since.
   Cotta. And by night too! Stay, sir;
I'll bear you company.
   Pomponius. Along then.   [*Exeunt.*

SCENE III—*A Room in* REGULUS' *House*

Enter MACRO, REGULUS, *and* Attendant.

   Macro. 'Tis Cæsar's will to have a frequent senate;
And therefore must your edict lay deep mulct
On such as shall be absent.
   Regulus. So it doth.
Bear it my fellow consul to adscribe.
   Macro. And tell him it must early be proclaimed:
The place Apollo's temple.   [*Exit* Attendant.
   Regulus. That's remembered.

Macro. And at what hour?

Regulus. Yes.

Macro. You do forget

To send one for the provost of the watch.

   Regulus. I have not: here he comes.

Enter LACO.

   Macro. Gracinus Laco,

You are a friend most welcome: by and by,

I'll speak with you. You must procure this list

Of the prætorian cohorts, with the names

Of the centurions, and their tribunes.

   Regulus. Ay.

   Macro. I bring you letters, and a health from Cæsar.

   Laco. Sir, both come well.

   Macro. And hear you? with your note,

Which are the eminent men, and most of action.

   Regulus. That shall be done you too.

   Macro. Most worthy Laco,

Cæsar salutes you. [*Exit* REGULUS.] Consul! death

    and furies!

Gone now! The argument will please you, sir,

Ho! Regulus! The anger of the gods

Follow your diligent legs, and overtake 'em,

In likeness of the gout!

Re-enter REGULUS.

        O, my good lord,

We lacked you present; I would pray you send

Another to Fulcinius Trio, straight,

To tell him you will come, and speak with him:

The matter we'll devise, to stay him there,

While I with Laco do survey the watch.

              [*Exit* REGULUS.

What are your strengths, Gracinus?

   Laco. Seven cohorts.

   Macro. You see what Cæsar writes; and—Gone again!

H' has sure a vein of mercury in his feet.

Know you what store of the prætorian soldiers

Sejanus holds about him, for his guard?

Laco. I cannot the just number; but I think
Three centuries.

Macro. Three! good.

Laco. At most not four.

Macro. And who be those centurions?

Laco. That the consul
Can best deliver you.

Macro. When he's away!
Spite on his nimble industry—Gracinus,
You find what place you hold, there, in the trust
Of royal Cæsar?

Laco. Ay, and I am——

Macro. Sir,
The honours there proposed are but beginnings
Of his great favours.

Laco. They are more——

Macro. I heard him
When he did study what to add.

Laco. My life,
And all I hold——

Macro. You were his own first choice!
Which doth confirm as much as you can speak;
And will, if we succeed, make more——Your guards
Are seven cohorts, you say?

Laco. Yes.

Macro. Those we must
Hold still in readiness and undischarged.

Laco. I understand so much. But how it can——

Macro. Be done without suspicion, you'll object?

Re-enter REGULUS.

Regulus. What's that?

Laco. The keeping of the watch in arms,
When morning comes.

Macro. The senate shall be met, and set
So early in the temple, as all mark
Of that shall be avoided.

Regulus. If we need,
We have commission to possess the palace,
Enlarge Prince Drusus, and make him our chief.

Macro. That secret would have burnt his reverend mouth,
Had he not spit it out now: by the gods,
You carry things too——Let me borrow a man
Or two, to bear these——That of freeing Drusus,
Cæsar projected as the last and utmost;
Not else to be remembered.

Enter Servants.

Regulus. Here are servants.
Macro. These to Arruntius, these to Lepidus.
This bear to Cotta, this to Latiaris.
If they demand you of me, say I have ta'en
Fresh horse and am departed. [*Exeunt* Servants.] You, my
    lord,
To your colleague, and be you sure to hold him
With long narration of the new fresh favours,
Meant to Sejanus, his great patron; I,
With trusted Laco, here, are for the guards:
Then to divide. For night hath many eyes,
Whereof, though most do sleep, yet some are spies.

                             [*Exeunt.*

SCENE IV—*A Sacellum* (*or Chapel*) *in* SEJANUS'
                    House

Enter Præcones, Flamen, Tubicines, Tibicines, Ministri,
    SEJANUS, TERENTIUS, NATTA, &c.

Præcones. "Be all profane far hence; fly, fly far off:
Be absent far; far hence be all profane!"
  [*Tubicines and* Tibicines *sound while the* Flamen
    washeth.
Flamen. We have been faulty, but repent us now.
And bring pure hands, pure vestments, and pure minds.
  1 *Minister.* Pure vessels.
  2 *Minister.* And pure offerings.
  3 *Minister.* Garlands pure.
  Flamen. Bestow your garlands: and, with reverence, place
The vervin on the altar.
  Præcones. Favour your tongues.

[*While they sound again, the* Flamen *takes of the honey with his finger, and tastes, then ministers to all the rest: so of the milk in an earthen vessel, he deals about; which done, he sprinkleth upon the altar, milk; then imposeth the honey, and kindleth his gums, and after censing about the altar, placeth his censer thereon, into which they put several branches of poppy, and the music ceasing, proceeds.*

Flamen. "Great mother Fortune, queen of human state,
Rectress of action, arbitress of fate,
To whom all sway, all power, all empire bows,
Be present, and propitious to our vows!"

Præcones. Favour it with your tongues.

Ministri. Be present, and propitious to our vows!

Omnes. Accept our offering, and be pleased, great goddess.

Terentius. See, see, the image stirs!

Satrius. And turns away!

Natta. Fortune averts her face!

Flamen. Avert, you gods,
The prodigy. Still! still! some pious rite
We have neglected. Yet, heaven be appeased,
And be all tokens false and void, that speak
Thy present wrath!

Sejanus. Be thou dumb, scrupulous priest:
And gather up thyself, with these thy wares,
Which I, in spite of thy blind mistress, or
Thy juggling mystery, religion, throw
Thus scorned on the earth.

[*Overturns the statue and the altar.*
                    Nay, hold thy look
Averted till I woo thee turn again;
And thou shalt stand to all posterity,
The eternal game and laughter, with thy neck
Writhed to thy tail, like a ridiculous cat.
Avoid these fumes, these superstitious lights,
And all these cosening ceremonies; you,
Your pure and spiced conscience!

[*Exeunt all but* SEJANUS, TERENTIUS, SATRIUS, *and* NATTA.

                                             I, the slave
And mock of fools, scorn on my worthy head!
That have been titled and adored a god,
Yea sacrificed unto, myself, in Rome,
No less than Jove: and I be brought to do
A peevish giglot[1] rites! perhaps the thought
And shame of that, made Fortune turn her face,
Knowing herself the lesser deity,
And but my servant.—Bashful queen, if so,
Sejanus thanks thy modesty. Who's that?

Enter POMPONIUS *and* MINUTIUS.

Pomponius. His fortune suffers, till he hears my news:
I have waited here too long. Macro, my lord——
  Sejanus. Speak lower and withdraw.   [*Takes him aside.*
  Terentius. Are these things true?
  Minutius. Thousands are gazing at it in the streets.
  Sejanus. What's that?
  Terentius. Minutius tells us here, my lord,
That a new head being set upon your statue,
A rope is since found wreathed about it! and,
But now a fiery meteor in the form
Of a great ball was seen to roll along
The troubled air, where yet it hangs unperfect,
The amazing wonder of the multitude!
  Sejanus. No more. That Macro's come, is more than all!
  Terentius. Is Macro come?
  Pomponius. I saw him.
  Terentius. Where? with whom?
  Pomponius. With Regulus.
  Sejanus. Terentius!
  Terentius. My lord.
  Sejanus. Send for the tribunes, we will straight have up
More of the soldiers for our guard. [*Exit* TERENTIUS.]
    Minutius,
We pray you go for Cotta, Latiaris,
Trio the consul, or what senators
You know are sure, and ours. [*Exit* MINUTIUS.] You, my
    good Natta,

---

[1] A wanton girl.

For Laco, provost of the watch. [*Exit* NATTA.] Now, Satrius,
The time of proof comes on; arm all our servants,
And without tumult. [*Exit* SATRIUS.] You, Pomponius,
Hold some good correspondence with the consul:
Attempt him, noble friend. [*Exit* POMPONIUS.] These things
    begin
To look like dangers, now, worthy my fates.
Fortune, I see thy worst: let doubtful states,
And things uncertain hang upon thy will;
Me surest death shall render certain still.
Yet, why is now my thought turned toward death,
Whom fates have let go on, so far in breath,
Unchecked or unreproved? I, that did help
To fell the lofty cedar of the world
Germanicus; that at one stroke cut down
Drusus, that upright elm; withered his vine;
Laid Silius and Sabinus, two strong oaks,
Flat on the earth; besides those other shrubs,
Cordus and Sosia, Claudia Pulchra,
Fernius and Gallus, which I have grubbed up;
And since, have set my axe so strong and deep
Into the root of spreading Agrippine;
Loft off and scattered her proud branches, Nero,
Drusus; and Caius too, although replanted.
If you will, Destinies, that after all,
I faint now ere I touch my period,
You are but cruel; and I already have done
Things great enough. All Rome hath been my slave;
The senate sate an idle looker-on,
And witness of my power; when I have blushed
More to command than it to suffer: all
The fathers have sat ready and prepared,
To give me empire, temples, or their throats,
When I would ask 'em; and, what crowns the top,
Rome, senate, people, all the world have seen
Jove but my equal; Cæsar but my second.
'Tis then your malice, Fates, who, but your own,
Envy and fear to have any power long known.   [*Exit.*

SCENE V—*A Room in the same*

Enter TERENTIUS *and* Tribunes.

Terentius. Stay here: I'll give his lordship you are come.

Enter MINUTIUS, *with* COTTA *and* LATIARIS.

Minutius. Marcus Terentius, pray you tell my lord
Here's Cotta, and Latiaris.
 Terentius. Sir, I shall.   [*Exit.*
 Cotta. My letter is the very same with yours;
Only requires me to be present there,
And give my voice to strengthen his design.
 Latiaris. Names he not what it is?
 Cotta. No, nor to you.
 Latiaris. 'Tis strange and singular doubtful!
 Cotta. So it is.
It may be all is left to lord Sejanus.

Enter NATTA *and* GRACINUS LACO.

Natta. Gentlemen, where's my lord?
Tribunes. We wait him here.
Cotta. The provost Laco! what's the news?
Latiaris. My lord——

Enter SEJANUS.

Sejanus. Now, my right dear, noble, and trusted friends,
How much I am a captive to your kindness!
Most worthy Cotta, Latiaris, Laco,
Your valiant hand; and, gentlemen, your loves.
I wish I could divide myself unto you;
Or that it lay within our narrow powers,
To satisfy for so enlarged bounty.
Gracinus, we must pray you, hold your guards
Unquit when morning comes. Saw you the consul?
 Minutius. Trio will presently be here, my lord.
 Cotta. They are but giving order for the edict,
To warn the senate?
 Sejanus. How! the senate?

Laco. Yes.

This morning in Apollo's temple——

    Cotta. We

Are charged by letter to be there, my lord.

    Sejanus. By letter! pray you let's see.

    Latiaris. Knows not his lordship?

    Cotta. It seems so!

    Sejanus. A senate warned! without my knowledge!

And on this sudden! Senators by letters

Required to be there! who brought these?

    Cotta. Macro.

    Sejanus. Mine enemy! and when?

    Cotta. This midnight.

    Sejanus. Time,

With every other circumstance, doth give

It hath some strain of engine in 't!—How now?

Enter SATRIUS.

    Satrius. My lord, Sertorius Macro is without,

Alone, and pray t' have private conference

In business of high nature with your lordship,

He says to me, and which regards you much.

    Sejanus. Let him come here.

    Satrius. Better, my lord, withdraw:

You will betray what store and strength of friends

Are now about you; which he comes to spy.

    Sejanus. Is he not armed?

    Satrius. We'll search him.

    Sejanus. No; but take,

And lead him to some room, where you concealed

May keep a guard upon us. [*Exit* SATRIUS.] Noble Laco,

You are our trust; and till our own cohorts

Can be brought up, your strengths must be our guard.

Now, good Minutius, honoured Latiaris,

[He salutes them humbly.

Most worthy and my most unwearied friends;

I return instantly.   [*Exit.*

    Latiaris. Most worthy lord!

    Cotta. His lordship is turned instant kind, methinks;

I have not observed it in him heretofore.

1 *Tribune.* 'Tis true, and it becomes him nobly.
Minutius. I
Am wrapt withal.
    2 *Tribune.* By Mars, he has my lives,
Were they a million, for this only grace.
    Laco. Ay, and to name a man!
    Latiaris. As he did me!
    Minutius. And me!
    Latiaris. Who would not spend his life and fortunes
To purchase but the look of such a lord?
    Laco. He that would nor be lord's fool, nor the world's.
                                                                    [*Aside.*

SCENE VI—*Another Room in the same*

Enter SEJANUS, MACRO, *and* SATRIUS.

Sejanus. Macro! most welcome, a most coveted friend!
Let me enjoy my longings. When arrived you?
    Macro. About the noon of night.
    Sejanus. Satrius, give leave.   [*Exit* SATRIUS.
    Macro. I have been, since I came, with both the consuls,
On a particular design from Cæsar.
    Sejanus. How fares it with our great and royal master?
    Macro. Right plentifully well; as with a prince
That still holds out the great proportion
Of his large favours, where his judgment hath
Made once divine election: like the god
That wants not, nor is wearied to bestow
Where merit meets his bounty, as it doth
In you, already the most happy, and ere
The sun shall climb the south, most high Sejanus.
Let not my lord be amused.[1] For to this end
Was I by Cæsar sent for to the isle,
With special caution to conceal my journey;
And thence had my despatch as privately
Again to Rome; charged to come here by night;
And only to the consuls make narration
Of his great purpose: that the benefit

---

[1] Amazed

Might come more full, and striking, by how much
It was less worked for, or aspired by you,
Or least informed to the common thought.

   Sejanus. What may this be? part of myself, dear Macro,
If good, speak out; and share with your Sejanus.

   Macro. If bad, I should for ever loathe myself
To be the messenger to so good a lord.
I do exceed my instructions to acquaint
Your lordship with thus much; but 'tis my venture
On your retentive wisdom: and because
I would no jealous scruple should molest
Or rack your peace of thought. For I assure
My noble lord, no senator yet knows
The business meant: though all by several letters
Are warned to be there, and give their voices,
Only to add unto the state and grace
Of what is purposed.

   Sejanus. You take pleasure, Macro,
Like a coy wench, in torturing your lover.
What can be worth this suffering?

   Macro. That which follows,
The tribunitial dignity and power:
Both which Sejanus is to have this day
Conferred upon him, and by public senate.

   Sejanus. Fortune be mine again! thou hast satisfied
For thy suspected loyalty.   [*Aside.*

   Macro. My lord,
I have no longer time, the day approacheth,
And I must back to Cæsar.

   Sejanus. Where's Caligula?

   Macro. That I forgot to tell your lordship. Why,
He lingers yonder about Capreæ,
Disgraced; Tiberius hath not seen him yet:
He needs would thrust himself to go with me,
Against my wish or will; but I have quitted
His forward trouble, with as tardy note
As my neglect or silence could afford him.
Your lordship cannot now command me aught,
Because I take no knowledge that I saw you;
But I shall boast to live to serve your lordship:

And so take leave.

   Sejanus. Honest and worthy Macro;

Your love and friendship. [*Exit* MACRO.] Who's there?
  Satrius,

Attend my honourable friend forth.—O!

How vain and vile a passion is this fear,

What base uncomely things it makes men do!

Suspect their noblest friends, as I did this,

Flatter poor enemies, entreat their servants,

Stoop, court, and catch at the benevolence

Of creatures unto whom, within this hour,

I would not have vouchsafed a quarter-look,

Or piece of face! By you that fools call gods,

Hang all the sky with your prodigious signs,

Fill earth with monsters, drop the scorpion down,

Out of the zodiac, or the fiercer lion,

Shake off the loosened globe from her long hinge,

Roll all the world in darkness, and let loose

The enraged winds to turn up groves and towns!

When I do fear again, let me be struck

With forked fire, and unpitied die:

Who fears, is worthy of calamity.   [*Exit.*

SCENE VII—*Another Room in the same*

Enter TERENTIUS, MINUTIUS, LACO, COTTA, LATIARIS,
and POMPONIUS; REGULUS, TRIO, *and others, on
different sides.*

  Pomponius. Is not my lord here?

  Terentius. Sir, he will be straight.

  Cotta. What news, Fulcinius Trio?

  Trio. Good, good tidings;

But keep it to yourself. My lord Sejanus

Is to receive this day in open senate

The tribunitial dignity.

  Cotta. Is't true?

  Trio. No words, not to your thought: but, sir, believe it.

  Latiaris. What says the consul?

Cotta. Speak it not again:
He tells me that to-day my lord Sejanus——
    Trio. I must entreat you, Cotta, on your honour
Not to reveal it.
    Cotta. On my life, sir.
    Latiaris. Say.
    Cotta. Is to receive the tribunitial power.
But, as you are an honourable man,
Let me conjure you not to utter it;
For it is trusted to me with that bond.
    Latiaris. I am Harpocrates.
    Terentius. Can you assure it?
    Pomponius. The consul told it me; but keep it close.
    Minutius. Lord Latiaris, what's the news?
    Latiaris. I'll tell you;
But you must swear to keep it secret.

Enter SEJANUS.

    Sejanus. I knew the Fates had on their distaff left
More of our thread, than so.
    Regulus. Hail, great Sejanus!
    Trio. Hail, the most honoured!
    Cotta. Happy!
    Latiaris. High Sejanus!
    Sejanus. Do you bring prodigies too?
    Trio. May all presage
Turn to those fair effects, whereof we bring
Your lordship news.
    Regulus. May't please my lord withdraw.
    Sejanus. Yes:—I will speak with you anon.
                        [To some that stand by.

    Terentius. My lord,
What is your pleasure for the tribunes?
    Sejanus. Why,
Let them be thanked and sent away.
    Minutius. My lord——
    Laco. Will't please my lordship to command me——
    Sejanus. No:
You are troublesome.
    Minutius. The mood is changed.

Trio. Not speak,
Nor look!

Laco. Ay, he is wise, will make him friends
Of such who never love but for their ends.   [*Exeunt.*

SCENE VIII—*A Space before the Temple of Apollo*

Enter ARRUNTIUS *and* LEPIDUS, *divers* Senators
passing by them.

Arruntius. Ay, go make haste; take heed you be not last
To tender your All Hail in the wide hall
Of huge Sejanus: run a lictor's pace:
Stay not to put your robes on; but away
With the pale troubled ensigns of great friendship
Stamped in your face! Now, Marcus Lepidus,
You still believe your former augury!
Sejanus must go downward! You perceive
His wane approaching fast!

Lepidus. Believe me, Lucius,
I wonder at this rising.

Arruntius. Ay, and that we
Must give our suffrage to it. You will say,
It is to make his fall more steep and grievous:
It may be so. But think it, they that can
With idle wishes 'say to bring back time:
In cases desperate, all hope is crime.
See, see! what troops of his officious friends
Flock to salute my lord, and start before
My great proud lord! to get a lord-like nod!
Attend my lord unto the senate-house!
Bring back my lord! like servile ushers, make
Way for my lord! proclaim his idol lordship,
More than ten criers, or six noise of trumpets!
Make legs, kiss hands, and take a scattered hair
From my lord's eminent shoulder! [SANQUINIUS *and*
        HATERIUS *pass over the stage.*] See, Sanquinius,
With his slow belly, and his dropsy! look,
What toiling haste he makes! yet here's another
Retarded with the gout, will be afore him.

Get thee Liburnian porters, thou gross fool,
To bear thy obsequious fatness, like thy peers.
They are met! the gout returns, and his great carriage.

[LICTORS, REGULUS, TRIO, SEJANUS, SATRIUS *and many other* Senators *pass over the stage.*

   Lictors. Give way, make place, room for the consul!
   Sanquinius. Hail,
Hail, great Sejanus!
   Haterius. Hail, my honoured lord!
   Arruntius. We shall be marked anon, for our not Hail.
   Lepidus. That is already done.
   Arruntius. It is a note.
Of upstart greatness, to observe and watch
For these poor trifles, which the noble mind
Neglects and scorns.
   Lepidus. Ay, and they think themselves
Deeply dishonoured where they are omitted,
As if they were necessities that helped
To the perfection of their dignities;
And hate the men that but refrain them.
   Arruntius. O!
There is a farther cause of hate. Their breasts
Are guilty that we know their obscure springs,
And base beginnings; thence the anger grows.
On. Follow.   [*Exeunt.*

SCENE IX—*Another Part of the same*

Enter MACRO *and* LACO.

   Macro. When all are entered, shut the temple doors;
And bring your guards up to the gate.
   Laco. I will.
   Macro. If you shall hear commotion in the senate,
Present yourself: and charge on any man
Shall offer to come forth.
   Laco. I am instructed.   [*Exeunt.*

SCENE X—*The Temple of Apollo*

Enter HATERIUS, TRIO, SANQUINIUS, COTTA, REGULUS,
SEJANUS, POMPONIUS, LATIARIS, LEPIDUS, ARRUNTIUS,
and divers other Senators; Præcones *and* Lictores.

Haterius. How well his lordship looks to-day!
Trio. As if
He had been born, or made for this hour's state.
  Cotta. Your fellow consul's come about, methinks?
  Trio. Ay, he is wise.
  Sanquinius. Sejanus trusts him well.
  Trio. Sejanus is a noble, bounteous lord.
  Haterius. He is so, and most valiant.
  Latiaris. And most wise.
  1 *Senator.* He's everything.
  Latiaris. Worthy of all, and more
Than bounty can bestow.
  Trio. This dignity
Will make him worthy.
  Pomponius. Above Cæsar.
  Sanquinius. Tut,
Cæsar is but the rector of an isle,
He of the Empire.
  Trio. Now he will have power
More to reward than ever.
  Cotta. Let us look
We be not slack in giving him our voices.
  Latiaris. Not I.
  Sanquinius. Nor I.
  Cotta. The readier we seem
To propagate his honours, will more bind
His thoughts to ours.
  Haterius. I think right with your lordship;
It is the way to have us hold our places.
  Sanquinius. Ay, and get more.
  Latiaris. More office and more titles.
  Pomponius. I will not lose the part I hope to share
In these his fortunes, for my patrimony.

Latiaris. See how Arruntius sits, and Lepidus!

Trio. Let them alone, they will be marked anon.

1 *Senator.* I'll do with others.

2 *Senator.* So will I.

3 *Senator.* And I.

Men grow not in the state but as they are planted
Warm in his favours.

Cotta. Noble Sejanus!

Haterius. Honoured Sejanus!

Latiaris. Worthy and great Sejanus!

Arruntius. Gods! how the sponges open and take in,
And shut again! look, look! is not he blest
That gets a seat in eye-reach of him? more
That comes in ear, or tongue-reach? O but most
Can claw his subtile elbow, or with a buz
Fly-bow his ears?

Præcones. Proclaim the senate's peace,
And give last summons by the edict.

Præcones. Silence!
In the name of Cæsar, and the senate, silence!

"Memmius Regulus, and Fulcinius Trio, consuls, these
present kalends of June, with the first light, shall hold a
senate, in the temple of Apollo Palatine: all that are fathers,
and are registered fathers, that have right of entering the
senate, we warn or command you be frequently present, take
knowledge the business is the commonwealth's: whosoever is
absent, his fine or mulct will be taken, his excuse will not be
taken."

Trio. Note who are absent, and record their names.

Regulus. Fathers conscript, may what I am to utter
Turn good and happy for the commonwealth!
And thou, Apollo, in whose holy house
We here are met, inspire us all with truth,
And liberty of censure to our thought!
The majesty of great Tiberius Cæsar
Propounds to this grave senate, the bestowing
Upon the man he loves, honoured Sejanus,
The tribunitial dignity and power:
Here are his letters, signed with his signet.

What pleaseth now the fathers to be done?

 Senators. Read, read them, open, publicly read them.

 Cotta. Cæsar hath honoured his own greatness much
In thinking of this act.

 Trio. It was a thought
Happy, and worthy Cæsar.

 Latiaris. And the lord
As worthy it, on whom it is directed!

 Haterius. Most worthy!

 Sanquinius. Rome did never boast the virtue
That could give envy bounds, but his: Sejanus——

 1 *Senator.* Honoured and noble!

 2 *Senator.* Good and great Sejanus!

 Arruntius. O, most tame slavery, and fierce flattery!

 Præcones. Silence!

"Tiberius Cæsar to the Senate greeting.
If you, conscript fathers, with your children, be in health,
it is abundantly well: we with our friends here are so. The
care of the commonwealth, howsoever we are removed in
person, cannot be absent to our thought: although, oftentimes, even to princes most present, the truth of their own
affairs is hid; than which nothing falls out more miserable
to a state, or makes the art of governing more difficult.
But since it hath been our easeful happiness to enjoy both
the aids and industry of so vigilant a senate, we profess to
have been the more indulgent to our pleasures, not as being
careless of our office, but rather secure of the necessity.
Neither do these common rumours of many, and infamous
libels published against our retirement, at all afflict us;
being born more out of men's ignorance than their malice:
and will, neglected, find their own grave quickly; whereas,
too sensibly acknowledged, it would make their obloquy
ours. Nor do we desire their authors, though found, be
censured, since in a free state, as ours, all men ought to
enjoy both their minds and tongues free."

 Arruntius. The lapwing, the lapwing!

"Yet in things which shall worthily and more near concern
the majesty of a prince, we shall fear to be so unnaturally

cruel to our own fame, as to neglect them. True it is, conscript fathers, that we have raised Sejanus from obscure,
and almost unknown gentry,"

Senator. How, how!

"to the highest and most conspicuous point of greatness,
and, we hope, deservingly; yet not without danger: it being
a most bold hazard in that sovereign who, by his particular
love to one, dares adventure the hatred of all his other
subjects."

Arruntius. This touches; the blood turns.
"But we affy in your loves and understandings, and do no
way suspect the merit of our Sejanus, to make our favours
offensive to any."

Senator. O! good, good.

"Though we could have wished his zeal had run a calmer
course against Agrippina and our nephews, howsoever the
openness of their actions declared them delinquents; and
that he would have remembered no innocence is so safe,
but it rejoiceth to stand in the sight of mercy: the use of
which in us he hath so quite taken away toward them, by
his loyal fury, as now our clemency would be thought but
wearied cruelty, if we should offer to exercise it."

Arruntius. I thank him; there I looked for 't.
A good fox!

"Some there be that would interpret this his public severity
to be particular ambition; and that, under a pretext of
service to us, he doth but remove his own lets: alleging
the strengths he hath made to himself, by the prætorian
soldiers, by his faction in court and senate, by the offices he
holds himself, and confers on others, his popularity and de-
pendents, his urging and almost driving us to this our unwilling retirement, and, lastly, his aspiring to be our son-
in-law."

Senators. This is strange!
Arruntius. I shall anon believe your vultures,[1] Marcus.

[1] Augury; vultures were one of the best known omens.

"Your wisdoms, conscript fathers, are able to examine, and censure these suggestions. But were they left to our absolving voice, we durst pronounce them, as we think them, most malicious."

 Senator. O, he has restored all; list!

"Yet are they offered to be averred, and on the lives of the informers. What we should say, or rather what we should not say, lords of the senate, if this be true, our gods and goddesses confound us if we know! Only we must think, we have placed our benefits ill; and conclude, that in our choice, either we were wanting to the gods, or the gods to us."   [*The* Senators *shift their places.*

 Arruntius. The place grows hot; they shift.

"We have not been covetous, honourable fathers, to change; neither is it now any new lust that alters our affection, or old loathing: but those needful jealousies of state, that warn wiser princes hourly to provide their safety; and do teach them how learned a thing it is to beware of the humblest enemy; much more of those great ones, whom their own employed favours have made fit for their fears."

 1 *Senator.* Away.
 2 *Senator.* Sit farther.
 Cotta. Let's remove——
 Arruntius. Gods! how the leaves drop off, this little wind!

"We therefore desire, that the office he holds be first seized by the senate; and himself suspended from all exercise of place or power——"

 Senator. How!
 Sanquinius [*thrusting by*]. By your leave.
 Arruntius. Come, porpoise; where's Haterius?
His gout keeps him most miserably constant!
Your dancing shows a tempest.
 Sejanus. Read no more.
 Regulus. Lords of the senate, hold your seats: read on.
 Sejanus. These letters they are forged.
 Regulus. A guard! sit still.

Enter LACO, *with the* Guards.

Arruntius. Here's change!

Regulus. Bid silence, and read forward.

Præcones. Silence—"and himself suspended from all exercise of place or power, but till due and mature trial be made of his innocency, which yet we can faintly apprehend the necessity to doubt. If, conscript fathers, to your more searching wisdoms, there shall appear farther cause—or of farther proceeding, either to seizure of lands, goods, or more —it is not our power that shall limit your authority, or our favour that must corrupt your justice: either were dishonourable in you, and both uncharitable to ourself. We would willingly be present with your counsels in this business; but the danger of so potent a faction, if it should prove so, forbids our attempting it: except one of the consuls would be entreated for our safety, to undertake the guard of us home; then we should most readily adventure. In the mean time, it shall not be fit for us to importune so judicious a senate, who know how much they hurt the innocent, that spare the guilty; and how grateful a sacrifice to the gods is the life of an ingrateful person. We reflect not in this on Sejanus (notwithstanding, if you keep an eye upon him— and there is Latiaris, a senator, and Pinnarius Natta, two of his most trusted ministers; and so professed, whom we desire not to have apprehended), but as the necessity of the cause exacts it."

Regulus. A guard on Latiaris!

Arruntius. O, the spy,
The reverend spy is caught! who pities him!
Reward, sir, for your service: now, you have done
Your property, you see what use is made!

　　　　　　　　　　[*Exeunt* LATIARIS *and* NATTA *guarded.*
Hang up the instrument.

Sejanus. Give leave.

Laco. Stand, stand!
He comes upon his death, that doth advance
An inch toward my point.

Sejanus. Have we no friends here?

Arruntius. Hushed!

Where now are all the hails and acclamations?

Enter Macro.

Macro. Hail to the consuls, and this noble senate!
Sejanus. Is Macro here? O, thou art lost, Sejanus!   [*Aside.*
Macro. Sit still, and unaffrighted, reverend fathers;
Macro, by Cæsar's grace, the new-made provost,
And now possest of the prætorian bands,
An honour late belonged to that proud man,
Bids you be safe: and to your constant doom
Of his deservings, offers you the surety
Of all the soldiers, tribunes, and centurions,
Received in our command.
    Regulus. Sejanus, Sejanus,
Stand forth, Sejanus!
    Sejanus. Am I called!
    Macro. Ay, thou,
Thou insolent monster, art bid stand.
    Sejanus. Why, Macro,
It hath been otherwise between you and I;
This court, that knows us both, hath seen a difference,
And can, if it be pleased to speak, confirm
Whose insolence is most.
    Macro. Come down, Typhœus.
If mine be most, lo! thus I make it more;
Kick up thy heels in air, tear off thy robe,
Play with thy beard and nostrils. Thus 'tis fit
(And no man take compassion of thy state)
To use th' ingrateful viper, tread his brains
Into the earth.
    Regulus. Forbear.
    Macro. If I could lose
All my humanity now, 'twere well to torture
So meriting a traitor.—Wherefore, fathers,
Sit you amazed and silent; and not censure
This wretch, who, in the hour he first rebelled
'Gainst Cæsar's bounty, did condemn himself?
Phlegra, the field where all the sons of earth
Mustered against the gods, did ne'er acknowledge
So proud and huge a monster.

Regulus. Take him hence;

And all the gods guard Cæsar!

    Trio. Take him hence.

    Haterius. Hence.

    Cotta. To the dungeon with him.

    Sanquinius. He deserves it.

    Senator. Crown all our doors with bays.

    Sanquinius. And let an ox,

With gilded horns and garlands, straight be led

Unto the Capitol.

    Haterius. And sacrificed

To Jove, for Cæsar's safety.

    Trio. All our gods

Be present still to Cæsar!

    Cotta. Phœbus.

    Sanquinius. Mars.

    Haterius. Diana.

    Sanquinius. Pallas.

    Senator. Juno, Mercury.

All guard him!

    Macro. Forth, thou prodigy of men.

                       [Exit SEJANUS, *guarded.*

    Cotta. Let all the traitor's titles be defaced.

    Trio. His images and statues be pulled down.

    Haterius. His chariot-wheels be broken.

    Arruntius. And the legs

Of the poor horses, that deserved nought,

Let them be broken too!

    [Exeunt Lictors, Præcones, MACRO, REGULUS, TRIO,

    HATERIUS, *and* SANQUINIUS: *manent* LEPIDUS, ARRUNTIUS,

    and a few Senators.

    Lepidus. O violent change,

And whirl of men's affections!

    Arruntius. Like, as both

Their bulks and souls were bound on Fortune's wheel,

And must act only with her motion.

    Lepidus. Who would depend upon the popular air,

Or voice of men, that have to-day beheld

That which, if all the gods had fore-declared,

Would not have been believed, Se¡anus' fall?

He that this morn rose proudly as the sun,
And, breaking through a mist of clients' breath,
Came on, as gazed at and admired as he,
When superstitious Moors salute his light!
That had our servile nobles waiting him
As common grooms; and hanging on his look
No less than human life on destiny!
That had men's knees as frequent as the gods;
And sacrifices more than Rome had altars:
And this man fall! fall? ay, without a look
That durst appear his friend, or lend so much
Of vain relief, to his changed state, as pity!

   Arruntius. They that before, like gnats, played in his
     beams,
And thronged to circumscribe him, now not seen,
Nor deign to hold a common seat with him!
Others, that waited him unto the senate,
Now inhumanely ravish him to prison,
Whom but this morn they followed as their lord!
Guard through the streets, bound like a fugitive,
Instead of wreaths give fetters, strokes for stoops:
Blind shames for honours, and black taunts for titles!
Who would trust slippery chance?

   Lepidus. They that would make
Themselves her spoil; and foolishly forget,
When she doth flatter, that she comes to prey.
Fortune, thou hadst no deity, if men
Had wisdom: we have placed thee so high,
By fond belief in thy felicity.

   [*Shout within.*] The gods guard Cæsar! All the gods
     guard Cæsar!

    Re-enter MACRO, REGULUS, *and divers* Senators.

   Macro. Now, great Sejanus, you that awed the state,
And sought to bring the nobles to your whip;
That would be Cæsar's tutor, and dispose
Of dignities and offices! that had
The public head still bare to your designs,
And made the general voice to echo yours!
That looked for salutations twelve score off,

And would have pyramids, yea, temples, reared
To your huge greatness; now you lie as flat
As was your pride advanced!

 Regulus. Thanks to the gods!

 Senator. And praise to Macro, that hath saved Rome!
Liberty, liberty, liberty! Lead on,
And praise to Macro, that hath saved Rome!

       [*Exeunt all but* ARRUNTIUS and LEPIDUS.

 Arruntius. I prophesy, out of the senate's flattery,
That this new fellow, Macro, will become
A greater prodigy in Rome than he
That now is fallen.

Enter TERENTIUS.

 Terentius. O you, whose minds are good,
And have not forced all mankind from your breasts;
That yet have so much stock of virtue left,
To pity guilty states, when they are wretched:
Lend your soft ears to hear, and eyes to weep,
Deeds done by men, beyond the acts of furies.
The eager multitude (who never yet
Knew why to love or hate, but only pleased
T' express their rage of power) no sooner heard
The murmur of Sejanus in decline,
But with that speed and heat of appetite,
With which they greedily devour the way
To some great sports, or a new theatre,
They filled the Capitol, and Pompey's Cirque
Where, like so many mastiffs, biting stones,
As if his statues now were sensitive
Of their wild fury; first, they tear them down;
Then fastening ropes, drag them along the streets,
Crying in scorn, This, this was that rich head
Was crowned with garlands, and with odours, this
That was in Rome so reverenced! Now
The furnace and the bellows shall to work,
The great Sejanus crack, and piece by piece
Drop in the founder's pit.

 Lepidus. O popular rage!

　　Terentius. The whilst the senate at the temple of Con-
　　　cord
Make haste to meet again, and thronging cry,
Let us condemn him, tread him down in water,
While he doth lie upon the bank; away!
While some more tardy, cry unto their bearers,
He will be censured ere we come; run, knaves,
And use that furious diligence, for fear
Their bondmen should inform against their slackness,
And bring their quaking flesh unto the hook:
The rout they follow with confused voice,
Crying they're glad, say they could ne'er abide him;
Inquire what man he was, what kind of face,
What beard he had, what nose, what lips? Protest
They ever did presage he'd come to this;
They never thought him wise, nor valiant; ask
After his garments, when he dies, what death;
And not a beast of all the herd demands
What was his crime, or who were his accusers,
Under what proof or testimony he fell?
There came, says one, a huge long-worded letter
From Capreæ against him. Did there so?
O, they are satisfied; no more.
　　Lepidus. Alas!
They follow Fortune, and hate men condemned,
Guilty or not.
　　Arruntius. But had Sejanus thrived
In his design, and prosperously opprest
The old Tiberius; then, in that same minute,
These very rascals, that now rage like furies,
Would have proclaimed Sejanus emperor.
　　Lepidus. But what hath followed?
　　Terentius. Sentence by the senate,
To lose his head; which was no sooner off,
But that and the unfortunate trunk were seized
By the rude multitude; who not content
With what the forward justice of the state
Officiously had done, with violent rage
Have rent it limb from limb. A thousand heads,

A thousand hands, ten thousand tongues and voices,
Employed at once in several acts of malice!
Old men not staid with age, virgins with shame,
Late wives with loss of husbands, mothers of children,
Losing all grief in joy of his sad fall,
Run quite transported with their cruelty!
These mounting at his head, these at his face,
These digging out his eyes, those with his brains
Sprinkling themselves, their houses and their friends;
Others are met, have ravished thence an arm,
And deal small pieces of the flesh for favours;
These with a thigh, this hath cut off his hands,
And this his feet; these fingers, and these toes;
That hath his liver, he his heart: there wants
Nothing but room for wrath, and place for hatred!
What cannot oft be done, is now o'erdone.
The whole, and all of what was great Sejanus,
And, next to Cæsar, did possess the world,
Now torn and scattered, as he needs no grave
Each little dust covers a little part:
So lies he nowhere, and yet often buried!

Enter NUNTIUS.

  Arruntius. More of Sejanus?
  Nuntius. Yes.
  Lepidus. What can be added?
We know him dead.
  Nuntius. Then there begin your pity.
There is enough behind to melt ev'n Rome,
And Cæsar into tears; since never slave
Could yet so highly offend, but tyranny,
In tormenting him, would make worth lamenting.
A son and daughter to the dead Sejanus,
(Of whom there is not now so much remaining
As would give fastening to the hangman's hook,)
Have they drawn forth for further sacrifice;
Whose tenderness of knowledge, unripe years,
And childish silly innocence was such,
As scarce would lend them feeling of their danger:
The girl so simple, as she often asked

"Where they would lead her? for what cause they dragged
    her?"
Cried, "She would do no more:" that she could take
"Warning with beating." And because our laws
Admit no virgin immature to die,
The wittily and strangely cruel Macro,
Delivered her to be deflowered and spoiled,
By the rude lust of the licentious hangman,
Then to be strangled with her harmless brother.
    Lepidus. O, act most worthy hell, and lasting night,
To hide it from the world!
    Nuntius. Their bodies thrown
Into the Gemonies (I know not how,
Or by what accident returned), the mother,
The expulsed Apicata, finds them there;
Whom when she saw lie spread on the degrees,
After a world of fury on herself,
Tearing her hair, defacing of her face,
Beating her breasts and womb, kneeling amazed,
Crying to heaven, then to them; at last,
Her drowned voice gat up above her woes,
And with such black and bitter execrations
As might affright the gods, and force the sun
Run backward to the east; nay, make the old
Deformed chaos rise again, to o'erwhelm
Them, us, and all the world, she fills the air,
Upbraids the heavens with their partial dooms,
Defies their tyrannous powers, and demands,
What she, and those poor innocents have transgressed,
That they must suffer such a share in vengeance,
Whilst Livia, Lygdus, and Eudemus live,
Who, as she says, and firmly vows to prove it
To Cæsar and the senate, poisoned Drusus?
    Lepidus. Confederates with her husband!
    Nuntius. Ay.
    Lepidus. Strange act!
    Arruntius. And strangely opened: what says now my
    monster,
The multitude? they reel now, do they not?
    Nuntius. Their gall is gone, and now they 'gin to weep

The mischief they have done.

Arruntius. I thank 'em, rogues.

Nuntius. Part are so stupid, or so flexible,
As they believe him innocent; all grieve:
And some, whose hands yet reek with his warm blood,
And grip the part which they did tear of him,
Wish him collected and created new.

Lepidus. How Fortune piles her sports, when she begins
To practise them! pursues, continues, adds,
Confounds with varying her impassioned moods!

Arruntius. Dost thou hope, Fortune, to redeem thy crimes,
To make amend for thy ill placed favours,
With these strange punishments! Forbear, you things
That stand upon the pinnacles of state,
To boast your slippery height; when you do fall,
You pash yourselves in pieces, ne'er to rise;
And he that lends you pity, is not wise.

Terentius. Let this example move the insolent man,
Not to grow proud and careless of the gods.
It is an odious wisdom to blaspheme,
Much more to slighten, or deny their powers:
For whom the morning saw so great and high,
Thus low and little, 'fore the even doth lie.   [*Exeunt.*

BARTHOLOMEW FAIR

This comedy was produced at the Hope Theatre (on the Bank-side), October 31, 1614, and acted, as Jonson tells us, by the Lady Elizabeth's servants. The Lady Elizabeth was the daughter of James I; she married the Elector Palatine, and saw many evil days both as a wife and mother: her descendants have been more fortunate, and are now on the throne of Great Britain.

The *Biographia Dramatica* speaks of an edition of this play in quarto, 1614. I know of no earlier one than the folio, 1631–1641, nor do I believe that it ever appeared in that form. In the title-page, it is said that it was dedicated in the year 1614 to King James; but by this expression no more is meant than that it was addressed to him in an occasional prologue, written for the purpose; though this probably led to the mistake just noticed. When this play was printed James was dead.

Bartholomew Fair was always a favourite with the people: this is easily accounted for from the ridicule with which it covers the Puritans. It was revived, as might naturally be expected, immediately after the Restoration, and was frequently honoured with a royal command by Charles, whom tradition represents as greatly delighted with the character of Cokes, which was, indeed, excellently played by Wintersel and afterwards by Nokes, the most celebrated comic performer of those days. To this comedy, Collin, the rustic champion of Puritanism, is taken, on his visit to London, and D'Urfey gives a humorous account of his zeal and fury at the scenical disgrace of Rabbi Busy. D'Urfey pays an incidental compliment to this piece, by representing Collin as completely deceived at first, and believing that what he saw and heard of the Puritans was a scene of real life.

I am sorry to observe that the excellent folio of 1616 deserts us here. Why this drama was not admitted into it, cannot now be told, unless, as I believe was really the case, that much of that volume was carried through the press some time before it was given to the public. Be this as it may, the subsequent plays do not exhibit, to my eye, the same marks of Jonson's care as those already given: nor do I think that he concerned himself with the revision of the

folio now before us, or, indeed, ever saw it, though many
of the pieces contained in it are dated several years antece‧
dent to his death.

To this comedy was prefixed the following apt motto:

> *Si foret in terris, rideret Democritus: nam*
> *Spectaret populum ludis attentius ipsis*
> *Ut sibi præbentem mimo spectacula plura.*
> *Scriptores autem narrare putaret asello*
> **Fabellam** *surdo.*
>
> —HOR. lib. ii. epist. I.

PROLOGUE

To the King's Majesty

Your Majesty is welcome to a Fair;
Such place, such men, such language, and such ware
You must expect: with these, the zealous noise
Of your land's faction, scandalized at toys,
As babies, hobby-horses, puppet-plays,
And such-like rage, whereof the petulant ways
Yourself have known, and have been vext with long.
These for your sport, without particular wrong,
Or just complaint of any private man,
Who of himself, or shall think well, or can,
The maker doth present: and hopes to-night
To give you for a fairing true delight.

DRAMATIS PERSONÆ

JOHN LITTLEWIT, a Proctor.
ZEAL-OF-THE-LAND BUSY, suitor to Dame Purecraft, a Banbury man.[1]
WINWIFE, his rival, a Gentleman.
TOM QUARLOUS, companion to Winwife, a Gamester.
BARTHOLOMEW COKES, an Esquire of Harrow.
HUMPHREY WASPE, his man.
ADAM OVERDO, a Justice of Peace.
LANTHORN LEATHERHEAD, a Hobby-horse Seller (toyman).
EZEKIEL EDGWORTH, a Cutpurse.
NIGHTINGALE, a Ballad-singer.
MOONCALF, Tapster to Ursula.
DAN JORDAN KNOCKEM, a horse-courser and a ranger of Turnbull.
VAL. CUTTING, a Roarer, or bully.
CAPTAIN WHIT, a Bawd.
TROUBLE-ALL, a Madman.
BRISTLE }
HAGGISE } Watchmen.
POCHER, a Beadle.
FILCHER }
SHARKWELL } Door-keepers to the puppet-show.
SOLOMON, Littlewit's man.
NORTHERN, a Clothier (a Northern man).
PUPPY, a Wrestler (a Western man).
WIN-THE-FIGHT LITTLEWIT.

DAME PURECRAFT, her Mother, and a Widow.
DAME OVERDO.
GRACE WELLBORN, Ward to Justice Overdo.
JOAN TRASH, a Gingerbread-woman.
URSULA, a Pig-woman.
ALICE, mistress o' the game.

Costardmonger, Mousetrap-man, Corncutter, Watch, Porters, Puppets, Passengers, Mob, Boys, &c.

[1] *I.e.,* a Puritan.

BARTHOLOMEW FAIR

THE INDUCTION

The Stage

Enter the STAGE-KEEPER.

STAGE-KEEPER. Gentlemen, have a little patience, they are e'en upon coming instantly. He that should begin the play, Master Littlewit, the proctor, has a stitch new fallen in his black silk stocking; 'twill be drawn up ere you can tell twenty: he plays one o' the Arches that dwells about the hospital, and he has a very pretty part. But for the whole play, will you have the truth on't?—I am looking, lest the poet hear me, or his man, Master Brome,[1] behind the arras —it is like to be a very conceited scurvy one, in plain English. When 't comes to the Fair once, you were e'en as good to Virginia, for anything there is of Smithfield. He has not hit the humours, he does not know them; he has not conversed with the Bartholomew birds, as they say; he has ne'er a sword and buckler-man in his Fair; nor a little Davy, to take toll o' the bawds there, as in my time; nor a Kindheart, if anybody's teeth should chance to ache, in his play; nor a juggler with a well-educated ape, to come over the chain for a King of England, and back again for the Prince, and sit still on his arse for the Pope and the King of Spain. None of these fine sights! Nor has he the canvas cut in the night, for a hobby-horse-man to creep into his she neighbour, and take his leap there. Nothing! No: an some writer that I know had had but the penning o' this matter, he would have made you such a jig-a-jog in the booths, you should have thought an earthquake had been in the Fair! But these master-poets, they will have their own absurd courses; they will be informed of nothing. He has (sir reverence) kicked me three or four times about the tiring-house, I thank him, for but offering to put in with my experience. I'll be judged by you, gen-

---

[1] The author's amanuensis.

tlemen, now, but for one conceit of mine: would not a fine
pump upon the stage have done well for a property now?
and a punk set under upon her head, with her stern upward, and have been soused by my witty young masters o'
the Inns of Court? What think you of this for a show, now?
he will not hear o' this! I am an ass! I! and yet I kept the
stage in Master Tarleton's time,[1] I thank my stars. Ho! an
that man had lived to have played in *Bartholomew Fair,*
you should have seen him have come in, and have been
cozened in the cloth-quarter, so finely! and Adams, the
rogue, have leaped and capered upon him, and have dealt
his vermin about, as though they had cost him nothing!
and then a substantial watch to have stolen in upon them,
and taken them away, with mistaking words, as the fashion
is in the stage-practice.

Enter the BOOKHOLDER[2] *with a* SCRIVENER.

Bookholder. How now! what rare discourse are you fallen
upon, ha? have you found any familiars here, that you are
so free? what's the business?

Stage-keeper. Nothing, but the understanding gentlemen
o' the ground [3] here asked my judgment.

Bookholder. Your judgment, rascal! for what? sweeping
the stage, or gathering up the broken apples for the bears
within? Away, rogue, it's come to a fine degree in these
spectacles, when such a youth as you pretend to a judgment.
[*Exit* STAGE-KEEPER.] And yet he may, in the most of this
matter, i' faith: for the author has writ it just to his
meridian, and the scale of the grounded judgments here,
his play-fellows in wit.—Gentlemen [*comes forward*], not
for want of a prologue, but by way of a new one, I am sent
out to you here, with a scrivener, and certain articles
drawn out in haste between our author and you; which if
you please to hear, and as they appear reasonable, to approve of; the play will follow presently—Read, scribe;
give me the counterpane.

Scrivener. "Articles of agreement, indented, between

[1] A celebrated comedian in the reign of Queen Elizabeth.
[2] I.e., the prompter.
[3] I.e., the pit.

the spectators or hearers, at the Hope on the Bankside in the county of Surrey, on the one party; and the author of *Bartholomew Fair,* in the said place and county, on the other party: the one and thirtieth day of October, 1614, and in the twelfth year of the reign of our sovereign lord, JAMES, by the grace of God, King of England, France, and Ireland, defender of the faith; and of Scotland the seven and fortieth.

"*Imprimis.* It is covenanted and agreed, by and between the parties aforesaid, and the said spectators and bearers, as well the curious and envious, as the favouring and judicious, as also the grounded judgments and understandings, do for themselves severally covenant and agree to remain in the places their money or friends have put them in, with patience, for the space of two hours and a half, and somewhat more. In which time the author promiseth to present them by us, with a new sufficient play, called *Bartholomew Fair,* merry, and as full of noise as sport: made to delight all, and to offend none; provided they have either the wit or the honesty to think well of themselves.

"It is further agreed, that every person here have his or their free-will of censure, to like or dislike at their own charge, the author having now departed with his right: it shall be lawful for any man to judge his sixpen'worth, his twelve pen'worth, so to his eighteen-pence, two shillings, half a crown, to the value of his place; provided always his place get not about his wit. And if he pay for half a dozen, he may censure for all them too, so that he will undertake that they shall be silent. He shall put in for censures here, as they do for lots at the lottery; marry, if he drop but sixpence at the door, and will censure a crown's-worth, it is thought there is no conscience or justice in that.

"It is also agreed, that every man here exercise his own judgment, and not censure by contagion, or upon trust, from another's voice or face, that sits by him, be he never so first in the commission of wit; as also, that he be fixed and settled in his censure, that what he approves or not approves to-day, he will do the same to-morrow; and if

to-morrow, the next day, and so the next week, if need
be; and not to be brought about by any that sits on the
bench with him, though they indite and arraign plays daily.
He that will swear *Jeronimo* or *Andronicus* are the best
plays yet, shall pass unexcepted at here, as a man whose
judgment shows it is constant, and hath stood still these
five and twenty or thirty years. Though it be an ignorance
it is a virtuous and staid ignorance; and next to truth, a
confirmed error does well; such a one the author knows
where to find him.

"It is further covenanted, concluded, and agreed, that
how great soever the expectation be, no person here is to
expect more than he knows, or better ware than a fair will
afford: neither to look back to the sword and buckler age
of Smithfield, but content himself with the present. Instead
of a little Davy, to take toll o' the bawds, the author doth
promise a strutting horse-courser, with a leer drunkard, two
or three to attend him, in as good equipage as you would
wish. And then for Kindheart, the tooth-drawer, a fine
oily pig-woman, with her tapster, to bid you welcome, and
a consort of roarers for music. A wise justice of peace
meditant, instead of a juggler with an ape. A civil cutpurse
searchant. A sweet singer of new ballads allurant: and as
fresh an hypocrite as ever was broached, rampant. If there
be never a servant monster in the fair, who can help it,
he says, nor a nest of antiques? he is loth to make nature
afraid in his plays, like those that beget tales, tempests,
and such like drolleries, to mix his head with other men's
heels; let the concupiscence of jigs and dances reign as
strong as it will amongst you; yet if the puppets will please
anybody they shall be intreated to come in.

"In consideration of which, it is finally agreed, by the
aforesaid hearers and spectators, That they neither in
themselves conceal, nor suffer by them to be concealed,
any state-decypherer, or politic picklock of the scene, so
solemnly ridiculous as to search out who was meant by the
gingerbread-woman, who by the hobby-horse man, who by
the costardmonger, nay, who by their wares. Or that will
pretend to affirm on his own inspired ignorance, what

Mirror of Magistrates[1] is meant by the justice, what great
lady by the pig-woman, what concealed statesman by the
seller of mouse-traps, and so of the rest. But that such
person, or persons, so found, be left discovered to the
mercy of the author, as a forfeiture to the stage, and your
laughter aforesaid. As also such as shall so desperately, or
ambitiously play the fool by his place aforesaid, to challenge the author of scurrility, because the language somewhere savours of Smithfield, the booth, and the pigbroth,
or of profaneness, because a madman cries, *God quit you,*
or *bless you!* In witness whereof, as you have preposterously
put to your seals already, which is your money, you will
now add the other part of suffrage, your hands. The play
shall presently begin. And though the Fair be not kept in
the same region that some here perhaps would have it, yet
think that therein the author hath observed a special
decorum, the place being as dirty as Smithfield, and as
stinking every whit.

"Howsoever, he prays you to believe his ware is still
the same, else you will make him justly suspect that he
that is so loth to look on a baby or an hobby-horse here,
would be glad to take up a commodity of them, at any
laughter or loss, in another place."   [*Exeunt.*

ACT THE FIRST

SCENE I—*A room in* LITTLEWIT'S

LITTLEWIT. A pretty conceit, and worth the finding! I have
such luck to spin out these fine things still, and like a silk-
worm, out of myself. Here's Master Bartholomew Cokes,
of Harrow o' the Hill, in the county of Middlesex, esquire,
takes forth his licence to marry Mistress Grace Wellborn,
of the said place and county: and when does he take it
forth? to-day! the four and twentieth of August! Bartholo-
mew-day! Bartholomew upon Bartholomew! there's the de-

[1] Alluding to the collection or series of poems so named, describing the
fall of the *Unfortunate Great.*

vice! who would have marked such a leap-frog chance now?
A very . . . less than amesace, on two dice! Well, go thy
ways, John Littlewit, proctor John Littlewit: one of the
pretty wits of Paul's, the Littlewit of London, so thou art
called, and something beside. When a quirk or a quiblin
does scape thee, and thou dost not watch and apprehend it,
and bring it afore the constable of conceit, (there now, I
speak quib too), let them carry thee out o' the archdeacon's
court into his kitchen, and make a Jack of thee, instead of
a John. There I am again la!—

Enter MRS. LITTLEWIT.

Win, good morrow, Win; ay marry, Win, now you look
finely indeed, Win! this cap does convince! You'd not have
worn it, Win, nor have had it velvet, but a rough country
beaver, with a copper band, like the coney-skin woman of
Budge-row: sweet Win, let me kiss it! And her fine high
shoes, like the Spanish lady! Good Win, go a little, I would
fain see thee pace, pretty Win; by this fine cap, I could
never leave kissing on't.

Mrs. Littlewit. Come indeed la, you are such a fool still!

Littlewit. No, but half a one, Win, you are the t'other
half: man and wife make one fool, Win. Good! Is there
the proctor, or doctor indeed, in the diocese, that ever had
the fortune to win him such a Win! There I am again!
I do feel conceits coming upon me, more than I am able
to turn tongue to. A pox o' these pretenders to wit! your
Three Cranes, Mitre, and Mermaid-men! not a corn of
true salt, not a grain of right mustard amongst them all.
They may stand for places, or so, again the next wit-fall,
and pay two-pence in a quart more for their canary than
other men. But give me the man can start up a justice of
wit out of six shillings beer, and give the law to all the
poets and poet-suckers in town:—because they are the
players' gossips! 'Slid, other men have wives as fine as the
players, and as well drest. Come hither, Win.   [*Kisses her.*

Enter WINWIFE.

Winwife. Why, how now, Master Littlewit! measuring of
lips, or moulding of kisses? which is it?

Littlewit. Troth, I am a little taken with my Win's dressing here: does it not fine, Master Winwife? How do you apprehend, sir? she would not have worn this habit. I challenge all Cheapside to show such another: Moon-fields, Pimlico-path, or the Exchange, in a summer evening, with a lace to boot, as this has. Dear Win, let Master Winwife kiss you. He comes a-wooing to our mother, Win, and may be our father perhaps, Win. There's no harm in him, Win.

Winwife. None in the earth, Master Littlewit.

[*Kisses her.*

Littlewit. I envy no man my delicates, sir.

Winwife. Alas, you have the garden where they grow still! A wife here with a strawberry breath, cherry-lips, apricot cheeks, and a soft velvet head, like a melicotton.

Littlewit. Good, i' faith! now dulness upon me, that I had not that before him, that I should not light on't as well as he! velvet head!

Winwife. But my taste, Master Littlewit, tends to fruit of a later kind; the sober matron, your wife's mother.

Littlewit. Ay, we know you are a suitor, sir; Win and I both wish you well. By this licence here, would you had her, that your two names were as fast in it as here are a couple! Win would fain have a fine young father i' law, with a feather; that her mother might hood it and chain it with Mistress Overdo. But you do not take the right course, Master Winwife.

Winwife. No, Master Littlewit, why?

Littlewit. You are not mad enough.

Winwife. How! is madness a right course?

Littlewit. I say nothing, but I wink upon Win. You have a friend, one Master Quarlous, comes here sometimes.

Winwife. Why, he makes no love to her, does he?

Littlewit. Not a tokenworth that ever I saw, I assure you: but——

Winwife. What?

Littlewit. He is the more madcap of the two. You do not apprehend me.

Mrs. Littlewit. You have a hot coal in your mouth now, you cannot hold.

Littlewit. Let me out with it, dear Win.

Mrs. Littlewit. I'll tell him myself.

Littlewit. Do, and take all the thanks, and much good do thy pretty heart, Win.

Mrs. Littlewit. Sir, my mother has had her nativity-water cast lately by the cunning-men in Cow-lane, and they have told her her fortune, and do ensure her, she shall never have happy hour, unless she marry within this sen'night; and when it is, it must be a madman, they say.

Littlewit. Ay, but it must be a gentleman madman.

Mrs. Littlewit. Yes, so the t'other man of Moor-fields says.

Winwife. But does she believe them?

Littlewit. Yes, and has been at Bedlam twice since every day, to inquire if any gentleman be there, or to come there mad.

Winwife. Why, this is a confederacy, a mere piece of practice upon her by these impostors.

Littlewit. I tell her so; or else, say I, that they mean some young madcap gentleman; for the devil can equivocate as well as a shopkeeper: and therefore would I advise you to be a little madder than Master Quarlous hereafter.

Winwife. Where is she, stirring yet?

Littlewit. Stirring! yes, and studying an old elder come from Banbury, a suitor that puts in here at meal tide, to praise the painful brethren, or pray that the sweet singers may be restored; says a grace as long as his breath lasts him! Sometime the spirit is so strong with him, it gets quite out of him, and then my mother, or Win, are fain to fetch it again with malmsey or aqua cœlestis.

Mrs. Littlewit. Yes, indeed, we have such a tedious life with him for his diet, and his clothes too! he breaks his buttons, and cracks seams at every saying he sobs out.

Littlewit. He cannot abide my vocation, he says.

Mrs. Littlewit. No; he told my mother, a proctor was a claw of the beast, and that she had little less than committed abomination in marrying me so as she has done.

Littlewit. Every line, he says, that a proctor writes, when it comes to be read in the bishop's court, is a long black hair, kembed out of the tail of Antichrist.

Winwife. When came this proselyte?

Littlewit. Some three days since.

Enter QUARLOUS.

Quarlous. O, sir, have you ta'en soil here? It's well a
man may reach you after three hours running yet! What
an unmerciful companion art thou, to quit thy lodging
at such ungentlemanly hours! none but a scattered covey
of fiddlers, or one of these rag-rakers in dunghills, or some
marrow-bone man at most, would have been up when thou
wert gone abroad, by all description. I pray thee what
ailest thou, thou canst not sleep? hast thou thorns in thy
eyelids, or thistles in thy bed?

Winwife. I cannot tell: it seems you had neither in your
feet, that took this pain to find me.

Quarlous. No, an I had, all the lime hounds o' the city
should have drawn after you by the scent rather.—Master
John Littlewit! God save you, sir. 'Twas a hot night with
some of us, last night, John: shall we pluck a hair of the
same wolf to-day,[1] Proctor John?

Littlewit. Do you remember, Master Quarlous, what we
discoursed on last night?

Quarlous. Not I, John, nothing that I either discourse
or do; at those times I forfeit all to forgetfulness.

Littlewit. No! not concerning Win? look you, there she
is, and drest, as I told you she should be: hark you, sir,
[*whispers him*] had you forgot?

Quarlous. By this head I'll beware how I keep you
company, John, when I drink, an you have this dangerous
memory: that's certain.

Littlewit. Why, sir?

Quarlous. Why! we were all a little stained last night,
sprinkled with a cup or two, and I agreed with Proctor
John here, to come and do somewhat with Win (I know
not what 'twas) to-day; and he puts me in mind on't now;
he says he was coming to fetch me. Before truth, if you
have that fearful quality, John, to remember when you
are sober, John, what you promise drunk, John; I shall

---

[1] A proverbial phrase for getting intoxicated again with the same liquor.

take heed of you, John. For this once I am content to
wink at you. Where's your wift? come hither, Win.

[Kisses her.

Mrs. Littlewit. Why, John! do you see this, John? look
you! help me, John.

Littlewit. O Win, fie, what do you mean, Win? be wom-
anly, Win; make an outcry to your mother, Win! Master
Quarlous is an honest gentleman, and our worshipful good
friend, Win; and he is Master Winwife's friend too; and
Master Winwife comes a suitor to your mother, Win; as
I told you before, Win, and may perhaps be our father,
Win: they'll do you no harm, Win; they are both our
worshipful good friends. Master Quarlous! you must know
Master Quarlous, Win; you must not quarrel with Master
Quarlous, Win.

Quarlous. No, we'll kiss again, and fall in.

[Kisses her again.

Littlewit. Yes, do, good Win.

Mrs. Littlewit. In faith, you are a fool, John.

Littlewit. A fool-John, she calls me; do you mark that,
gentlemen? pretty Littlewit of velvet! a fool-John.

Quarlous [*aside*]. She may call you an apple-John,[1] if you
use this.   [*Kisses her again.*

Winwife. Pray thee forbear, for my respect, somewhat.

Quarlous. Hoy-day! how respective you are become o'
the sudden! I fear this family will turn you reformed too;
pray you come about again. Because she is in possibility to
be your daughter-in-law, and may ask you blessing hereafter, when she courts it to Totenham to eat cream! Well,
I will forbear, sir; but, i' faith, would thou wouldst leave
thy exercise of widow-hunting once; this drawing after an
old reverend smock by the splay-foot! There cannot be an
ancient tripe or trillibub in the town, but thou art straight
nosing it, and 'tis a fine occupation thou'lt confine thyself
to when thou hast got one; scrubbing a piece of buff, as
if thou hadst the perpetuity of Pannier-alley to stink in;
or perhaps worse, currying a carcass that thou hast bound
thyself to alive. I'll be sworn, some of them that thou art,
or hast been a suitor to, are so old as no chaste or married

[1] A punning allusion to *apple-squire: i.e.,* pimp or procurer.

pleasure can ever become them; the honest instrument of
procreation has forty years since left to belong to them;
thou must visit them as thou wouldst do a tomb, with a
torch or three handfuls of link, flaming hot, and so thou
mayst hap to make them feel thee, and after come to inherit
according to thy inches. A sweet course for a man to waste
the brand of life for, to be still raking himself a fortune
in the old woman's embers! We shall have thee, after thou
hast been but a month married to one of them, look like
the quartan ague and the black jaundice met in a face,
and walk as if thou hadst borrowed legs of a spinner and
voice of a cricket. I would endure to hear fifteen sermons
a week for her, and such coarse and loud ones as some of
them must be! I would e'en desire of fate, I might dwell
in a drum and take in my sustenance with an old broken
tobacco-pipe and a straw. Dost thou ever think to bring
thine ears or stomach to the patience of a dry grace as
long as thy table-cloth; and droned out by thy son here
(that might be thy father) till all the meat on thy board
has forgot it was that day in the kitchen? or to brook the
noise made in a question of predestination by the good
labourers and painful eaters assembled together, put to
them by the matron your spouse; who moderates with a
cup of wine ever and anon, and a sentence out of Knox
between? Or the perpetual spitting before and after a
sober-drawn exhortation of six hours, whose better part
was the hum-ha-hum? or to hear prayers groaned out over
thy iron chests, as if they were charms to break them?
And all this for the hope of two apostle-spoons, to suffer!
and a cup to eat a caudle in! for that will be thy legacy.
She'll have conveyed her state safe enough from thee, an
she be a right widow.

Winwife. Alas, I am quite off that scent now.

Quarlous. How so?

Winwife. Put off by a brother of Banbury, one that, they
say, is come here, and governs all already.

Quarlous. What do you call him? I knew divers of those
Banburians when I was in Oxford.

Winwife. Master Littlewit can tell us.

Littlewit. Sir!—Good Win, go in, and if Master Bartholomew Cokes his man come for the licence (the little old
fellow), let him speak with me. [*Exit* Mrs. LITTLEWIT.]
What say you, gentlemen?

Winwife. What call you the reverend elder you told
me of, your Banbury man?

Littlewit. Rabbi Busy, sir; he is more than an elder, he
is a prophet, sir.

Quarlous. O, I know him! a baker, is he not?

Littlewit. He was a baker, sir, but he does dream now
and see visions; he has given over his trade.

Quarlous. I remember that too; out of a scruple he took
that, in spiced conscience, those cakes he made, were served
to bridales, maypoles, morrices, and such profane feasts and
meetings. His christian name is Zeal-of-the-land.

Littlewit. Yes, sir; Zeal-of-the-land Busy.

Winwife. How! what a name's there!

Littlewit. O, they have all such names, sir; he was witness for Win here,—they will not be called godfathers—
and named her Win-the-fight; you thought her name had
been Winnifred, did you not?

Winwife. I did indeed.

Littlewit. He would have thought himself a stark repro-
bate if it had.

Quarlous. Ay, for there was a blue-starch woman of the
name at the same time. A notable hypocritical vermin it is;
I know him. One that stands upon his face more than
his faith at all times: ever in seditious motion and re-
proving for vainglory; of a most lunatic conscience and
spleen, and affects the violence of singularity in all he does:
he has undone a grocer here in Newgate-market, that broke
with him, trusted him with currants, as arrant a zeal as
he, that's by the way. By his profession he will ever be in
the state of innocence though, and childhood; derides all
antiquity, defies any other learning than inspiration; and
what discretion soever years should afford him, it is all
prevented in his original ignorance: have not to do with
him, for he is a fellow of a most arrogant and invincible
dulness, I assure you.—Who is this?

Re-enter MRS. LITTLEWIT *with* WASPE.

Waspe. By your leave, gentlemen, with all my heart to
you; and God you good morrow! Master Littlewit, my
business is to you: is this licence ready?

Littlewit. Here, I have it for you in my hand, Master
Humphrey.

Waspe. That's well; nay, never open or read it to me,
it's labour in vain, you know. I am no clerk, I scorn to
be saved by my book, i' faith, I'll hang first; fold it up on
your word, and give it me. What must you have for it?

Littlewit. We'll talk of that anon, Master Humphrey.

Waspe. Now, or not at all, good Master Proctor; I am
for no anons, I assure you.

Littlewit. Sweet, Win, bid Solomon send me the little
black box within in my study.

Waspe. Ay, quickly, good mistress, I pray you; for I have
both eggs on the spit, and iron in the fire. [*Exit* MRS.
LITTLEWIT.] Say what you must have, good Master Littlewit.

Littlewit. Why, you know the price, Master Numps.

Waspe. I know! I know nothing, I: when tell you me of
knowing? Now I am in haste, sir, I do not know, and
I will not know, and I scorn to know, and yet, now I
think on't, I will, and do know as well as another; you
must have a mark for your thing here, and eightpence for
the box; I could have saved twopence in that, an I had
bought it myself; but here's fourteen shillings for you.
Good Lord, how long your little wife stays! pray God,
Solomon, your clerk, be not looking in the wrong box,
Master Proctor.

Littlewit. Good i' faith! no, I warrant you, Solomon is
wiser than so, sir.

Waspe. Fie, fie, fie, by your leave, Master Littlewit, this
is scurvy, idle, foolish, and abominable, with all my heart;
I do not like it.   [*Walks aside.*

Winwife. Do you hear! Jack Littlewit, what business
does thy pretty head think this fellow may have, that he
keeps such a coil with?

Quarlous. More than buying of gingerbread in the cloister
here, for that we allow him, or a gilt pouch in the Fair?

Littlewit. Master Quarlous, do not mistake him; he is his master's both-hands, I assure you.

Quarlous. What! to pull on his boots a-mornings, or his stockings, does he?

Littlewit. Sir, if you have a mind to mock him; mock him softly, and look t'other way: for if he apprehend you flout him once, he will fly at you presently. A terrible testy old fellow, and his name is Waspe too.

Quarlous. Pretty insect! make much on him.

Waspe. A plague o' this box, and the pox too, and on him that made it, and her that went for't, and all that should have sought it, sent it, or brought it! do you see, sir.

Littlewit. Nay, good Master Waspe.

Waspe. Good Master Hornet, t— in your teeth, hold you your tongue: do not I know you? your father was a 'pothecary, and sold clysters, more than he gave, I wusse; and t— in your little wife's teeth too—here she comes—

Re-enter MRS. LITTLEWIT *with the box.*

'twill make her spit, as fine as she is, for all her velvet custard on her head, sir.

Littlewit. O, be civil, Master Numps.

Waspe. Why, say I have a humour not to be civil; how then? who shall compel me, you?

Littlewit. Here is the box now.

Waspe. Why, a pox o' your box, once again! let your little wife stale in it, an she will. Sir, I would have you to understand, and these gentlemen too, if they please——

Winwife. With all our hearts, sir.

Waspe. That I have a charge, gentlemen.

Littlewit. They do apprehend, sir.

Waspe. Pardon me, sir, neither they nor you can apprehend me yet. You are an ass. I have a young master, he is now upon his making and marring; the whole care of his well-doing is now mine. His foolish schoolmasters have done nothing but run up and down the country with him to beg puddings and cakebread of his tenants, and almost spoiled him; he has learned nothing but to sing catches and repeat *Rattle bladder, rattle!* and *O, Madge!* I dare not let him walk alone for fear of learning of vile tunes,

which he will sing at supper, and in the sermon-times!
If he meet but a carman in the street, and I find him not
talk to keep him off on him, he will whistle him and all
his tunes over at night in his sleep! He has a head full
of bees! I am fain now, for this little time I am absent,
to leave him in charge with a gentlewoman: 'tis true, she
is a justice of peace his wife, and a gentlewoman of the
hood, and his natural sister; but what may happen under
a woman's government, there's the doubt. Gentlemen, you
do not know him; he is another manner of piece than you
think for: but nineteen years old, and yet he is taller than
either of you by the head, God bless him!

Quarlous. Well, methinks this is a fine fellow.

Winwife. He has made his master a finer by this description, I should think.

Quarlous. 'Faith, much about one, it is cross and pile,
whether for a new farthing.

Waspe. I'll tell you, gentlemen——

Littlewit. Will't please you drink, Master Waspe.

Waspe. Why, I have not talked so long to be dry, sir.
You see no dust or cobwebs come out o' my mouth, do you?
you'd have me gone, would you?

Littlewit. No, but you were in haste e'en now, Master
Numps.

Waspe. What an I were! so I am still, and yet I will
stay too; meddle you with your match, your Win there,
she has as little wit as her husband, it seems: I have others
to talk to.

Littlewit. She's my match indeed, and as *little wit* as I,
good!

Waspe. We have been but a day and a half in town,
gentlemen, 'tis true; and yesterday in the afternoon we
walked London, to show the city to the gentlewoman he
shall marry, Mistress Grace; but afore I will endure such
another half day with him, I'll be drawn with a good gib-
cat through the great pond at home, as his uncle Hodge
was. Why, we could not meet that heathen thing all the
day, but staid him: he would name you all the signs over,
as he went, aloud: and where he spied a parrot or a
monkey, there he was pitched, with all the little long coats

about him, male and female; no getting him away! I thought he would have run mad o' the black boy in Bucklersbury, that takes the scurvy, roguy tobacco there.

Littlewit. You say true, Master Numps; there's such a one indeed.

Waspe. It's no matter whether there be or no, what's that to you?

Quarlous. He will not allow of John's reading at any hand.

Enter COKES, MISTRESS OVERDO, *and* GRACE.

Cokes. O, Numps! are you here, Numps? look where I am, Numps, and Mistress Grace too! Nay, do not look angerly, Numps: my sister is here and all, I do not come without her.

Waspe. What the mischief do you come with her? or she with you?

Cokes. We come all to seek you, Numps.

Waspe. To seek me! why, did you all think I was lost, or run away with your fourteen shillings worth of small ware here? or that I had changed it in the Fair for hobby-horses? 'Sprecious——to seek me!

Mrs. Overdo. Nay, good Master Numps, do you show discretion, though he be exorbitant, as Master Overdo says, and it be but for conservation o' the peace.

Waspe. Marry gip, goody She-justice, Mistress French-hood! t— in your teeth, and t— in your Frenchhood's teeth too, to do you service, do you see! Must you quote your Adam to me! you think you are Madam Regent still, Mistress Overdo, when I am in place; no such matter, I assure you, your reign is out, when I am in, dame.

Mrs. Overdo. I am content to be in abeyance, sir, and be governed by you; so should he too, if he did well; but 'twill be expected you should also govern your passions.

Waspe. Will it so, forsooth! good Lord, how sharp you are, with being at Bedlam yesterday! Whetstone has set an edge upon you, has he?

Mrs. Overdo. Nay, if you know not what belongs to your dignity, I do yet to mine.

Waspe. Very well then.

Cokes. Is this the licence, Numps? for love's sake let me see't; I never saw a licence.

Waspe. Did you not so? why, you shall not see't then.

Cokes. An you love me, good Numps.

Waspe. Sir, I love you, and yet I do not love you in these fooleries: set your heart at rest, there's nothing in it but hard words; and what would you see it for?

Cokes. I would see the length and the breadth on't, that's all; and I will see it now, so I will.

Waspe. You shall not see it here.

Cokes. Then I'll see it at home, and I'll look upon the case here.

Waspe. Why, do so; a man must give way to him a little in trifles, gentlemen. These are errors, diseases of youth; which he will mend when he comes to judgment and knowledge of matters. I pray you conceive so, and I thank you: and I pray you pardon him, and I thank you again.

Quarlous. Well, this dry nurse, I say still, is a delicate man.

Mrs. Littlewit. And I am for the cosset his charge:[1] did you ever see a fellow's face more accuse him for an ass?

Quarlous. Accuse him! it confesses him one without accusing. What pity 'tis yonder wench should marry such a Cokes!

Winwife. 'Tis true.

Quarlous. She seems to be discreet, and as sober as she is handsome.

Winwife. Ay, and if you mark her, what a restrained scorn she casts upon all his behaviour and speeches?

Cokes. Well, Numps, I am now for another piece of business more, the Fair, Numps, and then——

Waspe. Bless me! deliver me! help, hold me! the Fair!

Cokes. Nay, never fidge up and down, Numps, and vex itself. I am resolute Bartholomew in this; I'll make no suit on't to you: 'twas all the end of my journey indeed, to show Mistress Grace my Fair. I call it my Fair, because of Bartholomew: you know my name is Bartholomew, and Bartholomew Fair.

Littlewit. That was mine afore, gentlemen; this morning.

[1] A cosset is a lamb, colt, &c., brought up by hand.

I had that, i' faith, upon his licence, believe me, there he comes after me.

Quarlous. Come, John, this ambitious wit of yours, I am afraid, will do you no good in the end.

Littlewit. No! why, sir?

Quarlous. You grow so insolent with it, and overdoing, John, that if you look not to it, and tie it up, it will bring you to some obscure place in time, and there 'twill leave you.

Winwife. Do not trust it too much, John, be more sparing, and use it but now and then; a wit is a dangerous thing in this age; do not over-buy it.

Littlewit. Think you so, gentlemen? I'll take heed on't hereafter.

Mrs. Littlewit. Yes, do, John.

Cokes. A pretty little soul, this same Mistress Littlewit, would I might marry her!

Grace. So would I; or anybody else, so I might scape you.   [*Aside.*

Cokes. Numps, I will see it, Numps, 'tis decreed: never be melancholy for the matter.

Waspe. Why, see it, sir, see it, do see it: who hinders you? why do you not go see it? 'slid, see it.

Cokes. The Fair, Numps, the Fair.

Waspe. Would the Fair, and all the drums and rattles in it, were in your belly for me! they are already in your brain. He that had the means to travel your head now, should meet finer sights than any are in the Fair, and make a finer voyage on't; to see it all hung with cockleshells, pebbles, fine wheat straws, and here and there a chicken's feather, and a cobweb.

Quarlous. Good faith, he looks, methinks, an you mark him, like one that were made to catch flies, with his Sir Cranion-legs.[1]

Winwife. And his Numps, to flap them away.

_____
[1] *I.e.*, small spider-like legs; but Cranion is the fairy appellation for a fly. Thus Drayton:

> "Four nimble gnats the horses were
>   Their harnesses of gossamere,
> Fly *Cranion,* her charioteer,
>   Upon the coach-box getting."
>   *Nimphidia.*

Waspe. God be wi' you, sir, there's your bee in a box, and much good do't you.

[*Gives* COKES *the box.*

Cokes. Why, your friend, and Bartholomew; an you be so contumacious.

Quarlous. What mean you, Numps?

[*Takes* WASPE *aside as he is going out.*

Waspe. I'll not be guilty, I, gentlemen.

Overdo. You will not let him go, brother, and lose him?

Cokes. Who can hold that will away? I had rather lose him than the Fair, I wusse.

Waspe. You do not know the inconvenience, gentlemen, you persuade to, nor what trouble I have with him in these humours. If he go to the Fair, he will buy of everything to a baby there; and household stuff for that too. If a leg or an arm on him did not grow on, he would lose it in the press. Pray heaven I bring him off with one stone! And then he is such a ravener after fruit!—you will not believe what a coil I had t'other day to compound a business between a Cather'ne-pear woman and him, about snatching: 'tis intolerable, gentlemen.

Winwife. O, but you must not leave him now to these hazards, Numps.

Waspe. Nay, he knows too well I will not leave him, and that makes him presume. Well, sir, will you go now? if you have such an itch in your feet, to foot it to the Fair, why do you stop, am I [o'] your tarriers? go, will you go, sir? why do you not go?

Cokes. O, Numps, have I brought you about? come, Mistress Grace, and sister, I am resolute Bat, i' faith still.

Grace. Truly, I have no such fancy to the Fair, nor ambition to see it; there's none goes thither of any quality or fashion.

Cokes. O Lord, sir! you shall pardon me, Mistress Grace, we are enow of ourselves to make it a fashion; and for qualities, let Numps alone, he'll find qualities.

Quarlous. What a rogue in apprehension is this, to understand her language no better!

Winwife. Ay, and offer to marry her! Well, I will leave the chase of my widow for to-day, and directly to the Fair.

These flies cannot, this hot season, but engender us excellent creeping sport.

Quarlous. A man that has but a spoonful of brain would think so.—Farewell, John. [*Exeunt* QUARLOUS *and* WINWIFE.

Littlewit. Win, you see 'tis in fashion to go to the Fair, Win; we must to the Fair too, you and I, Win. I have an affair in the Fair, Win, a puppet-play of mine own making, say nothing, that I writ for the motion-man, which you must see, Win.

Mrs. Littlewit. I would I might, John; but my mother will never consent to such a profane motion, she will call it.

Littlewit. Tut, we'll have a device, a dainty one. Now, Wit, help at a pinch, good Wit come, come good Wit, an it be thy will! I have it, Win, I have it, i' faith, and 'tis a fine one. Win, long to eat of a pig, sweet Win, in the Fair, do you see, in the heart of the Fair, not at Pye-corner. Your mother will do anything, Win, to satisfy your longing, you know; pray thee long presently; and be sick o' the sudden, good Win. I'll go in and tell her; cut thy lace in the meantime, and play the hypocrite, sweet Win.

Mrs. Littlewit. No, I'll not make me unready for it. I can be hypocrite enough, though I were never so straitlaced.

Littlewit. You say true, you have been bred in the family, and brought up to't. Our mother is a most elect hypocrite, and has maintained us all this seven year with it, like gentlefolks.

Mrs. Littlewit. Ay, let her alone, John, she is not a wise wilful widow for nothing; nor a sanctified sister for a song. And let me alone too, I have somewhat o' the mother in me, you shall see; fetch her, fetch her—[*Exit* LITTLEWIT.] Ah! ah!   [*Seems to swoon.*

Re-enter LITTLEWIT *with* DAME PURECRAFT.

Purecraft. Now the blaze of the beauteous discipline fright away this evil from our house! how now, Win-the-fight, child; how do you? sweet child, speak to me.

Mrs. Littlewit. Yes, forsooth.

Purecraft. Look up, sweet Win-the-fight, and suffer

not the enemy to enter you at this door, remember that your education has been with the purest. What polluted one was it, that named first the unclean beast, pig, to you, child?

Mrs. Littlewit. Uh, uh!

Littlewit. Not I, on my sincerity, mother; she longed above three hours ere she would let me know it.—Who was it, Win?

Mrs. Littlewit. A profane black thing with a beard, John.

Purecraft. O, resist it, Win-the-fight, it is the tempter, the wicked tempter, you may know it by the fleshly motion of pig; be strong against it, and its foul temptations, in these assaults, whereby it broacheth flesh and blood, as it were on the weaker side; and pray against its carnal provocations; good child, sweet child, pray.

Littlewit. Good mother, I pray you that she may eat some pig, and her belly full too; and do not you cast away your own child, and perhaps one of mine, with your tale of the tempter. How do you do, Win, are you not sick?

Mrs. Littlewit. Yes, a great deal, John, uh, uh!

Purecraft. What shall we do? Call our zealous brother Busy hither for his faithful fortification in this charge of the adversary. [*Exit* LITTLEWIT.] Child, my dear child, you shall eat pig; be comforted, my sweet child.

Mrs. Littlewit. Ay, but in the Fair, mother.

Purecraft. I mean in the Fair, if it can be any way made or found lawful.

Re-enter LITTLEWIT.

Where is our brother Busy? will he not come? Look up, child.

Littlewit. Presently, mother, as soon as he has cleansed his beard. I found him fast by the teeth in the cold turkey-pie in the cupboard, with a great white loaf on his left hand, and a glass of malmsey on his right.

Purecraft. Slander not the brethren, wicked one.

Littlewit. Here he is now, purified, mother.

Enter ZEAL-OF-THE-LAND BUSY.

Purecraft. O, brother Busy! your help here to edify and raise us up in a scruple: my daughter Win-the-fight is visited with a natural disease of women, called a longing to eat pig.

Littlewit. Ay, sir, a Bartholomew pig; and in the Fair.

Purecraft. And I would be satisfied from you, religiously-wise, whether a widow of the sanctified assembly, or a widow's daughter, may commit the act without offence to the weaker sisters.

Busy. Verily, for the disease of longing, it is a disease, a carnal disease, or appetite, incident to women; and as it is carnal and incident, it is natural, very natural; now pig, it is a meat, and a meat that is nourishing and may be longed for, and so consequently eaten; it may be eaten; very exceeding well eaten: but in the Fair, and as a Bartholomew pig, it cannot be eaten; for the very calling it a Bartholomew pig, and to eat it so, is a spice of idolatry, and you make the Fair no better than one of the high-places. This, I take it, is the state of the question: a high-place.

Littlewit. Ay, but in state of necessity, place should give place, Master Busy. I have a conceit left yet.

Purecraft. Good brother Zeal-of-the-land, think to make it as lawful as you can.

Littlewit. Yes, sir, and as soon as you can; for it must be, sir: you see the danger my little wife is in, sir.

Purecraft. Truly, I do love my child dearly, and I would not have her miscarry, or hazard her first-fruits, if it might be otherwise.

Busy. Surely, it may be otherwise, but it is subject to construction, subject, and hath a face of offence with the weak, a great face, a foul face; but that face may have a veil put over it, and be shadowed, as it were; it may be eaten, and in the Fair, I take it, in a booth, the tents of the wicked: the place is not much, not very much, we may be religious in the midst of the profane so it be eaten with a reformed mouth, with sobriety, and humbleness; not gorged in with gluttony or greediness, there's the fear: for, should she go there, as taking pride in the place, or delight in the unclean dressing, to feed the vanity of the eye, or lust of the palate, it were not well, it were not fit, it were abominable, and not good.

Littlewit. Nay, I knew that afore, and told her on't; but courage, Win, we'll be humble enough, we'll seek out the homeliest booth in the Fair, that's certain; rather than fail, we'll eat it on the ground.

Purecraft. Ay, and I'll go with you myself, Win-the-fight, and my brother Zeal-of-the-land shall go with us too, for our better consolation.

Mrs. Littlewit. Uh, uh!

Littlewit. Ay, and Solomon too, Win, the more the merrier. Win, we'll leave Rabbi Busy in a booth. [*Aside to* MRS. LITTLEWIT.]—Solomon! my cloak.

Enter SOLOMON *with the cloak.*

Solomon. Here, sir.

Busy. In the way of comfort to the weak, I will go and eat. I will eat exceedingly, and prophesy; there may be a good use made of it too, now I think on't: by the public eating of swine's flesh, to profess our hate and loathing of Judaism, whereof the brethren stand taxed. I will therefore eat, yea, I will eat exceedingly.

Littlewit. Good, i' faith, I will eat heartily too, because I will be no Jew, I could never away with that stiff-necked generation: and truly, I hope my little one will be like me, that cries for pig so in the mother's belly.

Busy. Very likely, exceeding likely, very exceeding likely.
[*Exeunt.*

ACT THE SECOND

SCENE I—*The Fair*

A number of Booths, Stalls, &c., set out, LANTHORN LEATHERHEAD, JOAN TRASH, *and others, sitting by their wares.*

Enter JUSTICE OVERDO, *at a distance, in disguise.*

OVERDO. Well, in justice' name and the king's, and for the commonwealth! defy all the world, Adam Overdo, for a disguise, and all story; for thou hast fitted thyself, I swear.

Fain would I meet the Linceus now, that eagle's eye, that
piercing Epidaurian serpent (as my Quintus Horace calls
him), that could discover a justice of peace (and lately of
the Quorum) under this covering. They may have seen
many a fool in the habit of a justice; but never till now, a
justice in the habit of a fool. Thus must we do though, that
wake for the public good; and thus hath the wise magistrate
done in all ages. There is a doing of right out of wrong, if
the way be found. Never shall I enough commend a
worthy worshipful man, sometimes a capital member of this
city, for his high wisdom in this point, who would take
you now the habit of a porter, now of a carman, now of the
dog-killer in this month of August; and in the winter, of a
seller of tinder-boxes. And what would he do in all these
shapes? marry, go you into every alehouse, and down into
every cellar; measure the length of puddings, take the gauge
of black pots and cans, ay, and custards, with a stick; and
their circumference with a thread; weigh the loaves of bread
on his middle finger; then would he send for them home;
give the puddings to the poor, the bread to the hungry, the
custards to his children; break the pots, and burn the cans
himself: he would not trust his corrupt officers, he would
do it himself. Would all men in authority would follow
this worthy precedent! for alas, as we are public persons,
what do we know? nay, what can we know? we hear with
other men's ears, we see with other men's eyes. A foolish
constable or a sleepy watchman, is all our information; he
slanders a gentleman by the virtue of his place, as he calls it,
and we, by the vice of ours, must believe him. As, awhile
agone, they made me, yea me, to mistake an honest zealous
pursuivant for a seminary; and a proper young bachelor
of musick, for a bawd. This we are subject to that live in
high place; all our intelligence is idle, and most of our in-
telligencers knaves; and by your leave, ourselves thought
little better, if not arrant fools, for believing them. I, Adam
Overdo, am resolved therefore to spare spy-money hereafter,
and make mine own discoveries. Many are the yearly
enormities of this Fair, in whose courts of Pie-poudres[1]

---

[1] From the French *Pied-poudreux*: a court held in fairs to do justice
to buyers and sellers, and for redress of all disorders committed in them.

I have had the honour, during the three days sometimes to sit as judge. But this is the special day for detection of those foresaid enormities. Here is my black book for the purpose; this the cloud that hides me; under this covert I shall see and not be seen. On, Junius Brutus. And as I began, so I'll end; in justice' name, and the king's, and for the commonwealth!

[*Advances to the booths, and stands aside.*

Leatherhead. The Fair's pestilence dead methinks; people come not abroad to-day, whatever the matter is. Do you hear, sister Trash, lady of the basket? sit farther with your gingerbread progeny there, and hinder not the prospect of my shop, or I'll have it proclaimed in the Fair, what stuff they are made on.

Trash. Why, what stuff are they made on, brother Leatherhead? nothing but what's wholesome, I assure you.

Leatherhead. Yes, stale bread, rotten eggs, musty ginger, and dead honey, you know.

Overdo. Ay! have I met with enormity so soon.

[*Aside.*

Leatherhead. I shall mar your market, old Joan.

Trash. Mar my market, thou too-proud pedler! do thy worst, I defy thee, I, and thy stable of hobby-horses. I pay for my ground as well as thou dost: an thou wrong'st me, for all thou art parcel-poet, and an inginer, I'll find a friend who shall right me, and make a ballad of thee, and thy cattle all over. Are you puft up with the pride of your wares? your arsedine?

Leatherhead. Go to, old Joan, I'll talk with you anon; and take you down too, afore Justice Overdo: he is the man must charm you, I'll have you in the Pie-poudres.

Trash. Charm me! I'll meet thee face to face, afore his worship, when thou darest: and though I be a little crooked o' my body, I shall be found as upright in my dealing as any woman in Smithfield, I; charm me!

Overdo. I am glad to hear my name is their terror yet; this is doing of justice.   [*Aside.*

[*A number of people pass over the stage.*

Leatherhead. What do you lack? what is't you buy? what

do you lack? rattles, drums, halberts, horses, babies o' the
best, fiddles of the finest?

Enter COSTARDMONGER, *followed by* NIGHTINGALE.

Costardmonger. Buy any pears, pears, fine, very fine pears!
Trash. Buy any gingerbread, gilt gingerbread.
Nightingale. Hey [*sings*]

>   Now the Fair's a filling!
>   O for a tune to startle
>   The birds o' the booths here billing,
>   Yearly with old saint Bartle!
>   The drunkards they are wading,
>   The punks and chapmen trading;
>   Who'd see the Fair without his lading?

Buy any ballads, new ballads?

Enter URSULA *from her booth.*

Ursula. Fie upon't: who would wear out their youth and
prime thus, in roasting of pigs, that had any cooler vocation? hell's a kind of cold cellar to't, a very fine vault,
o' my conscience!—What, Mooncalf!

Mooncalf [*within*]. Here, mistress.

Nightingale. How now, Ursula? in a heat, in a heat?

Ursula. My chair, you false faucet you; and my morning's draught quickly, a bottle of ale, to quench me, rascal.
I am all fire and fat, Nightingale, I shall e'en melt away
to the first woman, a rib again, I am afraid. I do water
the ground in knots, as I go, like a great garden pot; you
may follow me by the SS I make.

Nightingale. Alas, good Urse! was Zekiel here this
morning?

Ursula. Zekiel? what Zekiel?

Nightingale. Zekiel Edgworth, the civil cutpurse, you
know him well enough; he that talks bawdy to you still:
I call him my secretary.

Ursula. He promised to be here this morning, I remember.

Nightingale. When he comes, bid him stay: I'll be back
again presently.

Ursula. Best take your morning dew in your belly, Nightingale.——

Enter MOONCALF *with the chair.*

Come, sir, set it here; did not I bid you should get a chair let out o' the sides for me, that my hips might play? you'll never think of anything till your dame be rump-galled; 'tis well, changeling: because it can take in your grasshopper's thighs, you care for no more. Now, you look as you had been in the corner of the booth, fleaing your breech with a candle's end, and set fire o' the Fair. Fill, Stote, fill.

Overdo. This pig-woman do I know, and I will put her in, for my second enormity; she hath been before me, punk, pinnace, and bawd, any time these two and twenty years upon record in the Pie-poudres.   [*Aside.*

Ursula. Fill again, you unlucky vermin!

Mooncalf. Pray you be not angry, mistress, I'll have it widened anon.

Ursula. No, no, I shall e'en dwindle away to't, ere the Fair be done, you think, now you have heated me: a poor vexed thing I am, I feel myself dropping already as fast as I can; two stones o' suet a day is my proportion. I can but hold life and soul together with this (here's to you, Nightingale), and a whiff of tobacco at most. Where's my pipe now? not filled! thou arrant incubee.

Nightingale. Nay, Ursula, thou'lt gall between the tongue and the teeth, with fretting, now.

Ursula. How can I hope that ever he'll discharge his place of trust, tapster, a man of reckoning under me, that remembers nothing I say to him? [*Exit* NIGHTINGALE.] but look to't, sirrah, you were best. Threepence a pipe-full, I will have made, of all my whole half pound of tobacco, and a quarter of pound of colts-foot mixt with it too, to [eke] it out. I that have dealt so long in the fire, will not be to seek in smoke now. Then six and twenty shillings a barrel I will advance on my beer, and fifty shillings a hundred on my bottle-ale; I have told you the ways how to raise it. Froth your cans well in the filling, at length, rogue,

and jog your bottles o' the buttock, sirrah, then skink out
the first glass ever, and drink with all companies, though
you be sure to be drunk; you'll misreckon the better, and
be less ashamed on't. But your true trick, rascal, must be,
to be ever busy, and mistake away the bottles and cans, in
haste, before they be half drunk off, and never hear anybody call (if they should chance to mark you), till you have
brought fresh, and be able to forswear them. Give me a
drink of ale.

Overdo. This is the very womb and bed of enormity!
gross as herself! this must all down for enormity, all, every
whit on't.   [*Aside.*

                                          [*Knocking within.*

Ursula. Look who's there, sirrah: five shillings a pig is
my price, at least; if it be a sow pig, sixpence more; if she
be a great-bellied wife, and long for't, sixpence more for
that.

Overdo. O tempora! O mores! I would not have lost my
discovery of this one grievance, for my place and worship
o' the bench. How is the poor subject abused here! Well,
I will fall in with her, and with her Mooncalf, and win
out wonders of enormity! [*Comes forward.*]—By thy leave,
goodly woman, and the fatness of the Fair, oily as the
king's constable's lamp, and shining as his shooing-horn!
hath thy ale virtue or thy beer strength, that the tongue of
man may be tickled, and his palate pleased in the morning?
Let thy pretty nephew here go search and see.

Ursula. What new roarer is this?

Mooncalf. O Lord, do you not know him, mistress? 'tis
mad Arthur of Bradley, that makes the orations.—Brave
master, old Arthur of Bradley, how do you? welcome to
the Fair! when shall we hear you again, to handle your
matters, with your back against a booth, ha? I have been
one of your little disciples, in my days.

Overdo. Let me drink, boy, with my love, thy aunt here;
that I may be eloquent: but of thy best, lest it be bitter
in my mouth, and my words fall foul on the Fair.

Ursula. Why dost thou not fetch him drink, and offer
him to sit?

Mooncalf. Is it ale or beer, Master Arthur?

Overdo. Thy best, pretty stripling, thy best; the same thy dove drinketh, and thou drawest on holydays.

Ursula. Bring him a sixpenny bottle of ale; they say a fool's handsel is lucky.

Overdo. Bring both, child. [*Sits down in the booth.*] Ale for Arthur, and beer for Bradley. Ale for thine aunt, boy.[1] [*Exit* MOONCALF.] My disguise takes to the very wish and reach of it. I shall, by the benefit of this, discover enough and more: and yet get off with the reputation of what I would be: a certain middling thing, between a fool and a madman.   [*Aside.*

Enter KNOCKEM

Knockem. What! my little lean Ursula! my she-bear! art thou alive yet, with thy litter of pigs to grunt out another Bartholomew Fair? ha!

Ursula. Yes, and to amble a foot, when the Fair is done, to hear you groan out of a cart, up the heavy hill——

Knockem. Of Holbourn, Ursula, meanst thou so? for what, for what, pretty Urse?

Ursula. For cutting halfpenny purses, or stealing little penny dogs out o' the Fair.

Knockem. O! good words, good words, Urse.

Overdo. Another special enormity. A cutpurse of the sword, the boot, and the feather! those are his marks.
                                                        [*Aside.*

Re-enter MOONCALF *with the ale, &c.*

Ursula. You are one of those horse-leeches that gave out I was dead, in Turnbull-street, of a surfeit of bottle-ale and tripes?

Knockem. No, 'twas better meat, Urse: cows' udders, cows' udders!

Ursula. Well, I shall be meet with your mumbling mouth one day.

Knockem. What! thou'lt poison me with a newt in a bottle of ale, wilt thou? or a spider in a tobacco-pipe, Urse? Come, there's no malice in these fat folks, I never

[1] In the cant language of the age, *aunt* denoted a *bawd*.

fear thee, an I can scape thy lean Mooncalf here. Let's
drink it out, good Urse, and no vapours!

                                    [*Exit* URSULA.

  Overdo. Dost thou hear, boy? There's for thy ale, and
the remnant for thee.—Speak in thy faith of a faucet now;
is this goodly person before us here, this vapours, a knight
of the knife?

  Mooncalf. What mean you by that, Master Arthur?

  Overdo. I mean a child of the horn-thumb, a babe of
booty, boy, a cutpurse.

  Mooncalf. O Lord, sir! far from it. This is Master Daniel
Knockem Jordan: the ranger of Turnbull. He is a horse-
courser, sir.

  Overdo. Thy dainty dame, though, called him cutpurse.

  Mooncalf. Like enough, sir; she'll do forty such things
in an hour (an you listen to her) for her recreation, if the
toy take her in the greasy kerchief: it makes her fat, you
see; she battens with it.

  Overdo. Here I might have been deceived now, and
have put a fool's blot upon myself, if I had not played
an after game of discretion!   [*Aside.*

         Re-enter URSULA, *dropping.*

  Knockem. Alas, poor Urse! this is an ill season for thee.

  Ursula. Hang yourself, hackney-man!

  Knockem. How, how, Urse! vapours? motion breed
vapours.

  Ursula. Vapours! never tusk, nor twirl your dibble, good
Jordan, I know what you'll take to a very drop. Though
you be captain of the roarers, and fight well at the case
of piss-pots, you shall not fright me with your lion-chap,
sir, nor your tusks; you angry! you are hungry. Come, a
pig's head will stop your mouth, and stay your stomach
at all times.

  Knockem. Thou art such another mad, merry Urse,
still! troth I do make conscience of vexing thee, now in
the dog-days, this hot weather, for fear of foundering thee
in the body, and melting down a pillar of the Fair. Pray
thee take thy chair again, and keep state; and let's have
a fresh bottle of ale, and a pipe of tobacco; and no vapours.

I'll have this belly o' thine taken up, and thy grass scoured, wench.—

Enter EDGWORTH.

Look, here's Ezekiel Edgworth; a fine boy of his inches, as any is in the Fair! has still money in his purse, and will pay all, with a kind heart, and good vapours.

Edgworth. That I will indeed, willingly, Master Knockem; fetch some ale and tobacco.

[Exit MOONCALF—People cross the stage.

Leatherhead. What do you lack, gentlemen? maid, see a fine hobby-horse for your young master; cost you but a token a week his provender.

Re-enter NIGHTINGALE, with CORNCUTTER and
MOUSE-TRAP-MAN.

Corncutter. Have you any corns in your feet and toes?

Mouse-trap-man. Buy a mousetrap, a mousetrap, or a tormentor for a flea?

Trash. Buy some gingerbread?

Nightingale. Ballads, ballads! fine new ballads:—
"Hear for your love, and buy for your money.
A delicate ballad o' the ferret and the coney.
A preservative again' the punk's evil.
Another of goose-green starch, and the devil.[1]
A dozen of divine points, and the godly garters:
The fairing of good counsel, of an ell and three quarters."
What is't you buy?
"The windmill blown down by the witch's fart.
Or Saint George, that, O! did break the dragon's heart."

Re-enter MOONCALF, with ale and tobacco.

Edgworth. Master Nightingale, come hither, leave your mart a little.

Nightingale. O my secretary! what says my secretary?

[They walk into the booth.

Overdo. Child of the bottles, what's he? what's he?

[Points to EDGWORTH.

---

[1] This was "a goodly ballad against pride, showing how the devil appeared to a lady which was starching her ruff by night."

Mooncalf. A civil young gentleman, Master Arthur, that keeps company with the roarers, and disburses all still. He has ever money in his purse; he pays for them, and they roar for him; one does good offices for another. They call him the secretary, but he serves nobody. A great friend of the ballad-man's, they are never asunder.

Overdo. What pity 'tis, so civil a young man should haunt this debauched company? here's the bane of the youth of our time apparent. A proper penman, I see't in his countenance, he has a good clerk's look with him, and I warrant him a quick hand.

Mooncalf. A very quick hand, sir.   [*Exit.*

Edgworth [*whispering with* NIGHTINGALE *and* URSULA]. All the purses and purchases I give you to-day by convey-ance, bring hither to Ursula's presently. Here we will meet at night in her lodge, and share. Look you choose good places for your standing in the Fair, when you sing, Nightingale.

Ursula. Ay, near the fullest passages; and shift them often.

Edgworth. And in your singing, you must use your hawk's eye nimbly, and fly the purse to a mark still, where 'tis worn, and on which side; that you may give me the sign with your beak, or hang your head that way in the tune.

Ursula. Enough, talk no more on't: your friendship, masters, is not now to begin. Drink your draught of in-denture, your sup of covenant, and away: the Fair fills apace, company begins to come in, and I have ne'er a pig ready yet.

Knockem. Well said! fill the cups, and light the tobacco: let's give fire in the works, and noble vapours.

Edgworth. And shall we have smocks, Ursula, and good whimsies, ha?

Ursula. Come, you are in your bawdy vein!—the best the Fair will afford, Zekiel, if bawd Whit keep his word.—

Re-enter MOONCALF.

How do the pigs, Mooncalf?

Mooncalf. Very passionate, mistress, one of 'em has wept

out an eye.[1] Master Arthur o' Bradley is melancholy here, nobody talks to him. Will you any tobacco, Master Arthur?

Overdo. No, boy; let my meditations alone.

Mooncalf. He's studying for an oration now.

Overdo. If I can with this day's travail, and all my policy, but rescue this youth here out of the hands of the lewd man and the strange woman, I will sit down at night, and say with my friend Ovid,

Jamque opus exegi, quod nec Jovis ira, nec ignis, &c.

[*Aside.*

Knockem. Here, Zekiel, here's a health to Ursula, and a kind vapour; thou hast money in thy purse still, and store! how dost thou come by it? pray thee vapour thy friends some in a courteous vapour.

Edgworth. Half I have, Master Dan Knockem, is always at your service.   [*Pulls out his purse.*

Overdo. Ha, sweet nature! what goshawk would prey upon such a lamb?   [*Aside.*

Knockem. Let's see what 'tis, Zekiel; count it, come, fill him to pledge me.

Enter WINWIFE *and* QUARLOUS.

Winwife. We are here before them, methinks.

Quarlous. All the better; we shall see them come in now.

Leatherhead. What do you lack, gentlemen, what is't you lack! a fine horse? a lion? a bull? a bear? a dog or a cat? an excellent fine Bartholomew-bird? or an instrument? what is't you lack?

Quarlous. 'Slid! here's Orpheus among the beasts, with his fiddle and all!

Trash. Will you buy any comfortable bread,[2] gentlemen?

Quarlous. And Ceres selling her daughter's picture, in ginger-work.

Winwife. That these people should be so ignorant to think us chapmen for them! Do we look as if we would buy gingerbread or hobby-horses?

---

[1] When the eye of a pig in roasting drops out, it is a mark that the pig is almost roasted enough.

[2] *I.e.*, spiced gingerbread.

Quarlous. Why, they know no better ware than they have, nor better customers than come: and our very being here makes us fit to be demanded, as well as others. Would Cokes would come! there were a true customer for them.

Knockem [*to* EDGWORTH]. How much is't? thirty shillings? Who's yonder! Ned Winwife and Tom Quarlous, I think! yes: (give me it all, give it me all.)—Master Winwife! Master Quarlous! will you take a pipe of tobacco with us? —Do not discredit me now, Zekiel.

[EDGWORTH *gives him his purse.*

Winwife. Do not see him; he is the roaring horse-courser, pray thee let's avoid him: turn down this way.

Quarlous. 'Slud, I'll see him, and roar with him too, an he roared as loud as Neptune; pray thee go with me.

Winwife. You may draw me to as likely an inconvenience, when you please, as this.

Quarlous. Go to then, come along; we have nothing to do, man, but to see sights now.

[*They advance to the booth.*

Knockem. Welcome, Master Quarlous, and Master Winwife; will you take any froth and smoke with us?

Quarlous. Yes, sir; but you'll pardon us if we knew not of so much familiarity between us afore.

Knockem. As what, sir?

Quarlous. To be so lightly invited to smoke and froth.

Knockem. A good vapour! will you sit down, sir? this is old Ursula's mansion; how like you her bower? Here you may have your punk and your pig in state, sir, both piping hot.

Quarlous. I had rather have my punk cold, sir.

Overdo. There's for me: punk! and pig!   [*Aside.*

Ursula [*within*]. What, Mooncalf, you rogue!

Mooncalf. By and by, the bottle is almost off, mistress; here, Master Arthur.

Ursula [*within*]. I'll part you and your play fellow there, in the garded coat, an you sunder not the sooner.

Knockem. Master Winwife, you are proud, methinks, you do not talk, nor drink; are you proud?

Winwife. Not of the company I am in, sir, nor the place, I assure you.

Knockem. You do not except at the company, do you!
are you in vapours, sir?

Mooncalf. Nay, good Master Daniel Knockem, respect
my mistress's bower, as you call it; for the honour of our
booth, none o' your vapours here.

Enter URSULA *with a firebrand.*

Ursula. Why, you thin, lean polecat you, an they have
a mind to be in their vapours must you hinder 'em? What
did you know, vermin, if they would have lost a cloak,
or such trifle? must you be drawing the air of pacification
here, while I am tormented within i' the fire, you weasel?
                                        [*Aside to* MOONCALF.

Mooncalf. Good mistress, 'twas in behalf of your booth's
credit that I spoke.

Ursula. Why! would my booth have broke if they had
fallen out in't, sir? or would their heat have fired it? In,
you rogue, and wipe the pigs, and mend the fire that they
fall not, or I'll both baste and roast you till your eyes drop
out like them.—Leave the bottle behind you, and be curst
awhile!   [*Exit* MOON.

Quarlous. Body o' the Fair! what's this? mother of the
bawds?

Knockem. No, she's mother of the pigs, sir, mother of
the pigs.

Winwife. Mother of the furies I think, by her firebrand.

Quarlous. Nay, she is too fat to be a fury, sure some
walking sow of tallow!

Winwife. An inspired vessel of kitchen stuff!

Quarlous. She'll make excellent geer for the coachmakers
here in Smithfield to anoint wheels and axletrees with.
                                        [*She drinks this while.*

Ursula. Ay, ay, gamesters, mock a plain, plump, soft
wench of the suburbs, do, because she's juicy and wholesome; you must have your thin pinched ware pent up in
the compass of a dog-collar (or 'twill not do), that looks
like a long-laced conger set upright, and a green feather,
like fennel in the joll on't.

Knockem. Well said, Urse, my good Urse! to 'em, Urse!

Quarlous. Is she your quagmire, Daniel Knockem? is this your bog?

Nightingale. We shall have a quarrel presently.

Knockem. How! bog? quagmire? foul vapours! humph!

Quarlous. Yes, he that would venture for't, I assure him, might sink into her and be drowned a week ere any friend he had could find where he were.

Winwife. And then he would be a fortnight weighing up again.

Quarlous. 'Twere like falling into a whole shire of butter; they had need be a team of Dutchmen should draw him out.

Knockem. Answer 'em, Urse: where's thy Bartholomew wit now, Urse, thy Bartholomew wit?

Ursula. Hang 'em, rotten, roguy cheaters, I hope to see them plagued one day (poxed they are already, I am sure) with lean playhouse poultry, that has the bony rump sticking out like the ace of spades or the point of a partizan, that every rib of them is like the tooth of a saw; and will so grate them with their hips and shoulders as (take 'em altogether) they were as good lie with a hurdle.

Quarlous. Out upon her, how she drips! she's able to give a man the sweating sickness with looking on her.

Ursula. Marry look off, with a patch on your face and a dozen in your breech, though they be of scarlet, sir! I have seen as fine outsides as either of yours, bring lousy linings to the brokers, ere now, twice a week.

Quarlous. Do you think there may be a fine new cuckingstool [1] in the Fair, to be purchased; one large enough, I mean? I know there is a pond of capacity for her.

Ursula. For your mother, you rascal! Out you rogue, you hedge-bird, you pimp, you pannier-man's bastard, you!

Quarlous. Ha, ha, ha!

Ursula. Do you sneer, you dog's-head, you trendletail! you look as you were begotten a top of a cart in harvest time, when the whelp was hot and eager. Go, snuff after your brother's bitch, Mistress Commodity; that's the livery

[1] Now frequently corrupted into *ducking-stool.*

you wear, 'twill be out at the elbows shortly. It's time you went to't for the t'other remnant.

Knockem. Peace, Urse, peace, Urse;—they'll kill the poor whale and make oil of her. Pray thee go in.

Ursula. I'll see them poxed first, and piled and double piled.

Winwife. Let's away, her language grows greasier than her pigs.

Ursula. Does it so, snotty-nose? good Lord! are you snivelling? You were engendered on a she-beggar in a barn, when the bald thrasher, your sire, was scarce warm.

Winwife. Pray thee let's go.

Quarlous. No, faith; I'll stay the end of her now; I know she cannot last long: I find by her similes she wanes apace.

Ursula. Does she so? I'll set you gone. Give me my pig-pan hither a little: I'll scald you hence, an you will not go.
                                              [Exit.

Knockem. Gentlemen, these are very strange vapours, and very idle vapours, I assure you.

Quarlous. You are a very serious ass, we assure you.

Knockem. Hump, *ass!* and *serious!* nay, then pardon me my vapour. I have a foolish vapour, gentlemen. Any man that does vapour me the ass, Master Quarlous——

Quarlous. What then, Master Jordan?

Knockem. I do vapour him the lie.

Quarlous. Faith, and to any man that vapours me the lie, I do vapour that.   *[Strikes him.*

Knockem. Nay then, vapours upon vapours.

                                        [They fight.

          Re-enter URSULA *with the dripping-pan.*

Edgworth, Nightingale. 'Ware the pan, the pan, the pan! she comes with the pan, gentlemen! [URSULA *falls with the pan.*] God bless the woman.

   Ursula. Oh!   *[Exeunt* QUARLOUS *and* WINWIFE.
   Trash [runs in]. What's the matter?
   Overdo. Goodly woman!
   Mooncalf. Mistress!

Ursula. Curse of hell, that ever I saw these fiends! oh! I have scalded my leg, my leg, my leg, my leg! I have lost a limb in the service! run for some cream and salad oil, quickly. Are you under-peering, you baboon! rip off my hose, an you be men, men, men.

Mooncalf. Run you for some cream, good Mother Joan. I'll look to your basket. [*Exit* TRASH.

Leatherhead. Best sit up in your chair, Ursula. Help, gentlemen.

Knockem. Be of good cheer, Urse; thou hast hindered me the currying of a couple of stallions here, that abused the good racebawd of Smithfield; 'twas time for them to go.

Nightingale. I' faith, when the pan came,—they had made you run else. This had been a fine time for purchase, if you had ventured. [*Aside to* EDGWORTH.

Edgworth. Not a whit, these fellows were too fine to carry money.

Knockem. Nightingale, get some help to carry her leg out of the air: take off her shoes. Body o' me! she has the mallanders, the scratches, the crown scab, and the quitter bone in the t'other leg.

Ursula. Oh, the pox! why do you put me in mind of my leg thus, to make it prick and shoot? Would you have me in the hospital afore my time?

Knockem. Patience, Urse, take a good heart, 'tis but a blister as big as a windgall. I'll take it away with the white of an egg, a little honey and hog's grease, have thy pasterns well rolled, and thou shalt pace again by to-morrow. I'll tend thy booth, and look to thy affairs the while: thou shalt sit in thy chair, and give directions, an shine Ursa major.

[*Exeunt* KNOCKEM *and* MOONCALF *with* URSULA *in her chair.*

Overdo. These are the fruits of bottle-ale and tobacco! the foam of the one, and the fumes of the other! Stay, young man, and despise not the wisdom of these few hairs that are grown grey in care of thee.

Edgworth. Nightingale, stay a little. Indeed I'll hear some of this!

Enter Cokes, *with his box,* Waspe, Mistress Overdo, *and*
Grace.

Cokes. Come, Numps, come, where are you? Welcome
into the Fair, Mistress Grace.

Edgworth. 'Slight, he will call company, you shall see,
and put us into doings presently.

Overdo. Thirst not after that frothy liquor ale; for who
knows when he openeth the stopple, what may be in the
bottle? Hath not a snail, a spider, yea, a newt been found
there? thirst not after it, youth; thirst not after it.

Cokes. This is a brave fellow, Numps, let's hear him.

Waspe. 'Sblood! how brave is he? in a garded coat! You
were best truck with him; e'en strip, and truck presently, it
will become you. Why will you hear him? because he is an
ass, and may be akin to the Cokeses?

Cokes. O, good Numps.

Overdo. Neither do thou lust after that tawny weed
tobacco.

Cokes. Brave words!

Overdo. Whose complexion is like the Indian's that vents
it.

Cokes. Are they not brave words, sister?

Overdo. And who can tell, if before the gathering and
making up thereof, the Alligartha hath not pissed thereon?

Waspe. 'Heart! let 'em be brave words, as brave as they
will! an they were all the brave words in a country, how
then? Will you away yet, have you enough on him? Mistress
Grace, come you away; I pray you be not you accessary.
If you do lose your licence, or somewhat else, sir, with
listening to his fables, say Numps is a witch, with all my
heart, do, say so.

Cokes. Avoid in your satin doublet, Numps.

Overdo. The creeping venom of which subtle serpent,
as some late writers affirm, neither the cutting of the peril-
ous plant, nor the drying of it, nor the lighting or burning,
can any way persway[1] or assuage.

Cokes. Good, i' faith! is it not, sister?

Overdo. Hence it is that the lungs of the tobacconist

[1] Mitigate.

are rotted, the liver spotted, the brain smoked like the backside of the pig-woman's booth here, and the whole body within, black as her pan you saw e'en now without.

Cokes. A fine similitude that, sir! did you see the pan?

Edgworth. Yes, sir.

Overdo. Nay, the hole in the nose here of some tobacco-takers, or the third nostril, if I may so call it, which makes that they can vent the tobacco out, like the ace of clubs, or rather the flower-de-lis, is caused from the tobacco, the mere tobacco! when the poor innocent pox, having nothing to do there, is miserably and most unconscionably slandered.

Cokes. Who would have missed this, sister?

Mrs. Overdo. Not anybody but Numps.

Cokes. He does not understand.

Edgworth [*picks* COKES's *pocket of his purse*]. Nor you feel.   [*Aside.*

Cokes. What would you have, sister, of a fellow that knows nothing but a basket-hilt, and an old fox[1] in't? the best music in the Fair will not move a log.

Edgworth [*gives the purse aside to* NIGHTINGALE]. In, to Ursula, Nightingale, and carry her comfort: see it told. This fellow was sent to us by Fortune, for our first fairing.

[*Exit* NIGHTINGALE.

Overdo. But what speak I of the diseases of the body, children of the Fair?

Cokes. That's to us, sister. Brave, i' faith!

Overdo. Hark, O you sons and daughters of Smithfield! and hear what malady it doth the mind: it causeth swearing, it causeth swaggering, it causeth snuffing and snarling, and now and then a hurt.

Mrs. Overdo. He hath something of Master Overdo, methinks, brother.

Cokes. So methought, sister, very much of my brother Overdo: and 'tis when he speaks.

Overdo. Look into any angle of the town, the Streights, or the Bermudas,[2] where the quarrelling lesson is read, and

[1] *I.e.*, broadsword, as distinguished from the small (foreign) sword.
[2] Cant-names then given to the places frequented by bullies, knights of the post, and fencing masters.

how do they entertain the time, but with bottle-ale and
tobacco? The lecture is o' one side, and his pupils o' the
other; but the seconds are still bottle-ale and tobacco, for
which the lecturer reads, and the novices pay. Thirty
pound a week in bottle-ale! forty in tobacco! and ten more
in ale again. Then for a suit to drink in, so much, and,
that being slavered, so much for another suit, and then a
third suit, and a fourth suit! and still the bottle-ale
slavereth, and the tobacco stinketh.

Waspe. Heart of a madman! are you rooted here? will
you never away? what can any man find out in this bawling
fellow, to grow here for? He is a full handful higher sin'
he heard him. Will you fix here, and set up a booth, sir?

Overdo. I will conclude briefly——

Waspe. Hold your peace, you roaring rascal, I'll run
my head in your chaps else. You were best build a booth,
and entertain him; make your will, an you say the word,
and him your heir! heart, I never knew one taken with
a mouth of a peck afore. By this light, I'll carry you away
on my back, an you will not come.

                    [*He gets* Cokes *up on pick-back.*

Cokes. Stay, Numps, stay, set me down. I have lost my
purse, Numps. O my purse! One of my fine purses is gone!

Mrs. Overdo. Is it indeed, brother?

Cokes. Ay, as I am an honest man, would I were an
arrant rogue else! a plague of all roguy damned cutpurses
for me.   [*Examines his pockets.*

Waspe. Bless 'em with all my heart, with all my heart, do
you see! now, as I am no infidel, that I know of, I am
glad on't. Ay, I am (here's my witness), do you see, sir? I
did not tell you of his fables, I! no, no, I am a dull malt
horse, I, I know nothing. Are you not justly served, in your
conscience now, speak in your conscience? Much good do
you with all my heart, and his good heart that has it, with
all my heart again.

Edgworth. This fellow is very charitable, would he had a
purse too! but I must not be too bold all at a time. [*Aside.*

Cokes. Nay, Numps, it is not my best purse.

Waspe. Not your best! death! why should it be your

worst? why should it be any, indeed, at all? answer me to
that, give me a reason from you, why it should be any?

Cokes. Nor my gold, Numps; I have that yet, look here
else, sister.   [*Shows the other purse.*

Waspe. Why so, there's all the feeling he has!

Mrs. Overdo. I pray you have a better care of that,
brother.

Cokes. Nay, so I will, I warrant you; let him catch this
that catch can. I would fain see him get this, look you here.

Waspe. So, so, so, so, so, so, so, so! very good.

Cokes. I would have him come again now, and but
offer at it. Sister, will you take notice of a good jest? I will
put it just where the other was, and if we have good luck,
you shall see a delicate fine trap to catch the cutpurse
nibbling.

Edgworth. Faith, and he'll try ere you be out o' the Fair.
                                                  [*Aside.*

Cokes. Come, Mistress Grace, prithee be not melancholy
for my mischance; sorrow will not keep it, sweetheart.

Grace. I do not think on't, sir.

Cokes. 'Twas but a little scurvy white money, hang it! it
may hang the cutpurse one day. I have gold left to give thee
a fairing yet, as hard as the world goes. Nothing angers me
but that nobody here looked like a cutpurse, unless 'twere
Numps.

Waspe. How! I, I look like a cutpurse? death! your sister's
a cutpurse! and your mother and father, and all your kin,
were cutpurses! and here is a rogue is the bawd o' the
cutpurses, whom I will beat to begin with.   [*Beats* OVERDO.

Overdo. Hold thy hand, child of wrath, and heir of anger,
make it not Childermass day[1] in thy fury, or the feast of the
French Bartholomew, parent of the massacre.

Cokes. Numps, Numps!

Mrs. Overdo. Good Master Humphrey!

Waspe. You are the Patrico,[2] are you? the patriarch of
the cutpurses? You share, sir, they say; let them share this

---

[1] Innocent's day.
[2] Among strolling beggars and gipsies, the *patrico* is the orator of the
gang, the hedge priest who officiates at their ceremonies of marriage.

with you. Are you in your hot fit of preaching again? I'll
cool you.   [*Beats him again.*

Overdo. Murther, murther, murther!   [*Exeunt.*

ACT THE THIRD

SCENE I—*The Fair*

LANTHORN LEATHERHEAD, JOAN TRASH, *and others,
sitting by their wares, as before.*

Enter VAL., WHIT, HAGGISE, *and* BRISTLE.

WHIT. Nay, tish all gone, now! dish tish, phen tou wilt not
be phitin call, master offisher, phat ish a man te better to
lishen out noyshes for tee, and tou art in an oder orld,
being very shuffishient noyshes and gallantsh too? one o'
their brabblesh would have fed ush all dish fortnight, but
tou art so bushy about beggersh still, tou hast no leshure
to intend shentlemen, and 't be.

Haggise. Why, I told you, Davy Bristle.

Bristle. Come, come, you told me a pudding, Toby
Haggise; a matter of nothing; I am sure it came to nothing.
You said, let's go to Ursula's, indeed; but then you met the
man with the monsters, and I could not get you from him.
An old fool, not leave seeing yet!

Haggise. Why, who would have thought anybody would
have quarrelled so early; or that the ale o' the fair would
have been up so soon?

Whit. Phy, phat a clock toest tou tink it ish, man?

Haggise. I cannot tell.

Whit. Tou art a vish vatchman, i' te mean teem.

Haggise. Why, should the watch go by the clock, or the
clock by the watch, I pray?

Bristle. One should go by another, if they did well.

Whit. Tou art right now! phen didst tou ever know or
hear of a shuffishient vatchment, but he did tell the clock,
phat bushiness soever he had?

Bristle. Nay, that's most true, a sufficient watchman knows
what a clock it is.

Whit. Shleeping or vaking: ash well as te clock himshelf, or te Jack dat shtrikes him.

Bristle. Let's inquire of Master Leatherhead, or Joan Trash here.—Master Leatherhead, do you hear, Master Leatherhead?

Whit. If it be a Ledderhead, tish a very tick Ledderhead, tat sho mush noish vill not piersh him.

Leatherhead. I have a little business now, good friends, do not trouble me.

Whit. Phat, because o' ty wrought neet-cap, and ty phelvet sherkin, man? phy! I have sheene tee in ty ledder sherkin, ere now, mashter o' de hobby-horses, as bushy and stately as tou sheemest to be.

Trash. Why, what an you have, Captain Whit? he has his choice of jerkins, you may see by that, and his caps too, I assure you, when he pleases to be either sick or employed.

Leatherhead. God-a-mercy Joan, answer for me.

Whit. Away, be not sheen in my company, here be shentlemen, and men of vorship.

[*Exeunt* HAGGISE *and* BRISTLE.

Enter QUARLOUS *and* WINWIFE.

Quarlous. We had wonderful ill luck, to miss this prologue o' the purse; but the best is, we shall have five acts of him ere night: he'll be spectacle enough, I'll answer for't.

Whit. O creesh! Duke Quarlous, how dosht tou? tou dosht not know me, I fear: I am te vishesht man, but Justish Overdo, in all Bartholomew Fair now. Give me twelve pence from tee, I vill help tee to a vife vorth forty marks for't, and't be.

Quarlous. Away, rogue; pimp, away.

Whit. And she shall shew tee as fine cut orke for't in her shmock too as tou cansht vish, i' faith; vilt tou have her, vorshipful Vinvife? I vill help tee to her here, be an't be, into pig-quarter, gi' me ty twelve pence from tee.

Winwife. Why, there's twelve pence, pray thee wilt thou begone?

Whit. Tou art a vorthy man, and a vorshipful man still.

Quarlous. Get you gone, rascal.

Whit. I do mean it, man. Prinsh Quarlous, if tou hasht need on me, tou shalt find me here at Ursla's, I vill see phat ale and punque ish i' te pigsty for tee, bless ty good vorship.
[*Exit.*

Quarlous. Look! who comes here: John Littlewit!

Winwife. And his wife, and my widow, her mother: the whole family.

Quarlous. 'Slight, you must give them all fairings now.

Winwife. Not I, I'll not see them.

Quarlous. They are going a feasting. What schoolmaster's that is with 'em?

Winwife. That's my rival, I believe, the baker.

Enter RABBI BUSY, DAME PURECRAFT, JOHN LITTLEWIT, *and* MRS. LITTLEWIT.

Busy. So, walk on in the middle way, fore-right, turn neither to the right hand nor to the left; let not your eyes be drawn aside with vanity, nor your ear with noises.

Quarlous. O, I know him by that start.

Leatherhead. What do you lack, what do you buy, mistress? a fine hobby-horse, to make your son a tilter? a drum, to make him a soldier? a fiddle, to make him a reveller? what is't you lack? little dogs for your daughters? or babies, male or female?

Busy. Look not toward them, hearken not; the place is Smithfield, or the field of smiths, the grove of hobby-horses and trinkets, the wares are the wares of devils, and the whole Fair is the shop of Satan: they are hooks and baits, very baits, that are hung out on every side, to catch you, and to hold you, as it were, by the gills and by the nostrils, as the fisher doth; therefore you must not look nor turn toward them.—The heathen man could stop his ears with wax against the harlot of the sea; do you the like with your fingers against the bells of the beast.

Winwife. What flashes come from him!

Quarlous. O, he has those of his oven; a notable hot baker 'twas when he plied the peel [1]: he is leading his flock into the Fair now.

---

[1] The shovel-like instrument with which bakers withdraw their bread from the oven.

Winwife. Rather driving them to the pens; for he will let them look upon nothing.

Enter KNOCKEM *and* WHIT *from* URSULA'S *booth.*

Knockem. Gentlewomen, the weather's hot; whither walk you? have a care of your fine velvet caps, the Fair is dusty. Take a sweet delicate booth, with boughs, here in the way, and cool yourselves in the shade; you and your friends. The best pig and bottle-ale in the Fair, sir. Old Ursula is cook, there you may read; [*Points to the sign, a pig's head, with a large writing under it.*] the pig's head speaks it. Poor soul, she has had a stringhalt, the maryhinchco; but she's prettily amended.

Whit. A delicate show-pig, little mistress, with shweet sauce, and crackling, like de bay-leaf i' de fire, la! tou shalt hea' de clean side o' de tableclot, and di glass vashed with phatersh of Dame Annesh Cleare.[1]

Littlewit [*gazing at the inscription*]. This is fine verily. *Here be the best pigs, and she does roast them as well as ever she did,* the pig's head says.

Knockem. Excellent, excellent, mistress! with fire o' juniper and rosemary branches! the oracle of the pig's head, that, sir.

Purecraft. Son, were you not warned of the vanity of the eye? have you forgot the wholesome admonition so soon?

Littlewit. Good mother, how shall we find a pig, if we do not look about for't! will it run off o' the spit, into our mouths, think you, as in Lubberland, and cry *wee, wee!*

Busy. No, but your mother, religiously-wise conceiveth it may offer itself by other means to the sense, as by way of steam, which I think it doth here in this place—huh, huh— yes, it doth. [*He scents after it like a hound.*] And it were a sin of obstinacy, great obstinacy, high and horrible obstinacy, to decline or resist the good titillation of the famelic sense, which is the smell. Therefore be bold—huh, huh, huh—follow the scent: enter the tents of the unclean, for once, and satisfy your wife's frailty. Let your frail wife

---

[1] There was anciently near Hoxton a spring of water called *Agnes le Clare,* corrupted to *Annis the Clear.*

be satisfied; your zealous mother, and my suffering self, will also be satisfied.

Littlewit. Come, Win, as good winny here as go farther, and see nothing.

Busy. We scape so much of the other vanities, by our early entering.

Purecraft. It is an edifying consideration.

Mrs. Littlewit. This is scurvy, that we must come into the Fair, and not look on't.

Littlewit. Win, have patience, Win, I'll tell you more anon.

[*Exeunt into the booth,* LITTLEWIT, MRS. LITTLEWIT,
BUSY, *and* PURECRAFT.

Knockem. Mooncalf, entertain within there, the best pig in the booth, a pork-like pig. These are Banbury bloods, o' the sincere stud, come a pig-hunting. Whit, wait, Whit, look to your charge.   [*Exit* WHIT.

Busy. [*within.*] A pig prepare presently, let a pig be prepared to us.

Enter MOONCALF *and* URSULA.

Mooncalf. 'Slight, who be these?

Ursula. Is this the good service, Jordan, you'd do me?

Knockem. Why, Urse, why, Urse? thou'lt have vapours i' thy leg again presently, pray thee go in, it may turn to the scratches else.

Ursula. Hang your vapours, they are stale, and stink like you! Are these the guests o' the game you promised to fill my pit withal to-day?

Knockem. Ay, what ail they, Urse?

Ursula. Ail they! they are all sippers, sippers o' the city; they look as they would not drink off two pen'orth of bottle-ale amongst 'em.

Mooncalf. A body may read that in their small printed ruffs.

Knockem. Away, thou art a fool, Urse, and thy Mooncalf too: in your ignorant vapours now! hence; good guests, I say, right hypocrites, good gluttons. In, and set a couple o' pigs on the board, and half a dozen of the biggest bottles afore 'em, and call Whit. [*Exit* MOONCALF.] I do not love

to hear innocents abused: fine ambling hypocrites! and a
stone-puritan with a sorrel head and beard! good mouthed
glutton; two to a pig, away.

Ursula. Are you sure they are such?

Knockem. O' the right breed, thou shalt try 'em by the
teeth, Urse; where's this Whit?

Re-enter WHIT.

Whit.

"Behold, man, and see,
What a worthy man am ee!
With the fury of my sword,
And the shaking of my beard,
I will make ten thousand men afeard."

Knockem. Well said, brave Whit! in, and *fear* the ale
out o' the bottles into the bellies of the brethren, and . . .
the sisters drink to the cause, and pure vapours.

[*Exeunt* KNOCKEM, WHIT, *and* URSULA.

Quarlous. My roarer is turned tapster, methinks. Now
were a fine time for thee, Winwife, to lay aboard thy
widow, thou'lt never be master of a better season or place;
she that will venture herself into the Fair and a pig-box, will
admit any assault, be assured of that.

Winwife. I love not enterprises of that suddenness
though.

Quarlous. I'll warrant thee, then, no wife out of the
widow's hundred: if I had but as much title to her, as to
have breathed once on that straight stomacher of hers, I
would now assure myself to carry her yet ere she went
out of Smithfield; or she should carry me which were the
fitter sight, I confess. But you are a modest undertaker, by
circumstances and degrees; come, 'tis diseases in thee, not
judgment; I should offer at all together.—

Enter OVERDO.

Look, here's the poor fool again, that was stung by the
Wasp erewhile.

Overdo. I will make no more orations shall draw on these

tragical conclusions. And I begin now to think, that by a
spice of collateral justice, Adam Overdo deserved this
beating; for I, the said Adam, was one cause (a by-cause)
why the purse was lost; and my wife's brother's purse too,
which they know not of yet. But I shall make very good
mirth with it at supper, that will be the sport, and put my
little friend Master Humphrey Waspe's choler quite out of
countenance: when, sitting at the upper end of my table, as
I use, and drinking to my brother Cokes, and Mistress Alice
Overdo, as I will, my wife, for their good affection to old
Bradley, I deliver to them, it was I that was cudgelled, and
show them the marks. To see what bad events may peep out
o' the tail of good purposes! the care I had of that civil
young man I took fancy to this morning (and have not left
it yet), drew me to that exhortation, which drew the company indeed; which drew the cutpurse; which drew the
money; which drew my brother Cokes his loss; which drew
on Waspe's anger; which drew on my beating: a pretty
gradation! and they shall have it in their dish, i' faith, at
night for fruit; I love to be merry at my table. I had thought
once, at one special blow he gave me, to have revealed myself; but then (I thank thee, fortitude) I remembered that
a wise man, and who is ever so great a part of the commonwealth in himself, for no particular disaster ought to aban-
don a public good design. The husbandman ought not,
for one unthankful year, to forsake the plough; the shep-
herd ought not, for one scabbed sheep, to throw by his tar-
box; the pilot ought not, for one leak in the poop, to quit
the helm; nor the alderman ought not, for one custard more
at a meal, to give up his cloke; the constable ought not to
break his staff, and forswear the watch, for one roaring
night; nor the piper of the parish, *ut parvis componere
magna solebam,* to put up his pipes for one rainy Sunday.
These are certain knocking conclusions; out of which, I am
resolved, come what come can, come beating, come im-
prisonment, come infamy, come banishment, nay, come
the rack, come the hurdle (welcome all), I will not discover who I am, till my due time; and yet still, all shall
be, as I said ever, in justice' name, and the king's, and for
the commonwealth.

Winwife. What does he talk to himself, and act so seriously, poor fool!

Quarlous. No matter what. Here's fresher argument intend that.

Enter COKES, MISTRESS OVERDO, *and* GRACE WELLBORN,
followed by WASPE, *loaded with toys.*

Cokes. Come, Mistress Grace, come, sister, here's more fine sights yet, i' faith. Od's 'lid where's Numps?

Leatherhead. What do you lack, gentlemen? what is't you buy? fine rattles, drums, babies, little dogs, and birds for ladies? what do you lack?

Cokes. Good honest Numps, keep afore, I am so afraid thou'lt lose somewhat; my heart was at my mouth when I mist thee.

Waspe. You were best buy a whip in your hand to drive me.

Cokes. Nay, do not mistake, Numps; thou art so apt to mistake! I would but watch the goods. Look you now, the treble fiddle was e'en almost like to be lost.

Waspe. Pray you take heed you lose not yourself; your best way were e'en get up and ride for more surety. Buy a token's[1] worth of great pins, to fasten yourself to my shoulder.

Leatherhead. What do you lack, gentlemen? fine purses, pouches, pin-cases, pipes? what is't you lack? a pair o' smiths to wake you in the morning? or a fine whistling bird?

Cokes. Numps, here be finer things than any we have bought by odds! and more delicate horses, a great deal; good Numps, stay, and come hither.

Waspe. Will you scourse[2] with him? you are in Smithfield, you may fit yourself with a fine easy going street-nag, for your saddle, again Michaelmas term, do; has he ne'er a little odd cart for you to make a caroch on in the country, with four pied hobby-horses? Why the measles should you stand here, with your train, cheapning of dogs, birds, and babies? you have no children to bestow them on, have you?

[1] *I.e.*, A farthing's *worth.*
[2] *I.e., deal with* him for his horses?

Cokes. No, but again I have children, Numps, that's all one.

Waspe. Do, do, do, do; how many shall you have, think you? an I were as you, I'd buy for all my tenants too, they are a kind of civil savages, that will part with their children for rattles, pipes, and knives. You were best buy a hatchet or two, and truck with 'em.

Cokes. Good Numps, hold that little tongue o' thine, and save it a labour. I am resolute Bat, thou know'st.

Waspe. A resolute fool you are, I know, and a very sufficient coxcomb; with all my heart;—nay, you have it, sir, an you be angry, t— in your teeth, twice; if I said it not once afore, and much good do you.

Winwife. Was there ever such a self-affliction, and so impertinent?

Quarlous. Alas, his care will go near to crack him; let's in and comfort him.   [*They come forward.*

Waspe. Would I had been set in the ground, all but the head on me, and had my brains bowled at, or threshed out, when first I underwent this plague of a charge!

Quarlous. How now, Numps! almost tired in your protectorship? overparted, overparted?

Waspe. Why, I cannot tell, sir, it may be I am; does it grieve you?

Quarlous. No, I swear does't not, Numps; to satisfy you.

Waspe. Numps! 'sblood, you are fine and familiar: how long have we been acquainted, I pray you!

Quarlous. I think it may be remembered, Numps, that; 'twas since morning, sure.

Waspe. Why, I hope I know't well enough, sir; I did not ask to be told.

Quarlous. No! why, then?

Waspe. It's no matter why; you see with your eyes now, what I said to you to-day: you'll believe me another time?

Quarlous. Are you removing the Fair, Numps?

Waspe. A pretty question, and a civil one! yes, faith, I have my lading, you see, or shall have anon; you may know whose beast I am by my burden. If the pannier-man's jack were ever better known by his loins of mutton, I'll be flayed, and feed dogs for him when his time comes.

Winwife. How melancholic Mistress Grace is yonder! pray thee let's go enter ourselves in grace with her.

Cokes. Those six horses, friend, I'll have——

Waspe. How!

Cokes. And the three Jews-trumps; and half a dozen o' birds, and that drum (I have one drum already) and your smiths; I like that device of your smiths, very pretty well; and four halberts——and, let me see, that fine painted great lady, and her three women for state, I'll have.

Waspe. No, the shop; buy the whole shop, it will be best; the shop, the shop!

Leatherhead. If his worship please.

Waspe. Yes, and keep it during the Fair, Bobchin.

Cokes. Peace, Numps.—Friend, do not meddle with him, an you be wise, and would show your head above board; he will sting thorough your wrought nightcap, believe me. A set of these violins I would buy too, for a delicate young noise I have in the country, that are every one a size less than another, just like your fiddles. I would fain have a fine young masque at my marriage, now I think on't: but I do want such a number of things!—And Numps will not help me now, and I dare not speak to him.

Trash. Will your worship buy any gingerbread, very good bread, comfortable bread?

Cokes. Gingerbread! yes, let's see.

Waspe. There's the t' other springe.

[*Runs to her shop.*

Leatherhead. Is this well, goody Joan, to interrupt my market in the midst, and call away my customers? can you answer this at the Pie-poudres?

Trash. Why, if his mastership has a mind to buy, I hope my ware lies as open as another's; I may show my ware as well as you yours.

Cokes. Hold your peace; I'll content you both. I'll buy up his shop, and thy basket.

Waspe. Will you, i' faith?

Leatherhead. Why should you put him from it, friend.

Waspe. Cry you mercy! you'd be sold too, would you? what's the price on you, jerkin and all, as you stand? have you any qualities?

Trash. Yes, good-man, angry-man, you shall find he has qualities, if you cheapen him.

Waspe. Od's so, you have the selling of him! What are they, will they be bought for love or money?

Trash. No, indeed, sir.

Waspe. For what then, victuals?

Trash. He scorns victuals, sir; he has bread and butter at home, thanks be to God! and yet he will do more for a good meal, if the toy take him in the belly; marry then they must not set him at lower ends, if they do, he'll go away, though he fast: but put him a-top o' the table, where his place is, and he'll do you forty fine things. He has not been sent for, and sought out for nothing, at your great city-suppers, to put down Coriat and Cokely,[1] and been laughed at for his labour; he'll play you all the puppets in the town over, and the players, every company, and his own company too; he spares nobody.

Cokes. I' faith?

Trash. He was the first, sir, that ever baited the fellow in the bear's skin, an't like your worship: no dog ever came near him since. And for fine motions!

Cokes. Is he good at those too? can he set out a masque, trow?

Trash. O lord, master! sought to far and near for his inventions; and he engrosses all, he makes all the puppets in the Fair.

Cokes. Dost thou, in troth, old velvet jerkin? give me thy hand.

Trash. Nay, sir, you shall see him in his velvet jerkin, and a scarf too at night, when you hear him interpret Master Littlewit's motion.

Cokes. Speak no more, but shut up shop presently, friend, I'll buy both it and thee too, to carry down with me; and her hamper beside. Thy shop shall furnish out the masque, and hers the banquet. I cannot go less, to set out anything with credit. What's the price, at a word, of thy whole shop, case and all as it stands?

---

[1] *Coryat* was famous for his travels, an account of which he published under the title of *Coryat's Crudities. Cokely* was the master of a motion or puppet-show.

Leatherhead. Sir, it stands me in six-and-twenty shillings sevenpence halfpenny, besides three shillings for my ground.

Cokes. Well, thirty shillings will do all then! and what comes yours to?

Trash. Four shillings and elevenpence, sir, ground and all, an't like your worship.

Cokes. Yes, it does like my worship very well, poor woman; that's five shillings more: what a masque shall I furnish out, for forty shillings, twenty pound Scotch, and a banquet of gingerbread! there's a stately thing! Numps? sister? and my wedding gloves too! that I never thought on afore! All my wedding gloves, gingerbread? O me! what a device will there be, to make 'em eat their fingers' ends? and delicate brooches for the bridemen and all! and then I'll have this poesie put to them, *For the best grace,* meaning Mistress Grace, my wedding poesie.

Grace. I am beholden to you, sir, and to your Bartholomew wit.

Waspe. You do not mean this, do you? Is this your first purchase?

Cokes. Yes, faith; and I do not think, Numps, but thou'lt say, it was the wisest act that ever I did in my wardship.

Waspe. Like enough! I shall say anything, I!

Enter EDGWORTH, NIGHTINGALE, *and People, followed, at a distance, by* OVERDO.

Overdo. I cannot beget a project, with all my political brain yet: my project is how to fetch off this proper young man from his debauched company. I have followed him all the Fair over, and still I find him with this songster, and I begin shrewdly to suspect their familiarity; and the young man of a terrible taint, poetry! with which idle disease if he be infected, there's no hope of him in a state-course. *Actum est* of him for a commonwealth's-man, if he go to't in rhyme once.   [*Aside.*

Edgworth [*to* NIGHTINGALE]. Yonder he is buying of gingerbread; set in quickly, before he part with too much of his money.

Nightingale [*advancing and singing*]. *My masters and friends, and good people draw near——*

Cokes [*runs to the ballad-man*]. Ballads! hark, hark! pray thee, fellow, stay a little! good Numps, look to the goods. What ballads hast thou? let me see, let me see myself.

Waspe. Why so! he's flown to another lime-bush, there he will flutter as long more; till he have ne'er a feather left. Is there a vexation like this, gentlemen? will you believe me now, hereafter shall I have credit with you?

Quarlous. Yes, faith shalt thou, Numps, and thou art worthy on't, for thou sweatest for't. I never saw a young pimp-errant and his squire better matched.

Winwife. Faith, the sister comes after them well too.

Grace. Nay, if you saw the justice her husband, my guardian, you were fitted for the mess, he is such a wise one his way——

Winwife. I wonder we see him not here.

Grace. O! he is too serious for this place, and yet better sport then than the other three, I assure you, gentlemen, wherever he is, though it be on the bench.

Cokes. How dost thou call it? *A caveat against cutpurses!* a good jest, i' faith, I would fain see that demon, your cutpurse you talk of, that delicate-handed devil; they say he walks hereabout; I would see him walk now. Look you, sister, here, here—[*He shows his purse boastingly*]—let him come, sister, and welcome. Ballad-man, does any cutpurse haunt hereabout? Pray thee raise me one or two; begin, and show me one.

Nightingale. Sir, this is a spell against them, spick and span new; and 'tis made as 'twere in mine own person, and I sing it in mine own defence. But 'twill cost a penny alone, if you buy it.

Cokes. No matter for the price; thou dost not know me, I see, I am an odd Bartholomew.

Mrs. Overdo. Has it a fine picture, brother?

Cokes. O, sister, do you remember the ballads over the nursery chimney at home o' my own pasting up? there be brave pictures, other manner of pictures than these, friend.

Waspe. Yet these will serve to pick the pictures out of your pockets, you shall see.

Cokes. So I heard them say! Pray thee mind him not, fellow; he'll have an oar in everything.

Nightingale. It was intended, sir, as if a purse should chance to be cut in my presence, now, I may be blameless though; as by the sequel will more plainly appear.

Cokes. We shall find that in the matter: pray thee begin.

Nightingale. To the tune of Paggington's pound, sir.

Cokes [*sings*]. *Fa, la la la, la la la, fa la la la!* Nay, I'll put thee in tune and all! mine own country dance! Pray thee begin.

Nightingale. It is a gentle admonition, you must know, sir, both to the purse-cutter and the purse-bearer.

Cokes. Not a word more out of the tune, an thou lov'st me: *Fa, la la la, la la la, fa la la la.* Come, when?

Nightingale [*sings*]. "My masters, and friends, and good
    people, draw near,
And look to your purses, for that I do say;"

Cokes. Ha, ha, this chimes! Good counsel at first dash.

Nightingale. "And tho' little money in them you do bear,
It cost more to get, than to lose in a day."

Cokes. Good!

Nightingale. "You oft have been told,
        Both the young and the old,
And hidden beware of the cutpurse so bold;"

Cokes. Well said! he were to blame that would not, i' faith.

Nightingale. "Then if you take heed not, free me from
    the curse,
Who both give you warning, for, and the cutpurse.
Youth, youth, thou hadst better been starved by thy nurse,
Than live to be hanged for cutting a purse."

Cokes. Good i' faith; how say you, Numps, is there any harm in this?

Nightingale. "It hath been upbraided to men of my trade,
That oftentimes we are the cause of this crime;"

Cokes. The more coxcombs they that did it, I wusse.

Nightingale. "Alack and for pity, why should it be said?
As if they regarded or places, or time!
        Examples have been
        Of some that were seen

In Westminster-hall, yea, the pleaders between;

Then why should the judges be free from this curse,

More than my poor self, for cutting the purse?"

Cokes. God a mercy for that! why should they be more free indeed?

    Nightingale. "Youth, youth, thou hadst better been starved by thy nurse,

Than live to be hanged for cutting a purse."

Cokes. That again, good ballad-man, that again. [*He sings the burden with him.*] O, rare! I would fain rub mine elbow now, but I dare not pull out my hand. On, I pray thee; he that made this ballad shall be poet to my masque.

    Nightingale. "At Worc'ster 'tis known well, and even in the jail,

A knight of good worship did there show his face,

Against the foul sinners, in zeal for to rail,

And lost *ipso facto* his purse in the place."

    Cokes. Is it possible?

    Nightingale. "Nay, once from the seat

          Of judgment so great,

A judge there did lose a fair pouch of velvéte."

    Cokes. I' faith?

    Nightingale. "O Lord for thy mercy, how wicked or worse,

Are those that so venture their necks for a purse!

Youth, youth, thou hadst better been starved by thy nurse,

Than live to be hanged for cutting a purse."

    Cokes [*sings after him*]. *Youth, youth, &c.*—Pray thee stay a little, friend. Yet o' thy conscience, Numps, speak, is there any harm in this?

    Waspe. To tell you true, 'tis too good for you, less you had grace to follow it.

    Overdo. It doth discover enormity, I'll mark it more: I have not liked a paltry piece of poetry so well a good while.   [*Aside.*

    Cokes. Youth, youth, &c.; where's this youth now? a man must call upon him for his own good, and yet he will not appear. Look here, here's for him; [*Shows his purse.*] handy dandy, which hand will he have? On, I pray thee with the rest; I do hear of him, but I cannot see him, this master youth, the cutpurse.

   Nightingale. "At plays, and at sermons, and at the
      sessions,
'Tis daily their practice such booty to make;
Yea, under the gallows at executions,
They stick not the stare-abouts' purses to take.
        Nay, one without grace,
        At a [far] better place,
At court, and in Christmas, before the king's face";

   Cokes. That was a fine fellow! I would have him now.

   Nightingale. "Alack then for pity must I bear the curse,
That only belongs to the cunning cutpurse?"

   Cokes. But where's their cunning now, when they should use it? they are all chained now, I warrant you. [*Sings.*] *Youth, youth, thou hadst better*—The rat-catchers' charms are all fools and asses to this; a pox on them, that they will not come! that a man should have such a desire to a thing, and want it!

   Quarlous. 'Fore God I'd give half the Fair, and 'twere mine, for a cutpurse for him, to save his longing.

   Cokes. Look you, sister, [*shows his purse again*] here, here, where is't now? which pocket is't in, for a wager!

   Waspe. I beseech you leave your wagers, and let him end his matter, an't may be.

   Cokes. O, are you edified, Numps!

   Overdo. Indeed he does interrupt him too much: there Numps spoke to purpose.   [*Aside.*

   Cokes. Sister, I am an ass, I cannot keep my purse! [*Shows it again, and puts it up.*] On, on, I pray thee, friend.

   Nightingale. "Youth, youth, thou hadst better been
      starved by thy nurse,
Than live to be hanged for cutting a purse."

   [*As* NIGHTINGALE *sings,* EDGWORTH *gets up to* COKES *and
     tickles him in the ear with a straw twice to draw
     his hand out of his pocket.*

   Winwife. Will you see sport? look, there's a fellow gathers up to him, mark.

   Quarlous. Good, i' faith! O, he has lighted on the wrong pocket.

Winwife. He has it! 'fore God, he is a brave fellow: pity he should be detected.

Nightingale. "But O, you vile nation of cutpurses all,
Relent and repent, and amend and be sound,
And know that you ought not, by honest men's fall,
Advance your own fortunes, to die above ground;

      And though you go gay,

      In silks, as you may,

It is not the highway to heaven (as they say).
Repent then, repent you, for better, for worse,
And kiss not the gallows for cutting a purse.
Youth, youth, thou hadst better been starved by thy nurse,
Than live to be hanged for cutting a purse."

All. An excellent ballad! an excellent ballad!

Edgworth. Friend, let me have the first, let me have the first, I pray you.

[*As* NIGHTINGALE *reaches out the ballad,* EDGWORTH *slips the purse into his hand.*

Cokes. Pardon me, sir; first come first served; and I'll buy the whole bundle too.

Winwife. That conveyance was better than all, did you see't? he has given the purse to the ballad-singer.

Quarlous. Has he?

Edgworth. Sir, I cry you mercy, I'll not hinder the poor man's profit; pray you, mistake me not.

Cokes. Sir, I take you for an honest gentleman, if that be mistaking; I met you to-day afore: ha! humph! O Lord! my purse is gone, my purse, my purse, my purse!

Waspe. Come, do not make a stir, and cry yourself an ass thorough the Fair afore your time.

Cokes. Why, hast thou it, Numps? good Numps, how came you by it, I marle?

Waspe. I pray you seek some other gamester to play the fool with; you may lose it time enough, for all your Fair wit.

Cokes. By this good hand, glove and all, I have lost it already if thou hast it not; feel else, and Mistress Grace's handkerchief too, of the t'other pocket.

Waspe. Why, 'tis well, very well, exceeding pretty and well.

Edgworth. Are you sure you have lost it, sir?

Cokes. O Lord! yes; as I am an honest man, I had it but e'en now, at *Youth, youth.*

Nightingale. I hope you suspect not me, sir?

Edgworth. Thee! that were a jest indeed! dost thou think the gentleman is foolish? where hadst thou hands, I pray thee? Away, ass, away!   [*Exit* NIGHTINGALE.

Overdo. I shall be beaten again if I be spied.
                                              [*Aside, retiring.*

Edgworth. Sir, I suspect an odd fellow, yonder, is stealing away.

Mrs. Overdo. Brother, it is the preaching fellow: you shall suspect him. He was at your t'other purse, you know! [*Seizes* OVERDO.] Nay, stay, sir, and view the work you have done; an you be beneficed at the gallows, and preach there, thank your own handiwork.

Cokes. Sir, you shall take no pride in your preferment, you shall be silenced quickly.   [*They seize* OVERDO.

Overdo. What do you mean, sweet buds of gentility?

Cokes. To have my pennyworths out on you, bud. No less than two purses a day serve you! I thought you a simple fellow, when my man Numps beat you in the morning, and pitied you.

Mrs. Overdo. So did I. I'll be sworn, brother; but now I see he is a lewd and pernicious enormity, as Master Overdo calls him.

Overdo. Mine own words turned upon me like swords!
                                                        [*Aside.*

Cokes. Cannot a man's purse be at quiet for you in the master's pocket, but you must entice it forth, and debauch it?   [OVERDO *is carried off.*

Waspe. Sir, sir, keep your debauch, and your fine Bartholomew terms to yourself, and make as much on 'em as you please. But give me this from you in the meantime; I beseech you, see if I can look to this.

Cokes. Why, Numps?

Waspe. Why! because you are an ass, sir, there's a reason the shortest way, and you will needs have it: now you have got the trick of losing, you'd lose your breech an 'twere loose. I know you, sir, come, deliver [*takes the box from him*], you'll go and crack the vermin you breed now, will you? 'tis very fine; will you have the truth on't? they are such retchless flies as you are, that blow catpurses abroad in every corner; your foolish having of money makes them. An there were no wiser than I, sir, the trade should lie open for you, sir, it should, i' faith, sir. I would teach your wit to come to your head, sir, as well as your land to come into your hand, I assure you, sir.

Winwife. Alack, good Numps!

Waspe. Nay, gentlemen, never pity me, I am not worth it. Lord send me at home once to Harrow o' the Hill again, if I travel any more, call me Coriat with all my heart.

[*Exeunt* WASPE, COKES, *and* MRS. OVERDO, *followed by* EDGWORTH.

Quarlous [*stops* EDGWORTH]. Stay, sir, I must have a word with you in private. Do you hear?

Edgworth. With me, sir! what's your pleasure, good sir?

Quarlous. Do not deny it, you are a cutpurse, sir, this gentleman here and I saw you: nor do we mean to detect you, though we can sufficiently inform ourselves toward the danger of concealing you; but you must do us a piece of service.

Edgworth. Good gentlemen, do not undo me; I am a civil young man, and but a beginner indeed.

Quarlous. Sir, your beginning shall bring on your ending for us: we are no catchpoles nor constables. That you are to undertake is this; you saw the old fellow with the black box here?

Edgworth. The little old governor, sir?

Quarlous. That same: I see you have flown him to a mark already. I would have you get away that box from him, and bring it us.

Edgworth. Would you have the box and all, sir, or only that that is in't? I'll get you that, and leave him the box to play with still, which will be the harder of the two, because I would gain your worship's good opinion of me.

Winwife. He says well, 'tis the greater mastery, and 'twill make the more sport when 'tis mist.

Edgworth. Ay, and 'twill be the longer a missing, to draw on the sport.

Quarlous. But look you do it, now, sirrah, and keep your word, or——

Edgworth. Sir, if I break my word with a gentleman, may I never read word at my need. Where shall I find you?

Quarlous. Somewhere i' the Fair, hereabouts: dispatch it quickly. [*Exit* EDGWORTH.] I would fain see the careful fool deluded! Of all beasts, I love the serious ass; he that takes pains to be one, and plays the fool with the greatest diligence that can be.

Grace. Then you would not choose, sir, but love my guardian, Justice Overdo, who is answerable to that description in every hair of him.

Quarlous. So I have heard. But how came you, Mistress Wellborn, to be his ward, or have relation to him at first?

Grace. Faith, through a common calamity, he bought me, sir; and now he will marry me to his wife's brother, this wise gentleman that you see; or else I must pay value o' my land.

Quarlous. 'Slid, is there no device of disparagement, or so? talk with some crafty fellow, some picklock of the law: would I had studied a year longer in the Inns of Court, an't had been but in your case.

Winwife. Ay, Master Quarlous, are you proffering!
                                                    [*Aside.*

Grace. You'd bring but little aid, sir.

Winwife. I'll look to you, in faith, gamester.—[*Aside.*] An unfortunate foolish tribe you are fallen into, lady, I wonder you can endure them.

Grace. Sir, they that cannot work their fetters off must wear them.

Winwife. You see what care they have on you, to leave you thus.

Grace. Faith, the same they have of themselves, sir. I cannot greatly complain if this were all the plea I had against them.

Winwife. 'Tis true; but will you please to withdraw with us a little, and make them think they have lost you. I hope our manners have been such hitherto, and our language, as will give you no cause to doubt yourself in our company.

Grace. Sir, I will give myself no cause; I am so secure of mine own manners, as I suspect not yours.

Quarlous. Look where John Littlewit comes.

Winwife. Away, I'll not be seen by him.

Quarlous. No you were not best, he'd tell his mother, the widow.

Winwife. Heart! what do you mean?

Quarlous. Cry you mercy, is the wind there? must not the widow be named?   [*Exeunt.*

Enter LITTLEWIT *from* URSULA'S *booth, followed by* MRS. LITTLEWIT.

Littlewit. Do you hear, Win, Win?

Mrs. Littlewit. What say you, John?

Littlewit. While they are paying the reckoning, Win, I'll tell you a thing, Win; we shall never see any sights in the Fair, Win, except you long still, Win: good Win, sweet Win, long to see some hobby-horses, and some drums and rattles, and dogs, and fine devices, Win. The bull with the five legs, Win; and the great hog. Now you have begun with pig, you may long for anything, Win, and so for my motion, Win.

Mrs. Littlewit. But we shall not eat of the bull and the hog, John; how shall I long, then?

Littlewit. O yes, Win: you may long to see as well as to taste, Win: how did the pothecary's wife, Win, that longed to see the anatomy, Win? or the lady, Win, that desired to spit in the great lawyer's mouth, after an eloquent pleading? I assure you, they longed, Win; good Win, go in and long.   [*Exeunt* LITTLEWIT *and* MRS. LITTLEWIT.

Trash. I think we are rid of our new customer, brother Leatherhead, we shall hear no more of him.

Leatherhead. All the better; let's pack up all and begone, before he find us.

Trash. Stay a little, yonder comes a company; it may be we may take some more money.

Enter KNOCKEM *and* BUSY.

Knockem. Sir, I will take your counsel, and cut my hair,[1] and leave vapours: I see that tobacco, and bottle-ale and pig, and Whit, and very Ursla herself, is all vanity.

Busy. Only pig was not comprehended in my admonition, the rest were: for long hair, it is an ensign of pride, a banner; and the world is full of those banners, very full of banners. And bottle-ale is a drink of Satan's, a diet-drink of Satan's, devised to puff us up, and make us swell in this latter age of vanity; as the smoke of tobacco, to keep us in mist and error: but the fleshly woman, which you call Ursla, is above all to be avoided, having the marks upon her of the three enemies of man; the world, as being in the Fair; the devil, as being in the fire; and the flesh, as being herself.

Enter MRS. PURECRAFT.

Purecraft. Brother Zeal-of-the-land! what shall we do? my daughter Win-the-fight is fallen into her fit of longing again.

Busy. For more pig! there is no more, is there?

Purecraft. To see some sights in the Fair.

Busy. Sister, let her fly the impurity of the place swiftly, lest she partake of the pitch thereof. Thou art the seat of the beast, O Smithfield, and I will leave thee! Idolatry peepeth out on every side of thee.   [*Goes forward.*

Knockem. An excellent right hypocrite! now his belly is full, he falls a railing and kicking, the jade. A very good vapour! I'll in, and joy Ursla, with telling how her pig works; two and a half he eat to his share; and he has drunk a pail-full. He eats with his eyes as well as his teeth. [*Exit.*

Leatherhead. What do you lack, gentlemen? what is't you buy? rattles, drums, babies——

Busy. Peace, with thy apocryphal wares, thou profane publican; thy bells, thy dragons, and thy Tobie's dogs. Thy hobby-horse is an idol, a very idol, a fierce and rank idol; and thou the Nebuchadnezzar, the proud Nebuchadnezzar

[1] Close hair was at this time the distinguishing mark of a Puritan.

of the Fair, that sett'st it up, for children to fall down to, and worship.

Leatherhead. Cry you mercy, sir; will you buy a fiddle to fill up your noise?

Re-enter LITTLEWIT *and his* Wife.

Littlewit. Look, Win, do, look a God's name, and save your longing. Here be fine sights.

Purecraft. Ay, child, so you hate them, as our brother Zeal does, you may look on them.

Leatherhead. Or what do you say to a drum, sir?

Busy. It is the broken belly of the beast, and thy bellows there are his lungs, and these pipes are his throat, those feathers are of his tail, and thy rattles the gnashing of his teeth.

Trash. And what's my gingerbread, I pray you?

Busy. The provender that pricks him up. Hence with thy basket of popery, thy nest of images, and whole legend of ginger-work.

Leatherhead. Sir, if you be not quiet the quicklier, I'll have you clapped fairly by the heels, for disturbing the Fair.

Busy. The sin of the Fair provokes me, I cannot be silent.

Purecraft. Good brother Zeal!

Leatherhead. Sir, I'll make you silent, believe it.

Littlewit. I'd give a shilling you could, i' faith, friend.

[*Aside to* LEATHERHEAD.

Leatherhead. Sir, give me your shilling, I'll give you my shop, if I do not; and I'll leave it in pawn with you in the meantime.

Littlewit. A match, i' faith; but do it quickly then.

[*Exit* LEATHERHEAD.

Busy [*to* MRS. PURECRAFT]. Hinder me not, woman. I was moved in spirit, to be here this day, in this Fair, this wicked and foul Fair; and fitter may it be called a Foul than a Fair; to protest against the abuses of it, the foul abuses of it, in regard of the afflicted saints, that are troubled, very much troubled, exceedingly troubled, with the opening of the merchandise of Babylon again, and the peeping of popery upon the stalls here, here, in the

high places. See you not Goldylocks, the purple strumpet
there, in her yellow gown and green sleeves? the profane
pipes, the tinkling timbrels? a shop of relicks!

[Attempts to seize the toys.

Littlewit. Pray you forbear, I am put in trust with them.

Busy. And this idolatrous grove of images, this flasket
of idols, which I will pull down——

[Overthrows the gingerbread basket.

Trash. O my ware, my ware! God bless it!

Busy. In my zeal, and glory to be thus exercised.

Re-enter LEATHERHEAD, *with* BRISTLE, HAGGISE, *and other
Officers.*

Leatherhead. Here he is, pray you lay hold on his zeal;
we cannot sell a whistle for him in tune. Stop his noise
first.

Busy. Thou canst not; 'tis a sanctified noise. I will make
a loud and most strong noise, till I have daunted the
profane enemy. And for this cause——

Leatherhead. Sir, here's no man afraid of you, or your
cause. You shall swear it in the stocks, sir.

Busy. I will thrust myself into the stocks, upon the pikes
of the land.   *[They seize him.*

Leatherhead. Carry him away.

Purecraft. What do you mean, wicked men?

Busy. Let them alone, I fear them not.

[Exeunt Officers with BUSY, *followed by* DAME PURECRAFT.

Littlewit. Was not this shilling well ventured, Win, for
our liberty? now we may go play, and see over the Fair,
where we list ourselves: my mother is gone after him, and
let her e'en go, and lose us.

Mrs. Littlewit. Yes, John; but I know not what to do.

Littlewit. For what, Win?

Mrs. Littlewit. For a thing I am ashamed to tell you, i'
faith; and 'tis too far to go home.

Littlewit. I pray thee be not ashamed, Win. Come, i'
faith, thou shalt not be ashamed: is it anything about the
hobby-horse man? an't be, speak freely.

Mrs. Littlewit. Hang him, base Bobchin, I scorn him;

no, I have very great what sha' call 'um, John.

[*Whispers him.*

Littlewit. O, is that all, Win? we'll go back to Captain Jordan, to the pig-woman's, Win, he'll help us or she with a dripping-pan, or an old kettle, or something. The poor greasy soul loves you, Win; and after we'll visit the Fair all over, Win, and see my puppet-play, Win; you know it's a fine matter, Win.

[*Exeunt* LITTLEWIT *and* MRS. LITTLEWIT.

Leatherhead. Let's away: I counselled you to pack up afore, Joan.

Trash. A pox of his Bedlam purity! He has spoiled half my ware: but the best is, we lose nothing if we miss our first merchant.

Leatherhead. It shall be hard for him to find or know us, when we are translated, Joan.   [*Exeunt.*

ACT THE FOURTH

SCENE I—*The Fair*

Booths, Stalls, a Pair of Stocks, &c.

Enter COKES, BRISTLE, HAGGISE, *and* POCHER, *with* OVERDO, *followed by* TROUBLEALL.

TROUBLEALL. My masters, I do make no doubt but you are officers.

Bristle. What then, sir?

Troubleall. And the king's loving and obedient subjects.

Bristle. Obedient, friend! take heed what you speak, I advise you; Oliver Bristle advises you. His loving subjects, we grant you; but not his obedient, at this time, by your leave; we know ourselves a little better than so; we are to command, sir, and such as you are to be obedient. Here's one of his obedient subjects going to the stocks; and we'll make you such another, if you talk.

Troubleall. You are all wise enough in your places, I know.

Bristle. If you know it, sir, why do you bring it in question?

Troubleall. I question nothing, pardon me. I do only hope you have warrant for what you do, and so quit you, and so multiply you.   [*Exit.*

Haggise. What is he?—Bring him up to the stocks there. Why bring you him not up?   [OVERDO *is brought forward.*

Re-enter TROUBLEALL.

Troubleall. If you have Justice Overdo's warrant, 'tis well; you are safe: that is the warrant of warrants. I'll not give this button for any man's warrant else.

Bristle. Like enough, sir; but let me tell you, and you play away your buttons thus, you will want them ere night, for any store I see about you; you might keep them, and save pins, I wuss.   [*Exit* TROUBLEALL.

Overdo. What should he be, that doth so esteem and advance my warrant? he seems a sober and discreet person. It is a comfort to a good conscience to be followed with a good fame in his sufferings. The world will have a pretty taste by this, how I can bear adversity; and it will beget a kind of reverence towards me hereafter, even from mine enemies, when they shall see I carry my calamity nobly, and that it doth neither break me, nor bend me.   [*Aside.*

Haggise. Come, sir, here's a place for you to preach in. Will you put in your leg?

Overdo. That I will, cheerfully.

[*They put him in the stocks.*

Bristle. O' my conscience, a seminary![1] he kisses the stocks.

Cokes. Well, my masters, I'll leave him with you; now I see him bestowed, I'll go look for my goods, and Numps.

Haggise. You may, sir, I warrant you: where's the t'other bawler? fetch him too, you shall find them both fast enough.

[*Exit* COKES.

Overdo. In the midst of this tumult, I will yet be the author of mine own rest, and not minding their fury, sit in the stocks in that calm as shall be able to trouble a triumph.   [*Aside.*

---

[1] *I.e.,* A Romish priest educated in the *seminaries* abroad.

Re-enter TROUBLEALL.

Troubleall. Do you assure me upon your words? May I
undertake for you, if I be asked the question, that you
have this warrant?

Haggise. What's this fellow, for God's sake?

Troubleall. Do but show me Adam Overdo, and I am
satisfied.   [*Exit.*

Bristle. He is a fellow that is distracted, they say; one
Troubleall: he was an officer in the court of Pie-poudres
here last year, and put out of his place by Justice Overdo.

Overdo. Ha!   [*Aside.*

Bristle. Upon which he took an idle conceit, and is run
mad upon't: so that ever since he will do nothing but by
Justice Overdo's warrant; he will not eat a crust, nor drink
a little, nor make him in his apparel ready. His wife, sir
reverence, cannot get him make his water, or shift his
shirt, without his warrant.

Overdo. If this be true, this is my greatest disaster. How
am I bound to satisfy this poor man, that is of so good
a nature to me, out of his wits! where there is no room
left for dissembling.   [*Aside.*

Re-enter TROUBLEALL.

Troubleall. If you cannot show me Adam Overdo, I am
in doubt of you; I am afraid you cannot answer it.

[*Exit.*

Haggise. Before me, neighbour Bristle,—and now I think
on't better,—Justice Overdo is a very parantory person.

Bristle. O, are you advised of that! and a severe justicer,
by your leave.

Overdo. Do I hear ill o' that side too?   [*Aside.*

Bristle. He will sit as upright on the bench, an you mark
him, as a candle in the socket, and give light to the whole
court in every business.

Haggise. But he will burn blue, and swell like a boil,
God bless us, and he be angry.

Bristle. Ay, and he will be angry too, when he lists, that's
more; and when he is angry, be it right or wrong, he has
the law on's side ever: I mark that too.

Overdo. I will be more tender hereafter. I see compassion may become a justice, though it be a weakness, I confess, and nearer a vice than a virtue.   [*Aside.*

Haggise. Well, take him out o' the stocks again; we'll go a sure way to work, we'll have the ace of hearts of our side, if we can.   [*They take* Overdo *out.*

Enter Pocher, *and Officers with* Busy, *followed by* Mrs. Purecraft.

Pocher. Come, bring him away to his fellow there.— Master Busy, we shall rule your lags, I hope, though we cannot rule your tongue.

Busy. No, minister of darkness, no; thou canst not rule my tongue; my tongue it is mine own, and with it I will both knock and mock down your Bartholomew abominations, till you be made a hissing to the neighbouring parishes round about.

Haggise. Let him alone, we have devised better upon't.

Purecraft. And shall he not into the stocks then?

Bristle. No, mistress, we'll have them both to Justice Overdo, and let him do over 'em as is fitting; then I, and my gossip Haggise, and my beadle Pocher are discharged.

Purecraft. O, I thank you, blessed honest men!

Bristle. Nay, never thank us; but thank this madman that comes here; he put it in our heads.

Re-enter Troubleall.

Purecraft. Is he mad? now heaven increase his madness, and bless it, and thank it.—Sir, your poor handmaid, thanks you.

Troubleall. Have you a warrant? an you have a warrant, show it.

Purecraft. Yes, I have a warrant out of the word, to give thanks for removing any scorn intended to the brethren.
                                        [*Exeunt all but* Troubleall.

Troubleall. It is Justice Overdo's warrant that I look for; if you have not that, keep your word, I'll keep mine. Quit ye, and multiply ye.

Enter EDGWORTH *and* NIGHTINGALE.

Edgworth. Come away, Nightingale, I pray thee.

Troubleall. Whither go you? where's your warrant.

Edgworth. Warrant! for what, sir?

Troubleall. For what you go about, you know how fit it is; an you have no warrant, bless you, I'll pray for you, that's all I can do.   [*Exit.*

Edgworth. What means he?

Nightingale. A madman that haunts the Fair; do you not know him? It's marvel he has not more followers after his ragged heels.

Edgworth. Beshrew him, he startled me. I thought he had known of our plot. Guilt's a terrible thing. Have you prepared the costardmonger?

Nightingale. Yes, and agreed for his basket of pears; he is at the corner here, ready. And your prize, he comes down sailing that way all alone, without his protector; he is rid of him, it seems.

Edgworth. Ay, I know; I should have followed his protectorship, for a feat I am to do upon him: but this offered itself so in the way, I could not let scape: here he comes, whistle; be this sport called Dorring the Dotterel.

Re-enter COKES.

Nightingale. Wh, wh, wh, wh, &c.   [*Whistles.*

Cokes. By this light, I cannot find my gingerbread wife, nor my hobby-horse man, in all the Fair now, to have my money again: and I do not know the way out on't, to go home for more. Do you hear, friend, you that whistle? what tune is that you whistle?

Nightingale. A new tune I am practising, sir.

Cokes. Dost thou know where I dwell, I pray thee? nay, on with thy tune; I have no such haste for an answer: I'll practise with thee.

Enter Costardmonger *with a basket of Pears.*

Costardmonger. Buy any pears, very fine pears, pears fine! [NIGHTINGALE *sets his foot afore him and he falls with his basket.*

Cokes. Ods so! a muss, a muss, a muss, a muss! [1]

                  [*Falls a scrambling for the pears.*

Costardmonger. Good gentlemen, my ware, my ware; I am a poor man. Good sir, my ware.

Nightingale. Let me hold your sword, sir, it troubles you.

Cokes. Do, and my cloak an thou wilt, and my hat too.

Edgworth. A delicate great boy! methinks he outscrambles them all. I cannot persuade myself but he goes to grammar-school yet, and plays the truant to-day.

Nightingale. Would he had another purse to cut, Zekiel.

Edgworth. Purse! a man might cut out his kidneys, I think, and he never feel 'em, he is so earnest at the sport.

Nightingale. His soul is half-way out on's body at the game.

Edgworth. Away, Nightingale that way.

      [Nightingale *runs off with his sword, cloak, and hat.*

Cokes. I think I am furnished for cather'ne pears, for one undermeal.[2] Give me my cloak.

Costardmonger. Good gentleman, give me my ware.

Cokes. Where's the fellow I gave my cloak to? my cloak and my hat? ha! ods 'lid, is he gone? thieves, thieves! help me to cry, gentlemen.   [*Exit hastily.*

Edgworth. Away, costardmonger, come to us to Ursula's. [*Exit* Costardmonger.] Talk of him to have a soul! 'heart, if he have any more than a thing given him instead of salt, only to keep him from stinking, I'll be hanged afore my time presently: where should it be, trow? in his blood? he has not so much toward it in his whole body as will maintain a good flea! and if he take this course, he will not have so much land left as to rear a calf, within this twelvemonth. Was there ever green plover so pulled! That his little overseer had been here now, and been but tall enough to see him steal pears, in exchange for his beaver hat and his cloak thus! I must go find him out next, for his black box, and his patent, it seems, he has of his place; which I think the gentleman would have a reversion of, that spoke to me for it so earnestly.

                                    [*Exit.*

[1] *I.e.,* A scramble.
[2] *I.e.,* For an afternoon's meal.

Re-enter COKES.

Cokes. Would I might lose my doublet, and hose too, as I am an honest man, and never stir, if I think there be anything but thieving and cozening in this whole Fair. Bartholomew Fair, quoth he! an ever any Bartholomew had that luck in't that I have had, I'll be martyred for him, and in Smithfield too. I have paid for my pears, a rot on 'em! I'll keep them no longer; [*throws away his pears.*] you were choke-pears to me. I had been better have gone to num-chance for you, I wuss. Methinks the Fair should not have used me thus, an 'twere but for my name's-sake. I would not have used a dog o' the name so. O, Numps will triumph now!

Enter TROUBLEALL.

Friend, do you know who I am, or where I lie? I do not myself, I'll be sworn. Do but carry me home, and I'll please thee; I have money enough there. I have lost myself, and my cloak, and my hat, and my fine sword, and my sister, and Numps, and Mistress Grace, a gentlewoman that I should have married, and a cutwork handkerchief she gave me, and two purses, to-day; and my bargain of hobby-horses and gingerbread, which grieves me worst of all.

Troubleall. By whose warrant, sir, have you done all this?

Cokes. Warrant! thou art a wise fellow indeed; as if a man need a warrant to lose anything with.

Troubleall. Yes, Justice Overdo's warrant, a man may get and lose with, I'll stand to't.

Cokes. Justice Overdo! dost thou know him? I lie there; he is my brother-in-law; he married my sister: pray thee show me the way; dost thou know the house?

Troubleall. Sir, show me your warrant: I know nothing without a warrant, pardon me.

Cokes. Why, I warrant thee; come along: thou shalt see I have wrought pillows there, and cambric sheets, and sweet bags too. Pray thee guide me to the house.

Troubleall. Sir, I'll tell you; go you thither yourself first alone, tell your worshipful brother your mind, and but bring me three lines of his hand, or his clerk's, with Adam

Overdo underneath (here I'll stay you), I'll obey you, and I'll guide you presently.

Cokes. 'Slid, this is an ass, I have found him: pox upon me, what do I talking to such a dull fool! farewell! you are a very coxcomb, do you hear?

Troubleall. I think I am; if Justice Overdo sign to it, I am, and so we are all: he'll quit us all, multiply us all.

[*Exeunt.*

SCENE II—*Another part of the Fair*

Enter GRACE, QUARLOUS, *and* WINWIFE, *with their swords drawn.*

Grace. Gentlemen, this is no way that you take; you do but breed one another trouble and offence, and give me no contentment at all. I am no she that affects to be quarrelled for, or have my name or fortune made the question of men's swords.

Quarlous. 'Slood, we love you.

Grace. If you both love me, as you pretend, your own reason will tell you but one can enjoy me: and to that point there leads a directer line, than by my infamy, which must follow if you fight. 'Tis true, I have profest it to you ingenuously, that rather than to be yoked with this bridegroom is appointed me, I would take up any husband almost upon any trust; though subtlety would say to me, I know, he is a fool, and has an estate, and I might govern him, and enjoy a friend beside: but these are not my aims; I must have a husband I must love, or I cannot live with him. I shall ill make one of these politic wives.

Winwife. Why, if you can like either of us, lady, say which is he, and the other shall swear instantly to desist.

Quarlous. Content, I accord to that willingly.

Grace. Sure you think me a woman of an extreme levity, gentlemen, or a strange fancy, that meeting you by chance in such a place as this, both at one instant, and not yet of two hours' acquaintance, neither of you deserving afore the other of me, I should so forsake my modesty (though

I might affect one more particularly) as to say, this is he, and name him.

Quarlous. Why, wherefore should you not? What should hinder you?

Grace. If you would not give it to my modesty, allow it yet to my wit; give me so much of woman and cunning as not to betray myself impertinently. How can I judge of you, so far as to a choice, without knowing you more? You are both equal, and alike to me yet, and so indifferently affected by me, as each of you might be the man, if the other were away: for you are reasonable creatures, you have understanding and discourse; and if fate send me an understanding husband, I have no fear at all but mine own manners shall make him a good one.

Quarlous. Would I were put forth to making for you then.

Grace. It may be you are, you know not what is toward you: will you consent to a motion of mine, gentlemen?

Winwife. Whatever it be we'll presume reasonableness, coming from you.

Quarlous. And fitness too.

Grace. I saw one of you buy a pair of tables e'en now.

Winwife. Yes, here they be, and maiden ones too, unwritten in.

Grace. The fitter for what they may be employed in. You shall write either of you here a word or a name, what you like best, but of two or three syllables at most; and the next person that comes this way, because Destiny has a high hand in business of this nature, I'll demand which of the two words he or she doth approve and according to that sentence fix my resolution and affection without change.

Quarlous. Agreed; my word is conceived already.

Winwife. And mine shall not be long creating after.

Grace. But you shall promise, gentlemen, not to be curious to know which of you it is, taken; but give me leave to conceal that till you have brought me either home or where I may safely tender myself.

Winwife. Why, that's but equal.

Quarlous. We are pleased.

Grace. Because I will bind both your endeavours to work together friendly and jointly each to the other's fortune, and have myself fitted with some means to make him that is forsaken a part of amends.

Quarlous. These conditions are very courteous. Well, my word is out of the *Arcadia,* then; *Argalus*.

Winwife. And mine out of the play; *Palemon*.

[*They write.*

Enter TROUBLEALL.

Troubleall Have you any warrant for this, gentlemen.

Quarlous, Winwife. Ha!

Troubleall. There must be a warrant had, believe it.

Winwife. For what?

Troubleall. For whatsoever it is, anything indeed, no matter what.

Quarlous. 'Slight! here's a fine ragged prophet dropt down i' the nick!

Troubleall. Heaven quit you, gentlemen!

Quarlous. Nay, stay a little: good lady, put him to the question.

Grace. You are content then?

Winwife, Quarlous. Yes, yes.

Grace. Sir, here are two names written——

Troubleall. Is Justice Overdo one?

Grace. How, sir! I pray you read them to yourself; it is for a wager between these gentlemen; and with a stroke, or any difference, mark which you approve best.

Troubleall. They may be both worshipful names for aught I know, mistress; but Adam Overdo had been worth three of them, I assure you in this place, that's in plain English.

Grace. This man amazes me. I pray you like one of them, sir.

Troubleall [*marks the book*]. I do like him there, that has the best warrant, mistress, to save your longing, and (multiply him) it may be this. But I am still for Justice Overdo, that's my conscience; and quit you.

Winwife. Is it done, lady?

Grace. Ay, and strangely as ever I saw: what fellow is this, trow?

Quarlous. No matter what, a fortune-teller we have made him: which is it, which is it?

Grace. Nay, did you not promise not to inquire?

Enter EDGWORTH.

Quarlous. 'Slid, I forgot that, pray you pardon me. Look, here's our Mercury come; the licence arrives in the finest time too! 'tis but scraping out Cokes his name, and 'tis done.

Winwife. How now, lime-twig, hast thou touched?

Edgworth. Not yet, sir; except you would go with me and see it, it is not worth speaking on. The act is nothing without a witness. Yonder he is, your man with the box, fallen into the finest company, and so transported with vapours! they have got in a northern clothier, and one Puppy, a western man, that's come to wrestle before my Lord Mayor anon, and Captain Whit, and one Val Cutting, that helps Captain Jordan to roar, a circling boy; with whom your Numps is so taken that you may strip him of his clothes, if you will. I'll undertake to geld him for you, if you had but a surgeon ready to sear him. And Mistress Justice there is the goodest woman! she does so love them all over in terms of justice and the style of authority, with her hood upright that——I beseech you come away, gentlemen, and see't.

Quarlous. 'Slight, I would not lose it for the Fair; what will you do, Ned?

Winwife. Why, stay hereabout for you: Mistress Wellborn must not be seen.

Quarlous. Do so, and find out a priest in the meantime. I'll bring the licence.—Lead which way is't?

Edgworth. Here, sir, you are on the back o' the booth already; you may hear the noise.   [*Exeunt.*

SCENE III—*Another part of the Fair*

URSULA's *Booth, as before:* KNOCKEM, WHIT, NORTHERN,
PUPPY, CUTTING, WASPE, *and* MRS. OVERDO, *discovered,
all in a state of intoxication.*

Knockem. Whit, bid Val Cutting continue the vapours
for a lift, Whit, for a lift.   [*Aside to* WHIT.

Northern. I'll ne mare, I'll ne mare; the eale's too
meeghty.

Knockem. How now! my galloway nag the staggers, ha!
Whit, give him a slit in the forehead. Cheer up, man; a
needle and thread to stitch his ears. I'd cure him now,
an I had it, with a little butter and garlick, long pepper
and grains. Where's my horn? I'll give him a mash presently, shall take away this dizziness.

Puppy. Why, where are you, zurs? do you vlinch, and
leave us in the zuds now?

Northern. I'll ne mare, I is e'en as vull as a paiper's
bag, by my troth, I.

Puppy. Do my northern cloth zhrink i' the wetting, ha?

Knockem. Why, well said, old flea-bitten;[1] thou'le never
tire, I see.   [*They fall to their vapours again.*

Cutting. No, sir, but he may tire if it please him.

Whit. Who told dee sho, that he vuld never teer, man?

Cutting. No matter who told him so, so long as he
knows.

Knockem. Nay, I know nothing, sir, pardon me there.

Enter behind EDGWORTH *with* QUARLOUS.

Edgworth. They are at it still, sir; this they call vapours.

Whit. He shall not pardon dee, captain; dou shalt not
be pardoned. Pre'dee, shweetheart, do not pardon him.

Cutting. 'Slight, I'll pardon him, an I list, whosoever
says nay to't.

Quarlous. Where's Numps? I miss him.

Waspe. Why I say nay to't.

Quarlous. O, there he is.

[1] A familiar observation of the livery-stable. "A flea-bitten horse never
tires."

Knockem. To what do you say nay, sir?

Waspe. To anything, whatsoever it is, so long as I do not like it.

Whit. Pardon me, little man, dou musht like it a little.

Cutting. No, he must not like it at all, sir; there you are i' the wrong.

Whit. I tink I bee: he musht not like it indeed.

Cutting. Nay, then he both must and will like it, sir, for all you.

Knockem. If he have reason, he may like it, sir.

Whit. By no meensh, captain, upon reason, he may like nothing upon reason.

Waspe. I have no reason, nor I will hear of no reason, nor I will look for no reason, and he is an ass that either knows any, or looks for't from me.

Cutting. Yes, in some sense you may have reason, sir.

Waspe. Ay, in some sense, I care not if I grant you.

Whit. Pardon me, thou ougsht to grant him nothing in no shensh, if dou do love dyshelf, angry man.

Waspe. Why then, I do grant him nothing: and I have no sense.

Cutting. 'Tis true, thou hast no sense indeed.

Waspe. 'Slid, but I have sense, now I think on't better, and I will grant him anything, do you see.

Knockem. He is in the right, and does utter a sufficient vapour.

Cutting. Nay, it is no sufficient vapour neither, I deny that.

Knockem. Then it is a sweet vapour.

Cutting. It may be a sweet vapour.

Waspe. Nay, it is no sweet vapour neither, sir, it stinks, and I'll stand to't.

Whit. Yes, I tink it dosh shtink, captain: all vapour dosh shtink.

Waspe. Nay, then it does not stink, sir, and it shall not stink.

Cutting. By your leave, it may, sir.

Waspe. Ay, by my leave it may stink, I know that.

Whit. Pardon me, thou knowesht nothing, it cannot by thy leave, angry man.

Waspe. How can it not?

Knockem. Nay, never question him, for he is in the right.

Whit. Yesh, I am in de right, I confesh it, so ish de little man too.

Waspe. I'll have nothing confest that concerns me. I am not in the right, nor never was in the right, nor never will be in the right, while I am in my right mind.

Cutting. Mind! why, here's no man minds you, sir, nor anything else.   [*They drink again.*

Puppy. Vriend, will you mind this that we do?

                    [*Offering* NORTHERN *the cup.*

Quarlous. Call you this vapours! this is such belching of quarrel as I never heard. Will you mind your business, sir?

Edgworth. You shall see, sir.   [*Goes up to* WASPE.

Northern. I'll ne mare, my waimb warkes too mickle with this auready.

Edgworth. Will you take that, Master Waspe, that nobody should mind you?

Waspe. Why, what have you to do? is't any matter to you?

Edgworth. No, but methinks you should not be unminded, though.

Waspe. Nor I wu' not be, now I think on't. Do you hear, new acquaintance? does no man mind me, say you?

Cutting. Yes, sir, every man here minds you, but how?

Waspe. Nay, I care as little how as you do; that was not my question.

Whit. No, noting was ty question, tou art a learned man, and I am a valiant man, i' faith la, tou shalt speak for me, and I will fight for tee.

Knockem. Fight for him, Whit! a gross vapour, he can fight for himself.

Waspe. It may be I can, but it may be I wu' not, how then?

Cutting. Why, then you may choose.

Waspe. Why, then I'll choose whether I choose or no.

Knockem. I think you may, and 'tis true; and I allow it for a resolute vapour.

Waspe. Nay then, I do think you do not think, and it is no resolute vapour.

Cutting. Yes, in some sort he may allow you.

Knockem. In no sort, sir, pardon me, I can allow him nothing. You mistake the vapour.

Waspe. He mistakes nothing, sir, in no sort.

Whit. Yes, I pre dee now, let him mistake.

Waspe. A t— in your teeth, never pre dee me, for I will have nothing mistake.

Knockem. T—! ha, t—? a noisome vapour: strike, Whit.

[*Aside to* WHIT.

[*They fall together by the ears, while* EDGWORTH *steals the licence out of the box, and exit.*

Mrs. Overdo. Why, gentlemen, why, gentlemen, I charge you upon my authority, conserve the peace. In the king's name, and my husband's, put up your weapons, I shall be driven to commit you myself else.

Quarlous. Ha, ha, ha!

Waspe. Why do you laugh, sir?

Quarlous. Sir, you'll allow me my Christian liberty. I may laugh, I hope.

Cutting. In some sort you may, and in some sort you may not, sir.

Knockem. Nay, in some sort, sir, he may neither laugh nor hope in this company.

Waspe. Yes, then he may both laugh and hope in any sort, an't please him.

Quarlous. Faith, and I will then, for it doth please me exceedingly.

Waspe. No exceeding neither, sir.

Knockem. No, that vapour is too lofty.

Quarlous. Gentlemen, I do not play well at your game of vapours, I am not very good at it, but——

Cutting [*draws a circle on the ground*]. Do you hear, sir? I would speak with you in circle.

Quarlous. In circle, sir! what would you with me in circle?

Cutting. Can you lend me a piece, a Jacobus, in circle?

Quarlous. 'Slid, your circle will prove more costly than your vapours, then. Sir, no, I lend you none.

Cutting. Your beard's not well turned up, sir.

Quarlous. How, rascal! are you playing with my beard? I'll break circle with you.   [*They all draw and fight.*

Puppy, Northern. Gentlemen, gentlemen!

Knockem [*aside to Whit*]. Gather up, Whit, gather up, Whit, good vapours.

> [*Exit, while* WHIT *takes up the swords, cloaks, &c.,*
> *and conceals them.*

Mrs. Overdo. What mean you? are you rebels, gentlemen? shall I send out a serjeant-at-arms, or a writ of rebellion against you? I'll commit you upon my womanhood, for a riot, upon my justice-hood, if you persist.

> [*Exeunt* QUARLOUS *and* CUTTING.

Waspe. Upon my justice-hood! marry s— o' your hood: you'll commit! spoke like a true justice of peace's wife indeed, and a fine female lawyer! t— in your teeth for a fee, now.

Mrs. Overdo. Why, Numps, in Master Overdo's name I charge you.

Waspe. Good Mistress Underdo, hold your tongue.

Mrs. Overdo. Alas, poor Numps!

Waspe. Alas! and why *alas* from you, I beseech you? or why *poor* Numps, goody Rich? Am I come to be pitied by your tuft-taffata now? Why, mistress, I knew Adam the clerk, your husband, when he was Adam Scrivener,[1] and writ for twopence a sheet, as high as he bears his head now, or you your hood, dame——

Enter BRISTLE *and other* Watchmen.

What are you, sir?

Bristle. We be men, and no infidels; what is the matter here, and the noises, can you tell?

Waspe. Heart, what ha' you to do? cannot a man quarrel in quietness, but he must be put out on't by you? what are you?

Bristle. Why, we be his majesty's watch, sir.

Waspe. Watch! 'sblood, you are a sweet watch indeed. A body would think, an you watched well a-nights, you should be contented to sleep at this time a-day. Get you to your

---

[1] Numps had been reading Chaucer, who addresses his amanuensis by this name:

> "Adam Scrivenere, if ever it the befalle,
> Boece or Troiles for to write new," &c.

fleas and your flock-beds, you rogues, your kennels, and
lie down close.

Bristle. Down! yes, we will down, I warrant you: down
with him; in his majesty's name, down, down with him,
and carry him away to the pigeon-holes.

[*Some of the* Watch *seizes* WASPE, *and carry him off.*

Mrs. Overdo. I thank you, honest friends, in the behalf o'
the crown, and the peace, and in Master Overdo's name, for
suppressing enormities.

Whit. Stay, Bristle, here ish anoder brash of drunkards,
but very quiet, special drunkards, will pay de five shillings
very well. [*Points to* NORTHERN *and* PUPPY, *drunk and
asleep on the bench.*] Take 'em to de, in de graish o' God:
one of hem do's change cloth for ale in the Fair here; te
toder ish a strong man, a mighty man, my Lord Mayor's
man, and a wrastler. He has wrashled so long with the
bottle here, that the man with the beard hash almosht streek
up his heelsh.

Bristle. 'Slid, the clerk o' the market has been to cry him
all the Fair over here, for my lord's service.

Whit. Tere he ish, pre de taik him hensh, and make ty
best on him. [*Exeunt* BRISTLE *and the rest of the* Watch *with*
NORTHERN *and* PUPPY.]—How now, woman o'shilk, vot ailsh
ty shweet faish? art tou melancholy?

Mrs. Overdo. A little distempered with these enormities.
Shall I entreat a courtesy of you, captain?

Whit. Entreat a hundred, velvet voman, I vill do it,
shpeak out.

Mrs. Overdo. I cannot with modesty speak it out, but——
[*Whispers him.*

Whit. I vill do it, and more and more, for de. What
Ursla, an't be bitch, an't be bawd, an't be!

Enter URSULA.

Ursula. How now, rascal; what roar you for, old pimp?

Whit. Here, put de cloaks, Ursh; de purchase. Pre de
now, shweet Ursh, help dis good brave voman to a jordan,
an't be.

Ursula. 'Slid, call your Captain Jordan to her, can you
not?

Whit. Nay, pre de leave dy consheits, and bring the velvet woman to de——

Ursula. I bring her! hang her: heart, must I find a common pot for every punk in your purlieus?

Whit. O, good voordsh, Ursh, it ish a guest o' velvet, i' fait la.

Ursula. Let her sell her hood, and buy a sponge, with a pox to her! my vessel is employed, sir. I have but one, and 'tis the bottom of an old bottle. An honest proctor and his wife are at it within; if she'll stay her time, so.
                                                                    [*Exit.*

Whit. As soon as tou cansht, shweet Ursh. Of a valiant man I tink I am te patientsh man i' the world, or in all Smithfield.

Re-enter KNOCKEM.

Knockem. How now, Whit! close vapours, stealing your leaps! covering in corners, ha!

Whit. No, fait, captain, dough tou beesht a vishe man, dy vit is a mile hence now. I was procuring a shmall courtesie for a woman of fashion here.

Mrs. Overdo. Yes, captain, though I am a justice of peace's wife, I do love men of war, and the sons of the sword, when they come before my husband.

Knockem. Sayst thou so, filly? thou shalt have a leap presently, I'll horse thee myself else.

Ursula [*within*]. Come, will you bring her in now, and let her take her turn?

Whit. Grammercy, good Ursh, I tank de.

Mrs. Overdo. Master Overdo shall thank her.   [*Exit.*

Re-enter URSULA, *followed by* LITTLEWIT *and* MRS. LITTLEWIT.

Littlewit. Good ga'mere Urse, Win and I are exceedingly beholden to you, and to Captain Jordan, and Captain Whit.—Win, I'll be bold to leave you in this good company, Win; for half an hour or so, Win; while I go and see how my matter goes forward, and if the puppets be perfect; and then I'll come and fetch you, Win.

Mrs. Littlewit. Will you leave me alone with two men, John?

Littlewit. Ay, they are honest gentlemen, Win, Captain Jordan and Captain Whit; they'll use you very civilly, Win. God be wi' you, Win.   [*Exit.*

Ursula. What, is her husband gone?

Knockem. On his false gallop, Urse, away.

Ursula. An you be right Bartholomew birds, now show yourselves so: we are undone for want of fowl in the Fair here. Here will be Zekiel Edgworth, and three or four gallants with him at night, and I have neither plover nor quail for them: persuade this between you two, to become a bird o' the game, whilst I work the velvet woman within, as you call her.

Knockem. I conceive thee, Ursula: go thy ways. [*Exit* URSULA.] Dost thou hear, Whit? is't not pity, my delicate dark chestnut here, with the fine lean head, large forehead, round eyes, even mouth, sharp ears, long neck, thin crest, close withers, plain back, deep sides, short fillets, and full flanks; with a round belly, a plump buttock, large thighs, knit knees, straight legs, short pasterns, smooth hoofs, and short heels, should lead a full honest woman's life, that might live the life of a lady?

Whit. Yes, by my fait and trot it is, captain; de honest woman's life is a scurvy dull life indeed, la.

Mrs. Littlewit. How, sir, is an honest woman's life a scurvy life?

Whit. Yes fait, shweetheart, believe him, de leef of a bond-woman! but if dou vilt hearken to me, I vill make tee a free woman and a lady; dou shalt live like a lady, as te captain saish.

Knockem. Ay, and be honest too sometimes; have her wires and her tires, her green gowns and velvet petticoats.

Whit. Ay, and ride to Ware and Rumford in dy coash, shee de players, be in love vit 'em: sup vit gallantsh, be drunk, and cost de noting.

Knockem. Brave vapours!

Whit. And lie by twenty on 'em, if dou pleash, shweetheart.

Mrs. Littlewit. What, and be honest still! that were fine sport.

Whit. Tish common, shweetheart, tou mayst do it by my hand: it shall be justified to thy husband's faish, now: tou shalt be as honesht as the skin between his hornsh, la.

Knockem. Yes, and wear a dressing, top and top-gallant, to compare with e'er a husband on 'em all, for a foretop: it is the vapour of spirit in the wife to cuckold nowadays, as it is the vapour of fashion in the husband not to suspect. Your prying cat-eyed citizen is an abominable vapour.

Mrs. Littlewit. Lord, what a fool have I been!

Whit. Mend then, and do everything like a lady hereafter; never know ty husband from another man.

Knockem. Nor any one man from another, but in the dark.

Whit. Ay, and then it ish no digsrash to know any man.

Ursula [within]. Help, help here!

Knockem. How now? what vapour's there?

Re-enter URSULA.

Ursula. O, you are a sweet ranger, and look well to your walks! Yonder is your punk of Turnbull, ramping Alice, has fallen upon the poor gentlewoman within, and pulled her hood over her ears, and her hair through it.

Enter ALICE, *beating and driving in* MRS. OVERDO.

Mrs. Overdo. Help, help, in the king's name!

Alice. A mischief on you, they are such as you are that undo us and take our trade from us, with your tuft-taffata haunches.

Knockem. How now, Alice!

Alice. The poor common whores can have no traffic for the privy rich ones; your caps and hoods of velvet call away our customers, and lick the fat from us.

Ursula. Peace, you foul ramping jade, you——

Alice. Od's foot, you bawd in grease, are you talking?

Knockem. Why, Alice, I say.

Alice. Thou sow of Smithfield, thou!

Ursula. Thou tripe of Turnbull!

Knockem. Cat-a-mountain vapours, ha!

Ursula. You know where you were tawed lately; both lashed and slashed you were in Bridewell.

Alice. Ay, by the same token you rid that week,[1] and broke out the bottom of the cart, night-tub.

Knockem. Why, lion face, ha! do you know who I am? shall I tear ruff, slit waistcoat, make rags of petticoat, ha! go to, vanish for fear of vapours. Whit, a kick, Whit, in the parting vapour. [*They kick out* ALICE.] Come, brave woman, take a good heart, thou shalt be a lady too.

Whit. Yes, fait, dey shall all both be ladies, and write madam: I vill do't myself for dem. Do is the word, and D is the middle letter of madam, D D, put 'em together, and make deeds, without which all words are alike, la!

Knockem. 'Tis true: Ursula, take them in, open thy wardrobe, and fit them to their calling. Green gowns, crimson petticoats, green women, my lord mayor's green women! guests o' the game, true bred. I'll provide you a coach to take the air in.

Mrs. Littlewit. But do you think you can get one?

Knockem. O, they are common as wheelbarrows where there are great dunghills. Every pettifogger's wife has 'em; for first he buys a coach that he may marry, and then he marries that he may be made cuckold in't: for if their wives ride not to their cuckolding, they do them no credit. [*Exeunt* URSULA, MRS. LITTLEWIT, *and* MRS. OVERDO.] *Hide and be hidden, ride and be ridden,* says the vapour of experience.

Enter TROUBLEALL.

Troubleall. By what warrant does it say so?

Knockem. Ha, mad child o' the Pie-poudres! art thou there? fill us a fresh can, Urse, we may drink together.

Troubleall. I may not drink without a warrant, captain.

Knockem. 'Slod, thou'll not stale without a warrant shortly. Whit, give me pen, ink, and paper, I'll draw him a warrant presently.

Troubleall. It must be Justice Overdo's.

Knockem. I know, man; fetch the drink, Whit.

[1] *I.e.,* you were carted for a bawd.

Whit. I pre dee now, be very brief, captain; for de new ladies stay for dee.

> [*Exit, and re-enters with a can.*

Knockem. O, as brief as can be, here 'tis already. [*Gives* TROUBLEALL *a paper.*] *Adam Overdo.*

Troubleall. Why, now I'll pledge you, captain.

Knockem. Drink it off, I'll come to thee anon again.

> [*Exeunt.*

SCENE IV—*The back of* URSULA'S *Booth.* OVERDO
in the Stocks, People, &c.

Enter QUARLOUS *with the licence, and* EDGWORTH.

Quarlous. Well, sir, you are now discharged; beware of being spied hereafter.

Edgworth. Sir, will it please you enter in here at Ursula's, and take part of a silken gown, a velvet petticoat, or a wrought smock; I am promised such, and I can spare a gentleman a moiety.

Quarlous. Keep it for your companions in beastliness, I am none of them, sir. If I had not already forgiven you a greater trespass, or thought you yet worth my beating, I would instruct your manners to whom you made your offers. But go your ways, talk not to me, the hangman is only fit to discourse with you; the hand of beadle is too merciful a punishment for your trade of life. [*Exit* EDG-WORTH.] I am sorry I employed this fellow, for he thinks me such; *facinus quos inquinat, æquat.* But it was for sport; and would I make it serious, the getting of this licence is nothing to me, without other circumstances concur. I do think how impertinently I labour, if the word be not mine that the ragged fellow marked; and what advantage I have given Ned Winwife in this time now of working her, though it be mine. He'll go near to form to her what a debauched rascal I am, and fright her out of all good conceit of me. I should do so by him, I am sure, if I had the opportunity. But my hope is in her temper yet; and it must needs be next to despair, that is grounded on any part of a woman's discretion. I would give, by my troth

now, all I could spare, to my clothes and my sword, to
meet my tattered soothsayer again, who was my judge in
the question, to know certainly whose word he has damned
or saved; for till then I live but under a reprieve. I must
seek him. Who be these?

Enter BRISTLE *and some of the* Watch, *with* WASPE.

Waspe. Sir, you are a Welsh cuckold, and a prating runt,
and no constable.

Bristle. You say very well.—Come, put in his leg in the
middle roundel, and let him hole there.

                                        [*They put him in the stocks.*

Waspe. You stink of leeks, metheglin, and cheese, you
rogue.

Bristle. Why, what is that to you, if you sit sweetly in the
stocks in the meantime? if you have a mind to stink too,
your breeches sit close enough to your bum. Sit you merry,
sir.

Quarlous. How now, Numps?

Waspe. It is no matter how; pray you look off.

Quarlous. Nay, I'll not offend you, Numps; I thought you
had sat there to be seen.

Waspe. And to be sold, did you not? pray you mind your
business, an you have any.

Quarlous. Cry you mercy, Numps; does your leg lie high
enough?

Enter HAGGISE.

Bristle. How now, neighbour Haggise, what says Justice
Overdo's worship to the other offenders?

Haggise. Why, he says just nothing; what should he say,
or where should he say? He is not to be found, man; he
has not been seen in the Fair here all this livelong day,
never since seven o'clock i' the morning. His clerks know
not what to think on't. There is no court of Pie-poudres
yet. Here they be returned.

Enter others of the Watch *with* BUSY.

Bristle. What shall be done with them then, in your discretion?

Haggise. I think we were best put them in the stocks in discretion (there they will be safe in discretion) for the valour of an hour, or such a thing, till his worship come.

Bristle. It is but a hole matter if we do, neighbour Haggise; come, sir [*to* WASPE] here is company for you: heave up the stocks.

[*As they open the stocks,* WASPE *puts his shoe on his hand, and slips it in for his leg.*

Waspe. I shall put a trick upon your Welsh diligence perhaps.   [*Aside.*

Bristle. Put in your leg, sir.   [*To* BUSY.

Quarlous. What, Rabbi Busy! is he come?

Busy. I do obey thee; the lion may roar, but he cannot bite. I am glad to be thus separated from the heathen of the land, and put apart in the stocks, for the holy cause.

Waspe. What are you, sir?

Busy. One that rejoiceth in his affliction, and sitteth here to prophesy the destruction of fairs and May-games, wakes and Whitsun-ales, and doth sigh and groan for the reformation of these abuses.

Waspe [*to* OVERDO]. And do you sigh and groan too, or rejoice in your affliction?

Overdo. I do not feel it, I do not think of it, it is a thing without me. Adam, thou art above these batteries, these contumelies. *In te manca ruit fortuna,* as thy friend Horace says; thou art one, *Quem neque pauperies, neque mors, neque vincula terrent.* And therefore, as another friend of thine says, I think it be thy friend Persius, *Non te quæsiveris extra.*

Quarlous. What's here! a stoic in the stocks? the fool is turned philosopher.

Busy. Friend, I will leave to communicate my spirit with you, if I hear any more of those superstitious relics, those lists of Latin, the very rags of Rome, and patches of Popery.

Waspe. Nay, an you begin to quarrel, gentlemen, I'll leave you. I have paid for quarrelling too lately: look you, a device, but shifting in a hand for a foot. God be wi' you.
                                                      [*Slips out his hand.*

Busy. Wilt thou then leave thy brethren in tribution?

Waspe. For this once, sir.   [*Exit, running.*

Busy. Thou art a halting neutral: stay him there, stop him, that will not endure the heat of persecution.

Bristle. How now, what's the matter?

Busy. He is fled, he is fled, and dares not sit it out.

Bristle. What, has he made an escape! which way? follow, neighbour Haggise.   [*Exeunt* HAGGISE *and* Watch.

Enter DAME PURECRAFT.

Purecraft. O me, in the stocks! have the wicked prevailed?

Busy. Peace, religious sister, it is my calling, comfort yourself; an extraordinary calling, and done for my better standing, my surer standing, hereafter.

Enter TROUBLEALL, *with a can.*

Troubleall. By whose warrant, by whose warrant, this?

Quarlous. O, here's my man dropt in I looked for.

Overdo. Ha!

Purecraft. O, good sir, they have set the faithful here to be wondered at; and provided holes for the holy of the land.

Troubleall. Had they warrant for it? showed they Justice Overdo's hand? if they had no warrant, they shall answer it.

Re-enter HAGGISE.

Bristle. Sure you did not lock the stocks sufficiently, neighbour Toby.

Haggise. No! see if you can lock them better.

Bristle. They are very sufficiently locked, and truly; yet something is the matter.

Troubleall. True; your warrant is the matter that is in question; by what warrant?

Bristle. Madman, hold your peace, I will put you in his room else, in the very same hole, do you see?

Quarlous. How, is he a madman!

Troubleall. Show me Justice Overdo's warrant, I obey you.

Haggise. You are a mad fool, hold your tongue.
          [*Exeunt* HAGGISE *and* BRISTLE.

Troubleall. In Justice Overdo's name, I drink to you, and here's my warrant. [*Shows his can.*

Overdo. Alas, poor wretch! how it yearns my heart for him. [*Aside.*

Quarlous. If he be mad, it is in vain to question him. I'll try him though—Friend, there was a gentlewoman showed you two names some hours since, Argalus and Palemon, to mark in a book; which of them was it you marked.

Troubleall. I mark no name but Adam Overdo, that is the name of names, he only is the sufficient magistrate; and that name I reverence, show it me.

Quarlous. This fellow's mad indeed: I am further off now than afore.

Overdo. I shall not breathe in peace till I have made him some amends. [*Aside.*

Quarlous. Well, I will make another use of him is come in my head: I have a nest of beards in my trunk, one something like his.

Re-enter BRISTLE *and* HAGGISE.

Bristle. This mad fool has made me that I know not whether I have locked the stocks or no: I think I locked them. [*Tries the locks.*

Troubleall. Take Adam Overdo in your mind, and fear nothing.

Bristle. 'Slid, madness itself! hold thy peace, and take that. [*Strikes him.*

Troubleall. Strikest thou without a warrant? take thou that.

[*They fight, and leave open the stocks in the scuffle.*]

Busy. We are delivered by miracle; fellow in fetters, let us not refuse the means; this madness was of the spirit: the malice of the enemy hath mocked itself.

[*Exeunt* BUSY *and* OVERDO.

Purecraft. Mad do they call him! the world is mad in error, but he is mad in truth: I loved him o' the sudden (the cunning man said all true) and shall love him more and more. How well it becomes a man to be mad in truth! O that I might be his yoke-fellow, and be mad with him, what a many should we draw to madness in truth with us!

[*Exit.*

Bristle. How now, all scaped! where's the woman? it is
witchcraft! her velvet hat is a witch, o' my conscience, or
my key! the one.—The madman was a devil, and I am
an ass; so bless me, my place, and mine office!

[*Exit, affrighted.*

ACT THE FIFTH

SCENE I—*The Fair, as before. A Booth*

LANTHORN LEATHERHEAD, *dressed as a puppet showman*,
FILCHER, *and* SHARKWELL *with a flag.*

LEATHERHEAD. Well, luck and Saint Bartholomew! out with
the sign of our invention, in the name of wit, and do you
beat the drum the while: all the foul i' the Fair, I mean all
the dirt in Smithfield,—that's one of Master Littlewit's
carwhitchets now—will be thrown at our banner to-day, if
the matter does not please the people. O, the motions that I,
Lanthorn Leatherhead, have given light to, in my time,
since my Master Pod died! Jerusalem was a stately thing,
and so was Nineveh, and the City of Norwich, and Sodom
and Gomorrah, with the rising of the prentices, and pulling
down the bawdy-houses there upon Shrove Tuesday; but the
Gunpowder Plot, there was a getpenny? I have presented
that to an eighteen or twentypence audience, nine times in
an afternoon. Your home-born projects prove ever the best,
they are so easy and familiar; they put too much learning
in their things now o' days: and that I fear will be the spoil
of this. Littlewit! I say, Micklewit! if not too mickle! look
to your gathering there, goodman Filcher.

Filcher. I warrant you, sir.

Leatherhead. An there comes any gentlefolks, take twopence apiece, Sharkwell.

Sharkwell. I warrant you, sir, threepence an we can.

[*Exeunt.*

SCENE II—*Another part of the Fair*

Enter OVERDO, *disguised like a Porter.*

Overdo. This latter disguise, I have borrowed of a porter, shall carry me out to all my great and good ends; which however interrupted, were never destroyed in me: neither is the hour of my severity yet come to reveal myself, wherein, cloud-like, I will break out in rain and hail, lightning and thunder, upon the head of enormity. Two main works I have to prosecute: first, one is to invent some satisfaction for the poor kind wretch, who is out of his wits for my sake and yonder I see him coming, I will walk aside and project for it.

Enter WINWIFE *and* GRACE.

Winwife. I wonder where Tom Quarlous is, that he returns not; it may be he is struck in here to seek us.

Grace. See, here's our madman again.

Enter QUARLOUS, *in* TROUBLEALL'S *clothes, followed by* DAME PURECRAFT.

Quarlous. I have made myself as like him as his gown and cap will give me leave.

Purecraft. Sir, I love you, and would be glad to be mad with you in truth.

Winwife. How! My widow in love with a madman?

Purecraft. Verily, I can be as mad in spirit as you.

Quarlous. By whose warrant? leave your canting. Gentlewoman, have I found you? [*To* MISTRESS GRACE.] Save ye, quit ye, and multiply ye! Where's your book? 'twas a sufficient name I marked, let me see't, be not afraid to show't me.

Grace. What would you with it, sir?

Quarlous. Mark it again and again at your service.

Grace. Here it is, sir, this was it you marked.

Quarlous. Palemon! fare you well, fare you well.

Winwife. How, Palemon!

Grace. Yes, faith, he has discovered it to you now, and

therefore 'twere vain to disguise it longer; I am yours, sir,
by the benefit of your fortune.

Winwife. And you have him, mistress, believe it, that shall
never give you cause to repent her benefit; but make you
rather to think that in this choice she had both her eyes.

Grace. I desire to put it to no danger of protestation.

[*Exeunt* GRACE *and* WINWIFE.

Quarlous. Palemon the word, and Winwife the man!

Purecraft. Good sir, vouchsafe a yoke-fellow in your madness, shun not one of the sanctified sisters, that would draw
with you in truth.

Quarlous. Away, you are a herd of hypocritical proud
ignorants, rather wild than mad; fitter for woods, and the
society of beasts, than houses, and the congregation of men.
You are the second part of the society of canters, outlaws to
order and discipline, and the only privileged church-
robbers of Christendom. Let me alone: *Palemon* the word,
and Winwife the man!

Purecraft. I must uncover myself unto him, or I shall
never enjoy him, for all the cunning men's promises.
[*Aside.*] Good sir, hear me, I am worth six thousand pound,
my love to you is become my rack; I'll tell you all and
the truth, since you hate the hypocrisy of the party-coloured
brotherhood. These seven years I have been a wilful holy
widow, only to draw feasts and gifts from my entangled
suitors: I am also by office an assisting sister of the deacons,
and a devourer, instead of a distributor of the alms. I am
a special maker of marriages for our decayed brethren with
our rich widows, for a third part of their wealth, when
they are married, for the relief of the poor elect: as also
our poor handsome young virgins, with our wealthy
bachelors or widowers; to make them steal from their
husbands, when I have confirmed them in the faith, and
got all put into their custodies. And if I have not my
bargain, they may sooner turn a scolding drab into a
silent minister, than make me leave pronouncing reproba-
tion and damnation unto them. Our elder, Zeal-of-the-land,
would have had me, but I know him to be the capital knave
of the land, making himself rich by being made a feoffe
in trust to deceased brethren, and cozening their heirs by

swearing the absolute gift of their inheritance. And thus having eased my conscience, and uttered my heart with the tongue of my love; enjoy all my deceits together, I beseech you. I should not have revealed this to you, but that in time I think you are mad, and I hope you'll think me so too, sir?

Quarlous. Stand aside, I'll answer you presently. [*He walks by.*] Why should I not marry this six thousand pound, now I think on't, and a good trade too that she has beside, ha? The t'other wench Winwife is sure of; there's no expectation for me there. Here I may make myself some saver yet, if she continue mad, there's the question. It is money that I want, why should not I marry the money when 'tis offered me? I have a licence and all, it is but razing out one name, and putting in another. There's no playing with a man's fortune! I am resolved: I were truly mad an I would not!—Well, come your ways, follow me, an you will be mad, I'll show you a warrant.   [*Takes her along with him.*

Purecraft. Most zealously, it is that I zealously desire.

Overdo [*stopping him*]. Sir, let me speak with you.

Quarlous. By those warrant?

Overdo. The warrant that you tender, and respect so; Justice Overdo's. I am the man, friend Troubleall, though thus disguised (as the careful magistrate ought) for the good of the republic in the Fair, and the weeding out of enormity. Do you want a house, or meat, or drink, or clothes? speak whatsoever it is, it shall be supplied you; what want you?

Quarlous. Nothing but your warrant.

Overdo. My warrant! for what?

Quarlous. To be gone, sir.

Overdo. Nay, I pray thee stay; I am serious, and have not many words, nor much time to exchange with thee. Think what may do thee good.

Quarlous. Your hand and seal will do me a great deal of good; nothing else in the whole Fair that I know.

Overdo. If it were to any end, thou shouldst have it willingly.

Quarlous. Why, it will satisfy me, that's end enough to look on; an you will not give it me, let me go.

Overdo. Alas, thou shalt have it presently; I'll but step

into the scrivener's here by, and bring it. Do not go away.
                                                    [*Exit.*

Quarlous. Why, this madman's shape will prove a very
fortunate one, I think. Can a ragged robe produce these
effects? if this be the wise justice, and he bring me his
hand, I shall go near to make some use on't.

Re-enter OVERDO.

He is come already!

Overdo. Look thee! here is my hand and seal, Adam
Overdo; if there be anything to be written above in that
paper that thou wantest now, or at any time hereafter,
think on't, it is my deed, I deliver it so; can your friend
write?

Quarlous. Her hand for a witness, and all is well.

Overdo. With all my heart.   [*He urges her to sign it.*

Quarlous. Why should not I have the conscience to
make this a bond of a thousand pound now, or what I
would else?   [*Aside.*

Overdo. Look you, there it is, and I deliver it as my deed
again.

Quarlous. Let us now proceed in madness.

              [*Exeunt* QUARLOUS *and* DAME PURECRAFT.

Overdo. Well, my conscience is much eased; I have done
my part, though it doth him no good, yet Adam hath
offered satisfaction. The sting is removed from hence! Poor
man, he is much altered with his affliction, it has brought
him low. Now for my other work, reducing the young
man, I have followed so long in love, from the brink of his
bane to the centre of safety. Here, or in some such like vain
place, I shall be sure to find him. I will wait the good
time.   [*Exit.*

SCENE III—*Another part of the Fair*

The Puppet-show Booth, as before.

Enter SHARKWELL *and* FILCHER, *with bills and* COKES *in his doublet and hose, followed by the Boys of the Fair.*

Cokes. How now! what's here to do, friend? art thou the master of the monuments?

Sharkwell. 'Tis a motion, an't please your worship.

Enter OVERDO *behind.*

Overdo. My fantastical brother-in-law, Master Bartholo-mew Cokes!

Cokes. A motion! what's that? [*Reads.*] "The ancient modern history of Hero and Leander, otherwise called the Touchstone of true Love, with as true a trial of friend-ship between Damon and Pythias, two faithful friends o' the Bankside."—Pretty, i' faith, what's the meaning on't? is't an interlude, or what is't?

Filcher. Yes, sir, please you come near, we'll take your money within.

Cokes. Back with these children; they do so follow me up and down!

Enter LITTLEWIT.

Littlewit. By your leave, friend.

Filcher. You must pay, sir, an you go in.

Littlewit. Who, I! I perceive thou know'st not me; call the master of the motion.

Sharkwell. What, do you not know the author, fellow Filcher? You must take no money of him; he must come in gratis: Master Littlewit is a voluntary; he is the author.

Littlewit. Peace, speak not too loud, I would not have any notice taken that I am the author, till we see how it passes.

Cokes. Master Littlewit, how dost thou?

Littlewit. Master Cokes! you are exceeding well met: what, in your doublet and hose, without a cloak or a hat?

Cokes. I would I might never stir, as I am an *honest* man, and by that fire; I have lost all in the Fair, and all my acquaintance too: didst thou meet anybody that I know, Master Littlewit? my man Numps, or my sister Overdo, or Mistress Grace? Pray thee, Master Littlewit, lend me some money to see the interlude here; I'll pay thee again, as I am a gentleman. If thou'lt but carry me home, I have money enough there.

Littlewit. O, sir, you shall command it; what, will a crown serve you?

Cokes. I think it will; what do we pay for coming in, fellows?

Filcher. Twopence, sir.

Cokes. Twopence! there's twelvepence, friend; nay, I am a gallant, as simple as I look now; if you see me with my man about me, and my artillery again.

Littlewit. Your man was in the stocks e'en now, sir.

Cokes. Who, Numps?

Littlewit. Yes, faith.

Cokes. For what, i' faith? I am glad o' that; remember to tell me on't anon; I have enough now. What manner of matter is this, Master Littlewit? what kind of actors have you? are they good actors?

Littlewit. Pretty youths, sir, all children both old and young; here's the master of 'em——

Enter LEATHERHEAD.

Leatherhead [*aside to* LITTLEWIT]. Call me not Leather-head, but Lantern.

Littlewit. Master Lantern, that gives light to the business.

Cokes. In good time, sir! I would fain see them, I would be glad to drink with the young company; which is the tiring-house?

Leatherhead. Troth, sir, our tiring-house is somewhat little; we are but beginners yet, pray pardon us; you cannot go upright in't.

Cokes. No! not now my hat is off? what would you have done with me, if you had had me feather and all, as I was once to-day? Have you none of your pretty impudent boys now, to bring stools, fill tobacco, fetch ale, and beg money, as they have at other houses? Let me see some of your actors.

Littlewit. Show him them, show him them. Master Lantern, this is a gentleman that is a favourer of the quality.

[*Exit* LEATHERHEAD.

Overdo. Ay, the favouring of this licentious quality is the consumption of many a young gentleman; a pernicious enormity.   [*Aside.*

Re-enter LEATHERHEAD *with a basket.*

Cokes. What! do they live in baskets?

Leatherhead. They do lie in a basket, sir, they are o' the small players.

Cokes. These be players minors indeed. Do you call these players?

Leatherhead. They are actors, sir, and as good as any, none dispraised, for dumb shows: indeed, I am the mouth of them all.

Cokes. Thy mouth will hold them all. I think one tailor would go near to beat all this company with a hand bound behind him.

Littlewit. Ay, and eat them all too, an they were in cakebread.

Cokes. I thank you for that, Master Littlewit; a good jest! Which is your Burbage now?

Leatherhead. What mean you by that, sir?

Cokes. Your best actor, your Field?

Littlewit. Good, i' faith! you are even with me, sir.

Leatherhead. This is he, that acts young Leander, sir: he is extremely beloved of the womenkind, they do so affect his action, the green gamesters, that come here! and this is lovely Hero; this with the beard Damon; and this pretty Pythias: this is the ghost of king Dionysius in the habit of a scrivener; as you shall see anon at large.

Cokes. Well, they are a civil company, I like 'em for that; they offer not to fleer, nor jeer, nor break jests, as the great players do: and then, there goes not so much charge to the feasting of them, or making them drunk, as to the other, by reason of their littleness. Do they use to play perfect, are they never flustered?

Leatherhead. No, sir, I thank my industry and policy for it; they are as well governed a company, though I say it —And here is young Leander, is as proper an actor of his inches, and shakes his head like an hostler.

Cokes. But do you play it according to the printed book? I have read that.

Leatherhead. By no means, sir.

Cokes. No! how then?

Leatherhead. A better way, sir; that is too learned and poetical for our audience: what do they know what *Hellespont* is, *guilty of true love's blood?* or what *Abydos* is? or *the other, Sestos hight?*

Cokes. Thou art in the right; I do not know myself.

Leatherhead. No, I have entreated Master Littlewit to take a little pains to reduce it to a more familiar strain for our people.

Cokes. How, I pray thee, good Master Littlewit?

Littlewit. It pleases him to make a matter of it, sir; but there is no such matter, I assure you: I have only made it a little easy, and modern for the times, sir, that's all. As for the Hellespont, I imagine our Thames here; and then Leander I make a dyer's son about Puddle-wharf: and Hero a wench o' the Bankside, who going over one morning to Old Fish-street, Leander spies her land at Trig-stairs, and falls in love with her. Now do I introduce Cupid, having metamorphosed himself into a drawer, and he strikes Hero in love with a pint of sherry; and other pretty passages there are of the friendship, that will delight you, sir, and please you of judgment.

Cokes. I'll be sworn they shall: I am in love with the actors already, and I'll be allied to them presently.—They respect gentlemen, these fellows:—Hero shall by my fairing: but which of my fairings?—let me see—i' faith, my fiddle; and Leander my fiddlestick: then Damon my drum, and Pythias my pipe, and the ghost of Dionysius my hobby-horse. All fitted.

Enter WINWIFE *and* GRACE.

Winwife. Look, yonder's your Cokes gotten in among his playfellows; I thought we could not miss him at such a spectacle.

Grace. Let him alone, he is so busy he will never spy us.

Leatherhead. Nay, good sir!

                [To COKES, *who is handling the puppets.*

Cokes. I warrant thee I will not hurt her, fellow; what, dost thou think me uncivil? I pray thee be not jealous; I am toward a wife.

Littlewit. Well, good Master Lantern, make ready to begin, that I may fetch my wife; and look you be perfect, you undo me else, in my reputation.

Leatherhead. I warrant you, sir, do not you breed too great an expectation of it among your friends; that's the hurter of these things.

Littlewit. No, no, no.   *[Exit.*

Cokes. I'll stay here and see; pray thee let me see.

Winwife. How diligent and troublesome he is!

Grace. The place becomes him, methinks.

Overdo. My ward, Mistress Grace, in the company of a stranger! I doubt I shall be compelled to discover myself before my time.   *[Aside.*

Enter KNOCKEM, EDGWORTH, *and* MRS. LITTLEWIT, *followed by* WHIT *supporting* MRS. OVERDO, *masked.*

Filcher. Twopence a-piece, gentlemen, an excellent motion.

Knockem. Shall we have fine fireworks and good vapours?

Sharkwell. Yes, captain, and waterworks too.

Whit. I pree dee take care o' dy shmall lady there, Edgworth; I will look to dish tall lady myself.

Leatherhead. Welcome, gentlemen, welcome, gentlemen.

Whit. Predee mashter o' the monshtersh, help a very sick lady here to a chair to shit in.

Leatherhead. Presently, sir.

                [A chair is brought in for MRS. OVERDO.

Whit. Good fait now, Ursula's ale and aquavitæ ish to

blame for't: shit down, shweetheart, shit down and sleep a little.

Edgworth [*to* Mrs. Littlewit]. Madam, you are very welcome hither.

Knockem. Yes, and you shall see very good vapours.

Overdo. Here is my care come! I like to see him in so good company: and yet I wonder that persons of such fashion should resort hither.   [*Aside.*

Edgworth. There is a very private house, madam.

Mrs. Littlewit. Yes, good man. They do so all-to-be-madam me, I think they think me a very lady.

Edgworth. What else, madam?

Mrs. Littlewit. Must I put off my mask to him?

Edgworth. O, by no means.

Mrs. Littlewit. How should my husband know me then?

Knockem. Husband! an idle vapour; he must not know you, nor you him: there's the true vapour.

Overdo. Yea! I will observe more of this.   [*Aside.*
Is this a lady, friend?

Whit. Ay, and dat is anoder lady, shweetheart; if thou hasht a mind to 'em, give me twelvepence from tee, and dou shalt have eder oder on 'em.

Overdo. Ay! this will prove my chiefest enormity: I will follow this.   [*Aside.*

Edgworth. Is not this a finer life, lady, than to be clogged with a husband?

Mrs. Littlewit. Yes, a great deal. When will they begin, trow, in the name o' the motion?

Edgworth. By-and-by, madam; they stay but for company.

Knockem. Do you hear, puppet-master, these are tedious vapours, when begin you?

Leatherhead. We stay but for Master Littlewit, the author, who is gone for his wife; and we begin presently.

Mrs. Littlewit. That's I, that's I.

Edgworth. That was you, lady; but now you are no such poor thing.

Knockem. Hang the author's wife, a running vapour! here be ladies will stay for ne'er a Delia of them all.

Whit. But hear me now, here ish one o' de ladish ashleep, stay till shee but vake, man.

Enter WASPE.

Waspe. How now, friends! what's here to do?

Filcher. Twopence a-piece, sir, the best motion in the Fair.

Waspe. I believe you lie; if you do, I'll have my money again and beat you.

Mrs. Littlewit. Numps is come!

Waspe. Did you see a master of mine come in here, a tall young squire of Harrow-o'-the-Hill, Master Bartholomew Cokes?

Filcher. I think there be such a one within.

Waspe. Look he be, you were best: but it is very likely: I wonder I found him not at all the rest. I have been at the Eagle, and the Black Wolf, and the Bull with the Five Legs and Two Pizzles—he was a calf at Uxbridge Fair two years agone—and at the Dogs that dance the morrice, and the Hare of the Tabor; and mist him at all these! Sure this must needs be some fine sight that holds him so, if it have him.

Cokes. Come, come, are you ready now?

Leatherhead. Presently, sir.

Waspe. Hoyday, he's at work in his doublet and hose! Do you hear, sir, are you employed, that you are bare headed and so busy?

Cokes. Hold your peace, Numps; you have been in the stocks, I hear.

Waspe. Does he know that! nay, then the date of my authority is out; I must think no longer to reign, my government is at an end. He that will correct another must want fault in himself.

Winwife. Sententious Numps! I never heard so much from him before.

Leatherhead. Sure Master Littlewit will not come; please you take your place, sir; we'll begin.

Cokes. I pray thee do, mine ears long to be at it, and mine eyes too. O Numps, in the stocks, Numps! Where's your sword, Numps!

Waspe. I pray you intend your game, sir; let me alone.

Cokes. Well then, we are quit for all. Come, sit down,

Numps; I'll interpret to thee: did you see Mistress Grace?
It's no matter neither now I think on't, tell me anon.

Winwife. A great deal of love and care he expresses.

Grace. Alas, would you have him to express more than
he has? That were tyranny.

Cokes. Peace, ho! now, now.

Leatherhead. "Gentles, that no longer your expectations
    may wander,
Behold our chief actor, amorous Leander.
With a great deal of cloth, lapped about him like a scarf.
For he yet serves his father, a dyer at Puddle-wharf;
Which place we'll make bold with, to call it our Abydus,
As the Bankside is our Sestos; and let it not be denied us.
Now as he is beating to make the dye take the fuller,
Who chances to come by, but Fair Hero in a sculler;
And seeing Leander's naked leg and goodly calf,
Cast at him from the boat a sheep's eye and an half.
Now she is landed, and the sculler come back,
By-and-by you shall see what Leander doth lack.

Leander. Cole, Cole, old Cole!

Leatherhead. That is the sculler's name without control.

Leander. Cole, Cole, I say, Cole!

Leatherhead. We do hear you.

Leander. Old Cole!

Leatherhead. Old Cole! Is the dyer turned collier? How
do you sell?

Leander. A pox o' your manners, kiss my hole here, and
smell.

Leatherhead. Kiss your hole and smell! there's manners
indeed.

Leander. Why, Cole, I say, Cole!

Leatherhead. Is't the sculler you need?

Leander. Ay, and be hanged.

Leatherhead. Be hanged! look you yonder.
Old Cole, you must go hang with Master Leander.

Cole. Where is he?

Leander. Here, Cole: what fairest of fairs,
Was that fare that thou landest but now at Trig-stairs!"

Cokes. What was that, fellow? pray thee tell me, I scarce
understand them.

Leatherhead. "Leander does ask, sir, what fairest of fairs,
Was the fare he landed but now at Trig-stairs?

Cole. It is lovely Hero.

Leander. Nero?

Cole. No, Hero.

Leatherhead. It is Hero
Of the Bankside, he saith, to tell you truth without erring,
Is come over into Fish-street to eat some fresh herring.
Leander says no more, but as fast as he can,
Gets on all his best clothes, and will after to the Swan."

Cokes. Most admirable good, is't not?

Leatherhead. "Stay, sculler.

Cole. What say you?

Leatherhead. You must stay for Leander,
And carry him to the wench.

Cole. You rogue, I am no pander."

Cokes. He says he is no pander. 'Tis a fine language; I
understand it now.

Leatherhead. "Are you no pander, goodman Cole? here's
        no man says you are;
You'll grow a hot cole, it seems; pray you stay for your fare.

Cole. Will he come away?

Leatherhead. What do you say?

Cole. I'd have him come away.

Leatherhead. Would you have Leander come away? why,
        pray, sir, stay.
You are angry, goodman Cole; I believe the fair maid
Came over with you a' trust: tell us, sculler, are you paid?

Cole. Yes, goodman Hogrubber of Pickthatch.

Leatherhead. How, Hogrubber of Pickthatch.

Cole. Ay, Hogrubber of Pickthatch. Take you that.
                          [*Strikes him over the pate.*

Leatherhead. O, my head.

Cole. Harm watch, harm catch."

Cokes. *Harm watch, harm catch,* he says; very good, i'
faith: the sculler had like to have knocked you, sirrah.

Leatherhead. Yes, but that his fare called him away.

Leander. "Row apace, row apace, row, row, row, row,
        row.

Leatherhead. You are knavishly loaden, sculler, take heed
   where you go.

Cole. Knave in your face, goodman rogue.

Leander. Row, row, row, row, row."

Cokes. He said, knave in your face, friend.

Leatherhead. Ay, sir, I heard him; but there's no talking
to these watermen, they will have the last word.

Cokes. Od's my life! I am not allied to the sculler yet;
he shall be *Dauphin my boy.* But my fiddlestick does fiddle
in and out too much: I pray thee speak to him on't; tell him
I would have him tarry in my sight more.

Leatherhead. I pray you be content; you'll have enough
on him, sir.

"Now, gentles, I take it, here is none of you so stupid,
But that you have heard of a little god of love called
   Cupid;
Who out of kindness to Leander, hearing he but saw her,
This present day and hour doth turn himself to a drawer.
And because he would have their first meeting to be merry,
He strikes Hero in love to him with a pint of sherry;
Which he tells her from amorous Leander is sent her,
Who after him into the room of Hero doth venture.

               [LEANDER *goes into* MISTRESS HERO'S *room.*

Jonas. A pint of sack, score a pint of sack in the Coney."

Cokes. Sack! you said but e'en now it should be sherry.

Jonas. "Why, so it is; sherry, sherry, sherry!"

Cokes. Sherry, sherry, sherry! By my troth, he makes me
merry. I must have a name for Cupid too. Let me see, thou
might'st help me now, an thou wouldst, Numps, at a
dead lift; but thou art dreaming of the stocks still.—Do not
think on't, I have forgot it; 'tis but a nine days' wonder,
man; let it not trouble thee.

Waspe. I would the stocks were about your neck, sir;
condition I hung by the heels in them till the wonder wore
off from you, with all my heart.

Cokes. Well said, resolute Numps! but hark you, friend,
where's the friendship all this while between my drum
Damon and my pipe Pythias?

Leatherhead. You shall see by-and-by, sir.

Cokes. You think my hobby-horse is forgotten too; no,

I'll see them all enact before I go; I shall not know which
to love best else.

Knockem. This gallant has interrupting vapours, troublesome vapours; Whit, puff with him.

Whit. No, I pree dee, captain, let him alone; he is a
child, i' faith, la.

Leatherhead. "Now, gentles, to the friends, who in number are two,

And lodged in that alehouse in which fair Hero does do.
Damon, for some kindness done him the last week,
Is come, fair Hero, in Fish-street, this morning to seek:
Pythias does smell the knavery of the meeting,
And now you shall see their true-friendly greeting.

Pythias. You whore-masterly slave, you."

Cokes. Whore-masterly slave, you! very friendly and
familiar that.

Damon. "Whore-master in thy face,

Thou hast lain with her thyself, I'll prove it in this place."

Cokes. Damon says Pythias has lain with her himself,
he'll prove 't in this place.

Leatherhead. "They are whore-masters both, sir, that's a
plain case.

Pythias. You lie like a rogue.

Leatherhead. Do I lie like a rogue?

Pythias. A pimp and a scab.

Leatherhead. A pimp and a scab!

I say, between you, you have both but one drab.

Damon. You lie again.

Leatherhead. Do I lie again?

Damon. Like a rogue again.

Leatherhead. Like a rogue again!

Pythias. And you are a pimp again."

Cokes. And you are a pimp again, he says.

Damon. "And a scab again."

Cokes. And a scab again, he says.

Leatherhead. "And I say again, you are both whore-
masters again.

And you have both but one drab again.

Damon and Pythias. Dost thou, dost thou, dost thou?
                                    [*They fall upon him.*

Leatherhead. What, both at once?

Pythias. Down with him, Damon.

Damon. Pink his guts, Pythias.

Leatherhead. What, so malicious?

Will ye murder me, masters both, in my own house?"

Cokes. Ho! well acted, my drum, well acted, my pipe,
well acted still!

Waspe. Well acted, with all my heart.

Leatherhead. "Hold, hold your hands."

Cokes. Ay, both your hands, for my sake! for you have
both done well.

Damon. "Gramercy, pure Pythias.

Pythias. Gramercy, dear Damon."

Cokes. Gramercy to you both, my pipe and my drum.

Pythias and Damon. "Come, now we'll together to breakfast to Hero.

Leatherhead. 'Tis well you can now go to breakfast to
Hero.

You have given me my breakfast, with a hone and honero."

Cokes. How is't, friend, have they hurt thee?

Leatherhead. O no:

Between you and I, sir, we do but make show.—

"Thus, gentles, you perceive, without any denial,
'Twixt Damon and Pythias here, friendship's true trial.
Though hourly they quarrel thus, and roar each with other,
They fight you no more than does brother with brother;
But friendly together, at the next man they meet,
They let fly their anger, as here you might see't."

Cokes. Well, we have seen it, and thou hast felt it, whatsoever thou sayest. What's next, what's next?

Leatherhead. "This while young Leander with fair Hero
is drinking,

And Hero grown drunk to any man's thinking!
Yet was it not three pints of sherry could flaw her,
Till Cupid, distinguished like Jonas the drawer,
From under his apron, where his lechery lurks,
Put love in her sack. Now mark how it works.

Hero. O Leander, Leander, my dear, my dear Leander,
I'll for ever be thy goose, so thou'lt be my gander."

Cokes. Excellently well said, Fiddle, she'll ever be his

goose, so he'll be her gander: was't not so?

    Leatherhead. Yes, sir, but mark his answer now.

    Leander. "And sweetest of geese, before I go to bed,
I'll swim over the Thames, my goose, thee to tread."

    Cokes. Brave! he will swim over the Thames, and tread
his goose to-night, he says.

    Leatherhead. Ay, peace, sir, they'll be angry if they hear
you eavesdropping, now they are setting their match.

    Leander. "But lest the Thames should be dark, my goose,
    my dear friend,
Let thy window be provided of a candle's end.

    Hero. Fear not, my gander, I protest I should handle
My matters very ill, if I had not a whole candle.

    Leander. Well then, look to't, and kiss me to boot.

    Leatherhead. Now here come the friends again, Pythias
    and Damon,
And under their cloaks they have of bacon a gammon.

    Pythias. Drawer, fill some wine here."

    Leatherhead. How, some wine there!
There's company already, sir, pray forbear.

    Damon. " 'Tis Hero.

    Leatherhead. Yes, but she will not to be taken,
After sack and fresh-herring, with your Dunmow-bacon.

    Pythias. You lie, it's Westfabian.

    Leatherhead. Westphalian, you should say.

    Damon. If you hold not your peace, you are a coxcomb,
    I would say.   [LEADER *and* HERO *kiss.*
What's here, what's here? kiss, kiss, upon kiss.

    Leatherhead. Ay, wherefore should they not? what harm
    is in this?
'Tis Mistress Hero.

    Damon. Mistress Hero's a whore.

    Leatherhead. Is she a whore? keep you quiet, or, sir
    knave, out of door.

    Damon. Knave out of door!

    Hero. Yes, knave out of door.

    Damon. Whore out of door.

                           [They fall together by the ears.

    Hero. I say, knave out of door.

    Damon. I say, whore out of door.

Pythias. Yea, so say I too.

Hero. Kiss the whore o' the a——.

Leatherhead. Now you have something to do.
You must kiss her o' the a——, she says.

Damon and Pythias. So we will, so we will.

> *[They kick her.*

Hero. O my haunches, O my haunches, hold, hold.

Leatherhead. Stand'st thou still!
Leander, where art thou? stand'st thou still like a sot,
And not offerest to break both their heads with a pot?
See who's at thine elbow there! puppet Jonas and Cupid.

Jonas. Upon 'em, Leander, be not so stupid.

Leander. You goat-bearded slave!

Damon. You whore-master knave!   *[They fight.*

Leander. Thou art a whore-master.

Jonas. Whore-masters all.

Leatherhead. See, Cupid with a word has tane up the
    brawl."

Knockem. These be fine vapours.

Cokes. By this good day, they fight bravely; do they not,
Numps?

Waspe. Yes, they lacked but you to be their second all
this while.

Leatherhead. "This tragical encounter falling out thus
    to busy us,
It raises up the ghost of their friend Dionysius;
Not like a monarch, but the master of a school,
In a scrivener's furred gown, which shows he is no fool:
For therein he hath wit enough to keep himself warm.
O Damon, he cries, and Pythias, what harm
Hath poor Dionysius done you in his grave,
That after his death you should fall out thus and rave,
And call amorous Leander whore-master knave?

Damon. I cannot, I will not, I promise you, endure it."

RABBI BUSY *rushes in.*

Busy. Down with Dagon! down with Dagon! 'tis I, I will
no longer endure your profanations.

Leatherhead. What mean you, sir?

Busy. I will remove Dagon there, I say, that idol, that

heathenish idol, that remains, as I may say, a beam, a very beam,—not a beam of the sun, nor a beam of the moon, nor a beam of a balance, neither a house-beam, nor a weaver's beam, but a beam in the eye, in the eye of the brethren; a very great beam, an exceedingly great beam; such as are your stageplayers, rimers, and morrice-dancers, who have walked hand in hand, in contempt of the brethren, and the cause; and been borne out by instruments of no mean countenance.

Leatherhead. Sir, I present nothing but what is licensed by authority.

Busy. Thou art all licence, even licentiousness itself, Shimei!

Leatherhead. I have the Master of the Revels' hand for't, sir.

Busy. The master of the rebel's hand thou hast, Satan's! hold thy peace, thy scurrility, shut up thy mouth, thy profession is damnable, and in pleading for it thou dost plead for Baal. I have long opened my mouth wide, and gaped. I have gaped as the oyster for the tide, after thy destruction: but cannot compass it by suit or dispute; so that I look for a bickering ere long, and then a battle.

Knockem. Good Banbury vapours!

Cokes. Friend, you'd have an ill match on't, if you bicker with him here; though he be no man of the fist, he has friends that will to cuffs for him. Numps, will not you take our side?

Edgworth. Sir, it shall not need; in my mind he offers him a fairer course, to end it by disputation: hast thou nothing to say for thyself, in defence of thy quality?

Leatherhead. Faith, sir, I am not well-studied in these controversies between the hypocrites and us. But here's one of my motion, puppet Dionysius, shall undertake him, and I'll venture the cause on't.

Cokes. Who, my hobby-horse! will be dispute with him?

Leatherhead. Yes, sir, and make a hobby-ass of him, I hope.

Cokes. That's excellent! indeed he looks like the best scholar of them all. Come, sir, you must be as good as your word now.

Busy. I will not fear to make my spirit and gifts known: assist me, zeal, fill me, fill me, that is, make me full!

Winwife. What a desperate, profane wretch is this! is there any ignorance or impudence like his, to call his zeal to fill him against a puppet?

Quarlous. I know no fitter match than a puppet to commit with an hypocrite!

Busy. First, I say unto thee, idol, thou hast no calling.

Dionysius. "You lie, I am called Dionysius."

Leatherhead. The motion says, you lie, he is called Dionysius in the matter, and to that calling he answers.

Busy. I mean no vocation, idol, no present lawful calling.

Dionysius. "Is yours a lawful calling?"

Leatherhead. The motion asketh, if yours be a lawful calling.

Busy. Yes, mine is of the spirit.

Dionysius. "Then idol is a lawful calling."

Leatherhead. He says, then idol is a lawful calling; for you called him idol, and your calling is of the spirit.

Cokes. Well disputed, hobby-horse.

Busy. Take not part with the wicked, young gallant: he neigheth and hinnieth; all is but hinnying sophistry. I call him idol again; yet, I say, his calling, his profession is profane, it is profane, idol.

Dionysius. "It is not profane."

Leatherhead. It is not profane, he says.

Busy. It is profane.

Dionysius. "It is not profane."

Busy. It is profane.

Dionysius. "It is not profane."

Leatherhead. Well said, confute him with *Not* still. You cannot bear him down with your base noise, sir.

Busy. Nor he me, with his treble creeking, though he creek like the chariot wheels of Satan; I am zealous for the cause——

Leatherhead. As a dog for a bone.

Busy. And I say it is profane, as being the page of Pride, and the waiting-woman of Vanity.

Dionysius. "Yea! what say you to your tire-women then?"

Leatherhead. Good.

Dionysius. "Or feather-makers in the Friers, that are of your faction of faith? are not they, with their perukes, and their puffs, their fans, and their huffs, as much pages of Pride, and waiters upon Vanity? What say you, what say you, what say you?"

Busy. I will not answer for them.

Dionysius. "Because you cannot, because you cannot. Is a bugle-maker a lawful calling? or the confect-makers? such you have there; or your French fashioner? you would have all the sin within yourselves, would you not, would you not?"

Busy. No, Dagon.

Dionysius. "What then, Dagonet? is a puppet worse than these?"

Busy. Yes, and my main argument against you is, that you are an abomination; for the male among you putteth on the apparel of the female, and the female of the male.

Dionysius. "You lie, you lie, you lie abominably."

Cokes. Good, by the troth, he has given him the lie thrice.

Dionysius. "It is your old stale argument against the players, but it will not hold against the puppets; for we have neither male nor female amongst us. And that thou mayst see, if thou wilt, like a malicious purblind zeal as thou art!"   [*Takes up his garment.*

Edgworth. By my faith, there he has answered you, friend, a plain demonstration.

Dionysius. "Nay, I'll prove, against e'er a Rabbin of them all, that my standing is as lawful as his; that I speak by inspiration, as well as he; that I have as little to do with learning as he; and do scorn her helps as much as he."

Busy. I am confuted, the cause hath failed me.

Dionysius. "Then be converted, be converted."

Leatherhead. Be converted, I pray you, and let the play go on!

Busy. Let it go on; for I am changed, and will become a beholder with you.

Cokes. That's brave, i' faith, thou hast carried it away, hobby-horse; on with the play.

Overdo [*discovering himself*]. Stay, now do I forbid; I am Adam Overdo! sit still, I charge you.

Cokes. What, my brother-in-law!

Grace. My wise guardian!

Edgworth. Justice Overdo!

Overdo. It is time to take enormity by the forehead, and brand it; for I have discovered enough.

Enter QUARLOUS *in* TROUBLEALL'S *clothes, as before, and* DAME PURECRAFT.

Quarlous. Nay, come, mistress bride; you must do as I do, now. You must be mad with me, in truth. I have here Justice Overdo for it.

Overdo. Peace, good Troubleall; come hither, and you shall trouble none. I will take the charge of you, and your friend too; you also, young man [*to* EDGWORTH] shall be my care; stand there.

Edgworth. Now, mercy upon me.

Knockem. Would we were away, Whit, these are dangerous vapours, best fall off with our birds for fear o' the cage.   [*They attempt to steal away.*

Overdo. Stay, is not my name your terror?

Whit. Yesh, fait, man, and it ish for tat we would begone, man.

Enter LITTLEWIT.

Littlewit. O, gentlemen! did you not see a wife of mine? I have lost my little wife, as I shall be trusted; my little pretty Win. I left her at the great woman's house in trust yonder, the pig-woman's, with Captain Jordan and Captain Whit, very good men, and I cannot hear of her. Poor fool, I fear she's stepped aside. Mother, did you not see Win?

Overdo. If this grave matron be your mother, sir, stand by her, *et digito compesce labellum;* I may perhaps spring a wife for you anon. Brother Bartholomew, I am sadly sorry to see you so lightly given, and such a discipline of enormity with your grave governor Humphrey; but stand you both there, in the middle place; I will reprehend you in your course. Mistress Grace, let me rescue you out of the hands of the stranger.

Winwife. Pardon me, sir, I am a kinsman of hers.

Overdo. Are you so! of what name, sir?

Winwife. Winwife, sir.

Overdo. Master Winwife! I hope you have won no wife of her, sir; if you have, I will examine the possibility of it at fit leisure. Now to my enormities: look upon me, O London! and see me, O Smithfield! the example of justice, and Mirror of Magistrates; the true top of formality and scourge of enormity. Hearken unto my labours, and but observe my discoveries; and compare Hercules with me, if thou dar'st, of old; or Columbus, Magellan, or our countryman Drake, of later times. Stand forth, you weeds of enormity, and spread. First Rabbi Busy, thou superlunatical hypocrite;—[*to* LEATHERHEAD.] Next thou other extremity, thou profane professor of puppetry, little better than poetry:—[*to* WHIT.] Then thou strong debaucher and seducer of youth; witness this easy and honest young man, [*pointing to* EDGWORTH.]—[*to* KNOCKEM.] Now, thou esquire of dames, madams, and twelvepenny ladies;—Now, my green madam herself of the price; let me unmask your ladyship.

                              [*Discovers* MRS. LITTLEWIT.

Littlewit. O my wife, my wife, my wife!

Overdo. Is she your wife? *redde te Harpocratem.*

Enter TROUBLEALL, *with a dripping-pan, followed by* URSULA *and* NIGHTINGALE.

Troubleall. By your leave, stand by, my masters, be uncovered.

Ursula. O stay him, stay him, help to cry, Nightingale; my pan, my pan!

Overdo. What's the matter?

Nightingale. He has stolen gammar Ursula's pan.

Troubleall. Yes, and I fear no man but Justice Overdo.

Overdo. Ursula! where is she? O the sow of enormity, this! welcome, stand you there; you songster, there.

Ursula. An't please your worship, I am in no fault: a gentleman stripped him in my booth, and borrowed his gown, and his hat; and he ran away with my goods here for it.

Overdo [*to* QUARLOUS]. Then this is the true madman, and you are the enormity!

Quarlous. You are in the right; I am mad but from the gown outward.

Overdo. Stand you there.

Quarlous. Where you please, sir.

Mrs. Overdo. [*waking*]. O, lend me a bason, I am sick, I am sick! where's Master Overdo? Bridget, call hither my Adam.

Overdo. How!   [*He is shamed and silenced.*

Whit. Dy very own wife, i' fait, worshipful Adam.

Mrs. Overdo. Will not my Adam come at me! shall I see him no more, then?

Quarlous. Sir, why do you not go with the enormity? are you oppressed with it? I'll help you: hark you, sir, in your ear—Your innocent young man, you have ta'en such care of all this day, is a cutpurse, and hath got all your brother Cokes's things, and helped you to your beating and the stocks; if you have a mind to hang him now, and show him your magistrate's wit, you may: but I should think it were better recovering the goods, and to save your estimation in him. I thank you, sir, for the gift of your ward, Mistress Grace; look you, here is your hand and seal, by the way. Master Winwife, give you joy, you are *Palemon,* you are possessed of the gentlewoman, but she must pay me value, here's warrant for it. And, honest madman, there's thy gown and cap again; I thank thee for my wife. Nay, I can be made, sweetheart [*to* Mrs. Purecraft], when I please still; never fear me; and careful Numps, where's he? I thank him for my licence.

Waspe. How!

Quarlous. 'Tis true, Numps.

Waspe. I'll be hanged then.

Quarlous. Look in your box, Numps.—Nay, sir [*to* Overdo], stand not you fixed here, like a stake in Finsbury, to be shot at, or the whipping-post in the Fair, but get your wife out o' the air, it will make her worse else: and remember you are but Adam, flesh and blood! you have your frailty, forget your other name of Overdo, and invite us all to supper. There you and I will compare our discoveries; and drown the memory of all enormity in your biggest bowl at home.

Cokes. How now, Numps, have you lost it? I warrant 'twas when thou wert in the stocks. Why dost not speak!

Waspe. I will never speak while I live again, for aught I know.

Overdo. Nay, Humphrey, if I be patient, you must be so too; this pleasant conceited gentleman hath wrought upon my judgment, and prevailed. I pray you take care of your sick friend, Mistress Alice, and my good friends all——

Quarlous. And no *enormities.*

Overdo. I invite you home with me to my house to supper: I will have none fear to go along, for my intents are *ad correctionem, non ad destructionem; ad ædificandum, non ad diruendum:* so lead on.

Cokes. Yes, and bring the actors along, we'll have the rest of the play at home.   [*Exeunt.*

EPILOGUE

Your Majesty hath seen the play, and you
Can best allow it from your ear and view.
You know the scope of writers, and what store
Of leave is given them, if they take not more,
And turn it into licence: you can tell
If we have used that leave you gave us well:
Or whether we to rage or license break,
Or be profane, or make profane men speak:
This is your power to judge, great sir, and not
The envy of a few. Which if we have got,
We value less what their dislike can bring,
If it so happy be, t' have pleased the King.

THE MERMAID SERIES

THE MERMAID SERIES of English dramatists was the brain-child of a twenty-six year old medical student, later a famous sexologist. "At that time," Havelock Ellis writes in his autobiography,* speaking of the year 1886, "it happened that a London publisher, Henry Vizetelly, was conspicuous by the way in which he had published fairly literal translations of the chief contemporary French novelists. My friend Eleanor Marx Aveling [daughter of Karl Marx] had translated *Madame Bovary* for him, and he had issued translations—it is true by no means always literal—of a large number of Zola's novels. He had himself been a distinguished journalist in earlier days, he was familiar with France, and he was really engaged in a quite honorable and useful work. It occurred to me that a series of volumes of the best plays, unexpurgated, of the Elizabethan dramatists—for which I devised at the suggestion of Beaumont's poem the name Mermaid Series—would be an excellent scheme for Vizetelly to undertake. I had no idea of proposing myself for editor, and indeed could hardly feel competent for the post. I wrote to Vizetelly putting the scheme before him, and almost by return of post he replied accepting it, asking me to undertake the work of general editor, and inquiring what remuneration I would wish to receive. Such a proposal seemed too tempting for a young unknown man to put aside, whatever his disabilities, and even though he was in the midst of training for an arduous profession. I accepted with alacrity, and speedily repaired, so far as I could, my incompetence. I knew nothing as to what fees a general editor was entitled, and the sum I asked (three guineas per volume) was, no doubt, too small . . . I selected the dramatists, the space to be devoted to each, and I chose the editors [though Vizetelly told Ellis that he needed 'one or two names of mark' to launch the project] cooperating in their work, besides myself editing Marlowe, Middleton, Ford and Porter. . . ." Ellis goes on to describe the bowdlerizing of the Baines note at the hands of his publisher and assorted associates—including, surprisingly enough, Swinburne and Symonds.†

Ellis then relates how Vizetelly was sent to jail as the publisher of that famous pornographer, Emile Zola; and how, soon afterwards, he died. At this point, Ellis continues, "the Mermaid Series was taken over [by T. Fisher Unwin, a publisher], without any word of explanation or apology to me, or any word of protest from me, though I do not flatter myself he [Unwin] knew that my silence was contempt. I was well aware that for a publisher the editor of a series is an insignificant figure even though he may be altogether responsible for its conception, mainly responsible for its production, and largely responsible for its success. I had, of course, arranged for volumes ahead, many of them nearly ready for publication; the editors of these were equally disregarded by the new publisher. . . . The Mermaid Series swiftly passed away so far as I was concerned, and languished to death after it was taken out of my hands. But it was not superseded. I am pleased to be assured—as I revise these lines some forty years later, a paper on 'Havelock Ellis and the English Drama' comes to

---

* *My Life,* by Havelock Ellis. Quoted by permission of the publisher, Houghton Mifflin Co.

† Instigated, as Houston Peterson tells in his life of Ellis, by the protest of "a well-meaning woman" but put through with rather hysterical despatch by Vizetelly.

hand, written by a devoted student of the drama, Montague Summers
—that 'the Mermaid Series remains a magnificent service rendered to
the English drama, a pioneer work, a work that demanded courage,
scholarship, and enthusiasm.' "

In 1917, the firm of T. Fisher Unwin arranged for publication of
the Mermaid Series in the United States by Charles Scribner's Sons.
In 1926 Unwin was absorbed by Ernest Benn Limited who continued
supplying Scribner's with the Mermaid volumes until 1945. After the
Second World War some 12 of the Mermaid volumes were re-issued
in London by Ernest Benn Limited and A. A. Wyn Incorporated in
New York. On this occasion, the Curator of the Brander Matthews
Dramatic Museum at Columbia University (Henry W. Wells) wrote:
"If a class of students in our century was to know the Elizabethan
drama through any more attractive medium than an anthology, this
series provided the almost certain means. Earlier editions . . . were
directed to . . . British gentlemen. The new library . . . was addressed to a very much larger and democratic public. It always sold
well in America. Yet one by one these books went out of print. . . .
The gradual strangulation of the Mermaid Series seemed a mark of
doom upon the popular success of Elizabethan studies themselves. . . .
But lovers of the most humane movement in all English literature
have at present cause for congratulation . . . the Mermaid Series is
being re-issued." But the price of this 1948-49 hard-back edition was
beyond the means of the academic and democratic public Mr. Wells
speaks about. The necessary next step was to issue the books—completely reset—in paper-back form at little more than one dollar each.

It also seemed high time to continue the work itself where Ellis, so
long ago, had left off. In 1887 were issued the Marlowe, the Dekker,
the Congreve, Middleton Volume I, and Massinger Volume I. In 1888
followed Heywood, Ford, Shirley, Wycherley, Otway, Webster and
Tourneur, and an anthology entitled *Nero and Other Plays;* in 1889-90,
the second volumes of Middleton and Massinger, respectively. In the
nineties came Steele, Chapman, Vanbrugh, and three volumes of Jonson.
In the nineteen-hundreds, Shadwell, Farquhar, Greene, and two volumes each of Dryden and Beaumont & Fletcher. The rest was silence.*

In addition to reprinting the original Mermaids, Hill and Wang Inc.
is issuing several new Mermaids a year.

As published by Hill and Wang Inc., the Mermaid Series is a section
of a still larger series, *Dramabooks,* which also includes books old and
new *about* theatre and drama.

The Publishers

---

* Ellis's editors—aside from those whose work never appeared—were Alexander
C. Ewald, H. P. Horne, Edmund Gosse, Roden Noel, Ernest Rhys, A. C. Swin-
burne, John Addington Symonds, Arthur Symons, A. W. Verity, and W. C. Ward.
The choice of editors after 1890 was presumably made by T. Fisher Unwin. Those
chosen were: G. A. Aitken, William Archer, T. H. Dickinson, C. H. Herford,
Brinsley Nicholson, William Lyon Phelps, George Saintsbury, J. St. Loe Strachey,
A. E. H. Swaen.

DRAMABOOKS

PLAYS

MD 1   *Christopher Marlowe* edited by Havelock Ellis. Introduction by John Addington Symonds (Tamburlaine the Great, Parts I & II, Doctor Faustus, The Jew of Malta, Edward the Second)

MD 2   *William Congreve* edited by Alexander Charles Ewald. Introduction by Macaulay (Complete Plays)

MD 3   *Webster and Tourneur* Introduction by John Addington Symonds (The White Devil, The Duchess of Malfi, The Atheist's Tragedy, The Revenger's Tragedy)

MD 4   *John Ford* edited by Havelock Ellis (The Lover's Melancholy, 'Tis Pity She's a Whore, The Broken Heart, Love's Sacrifice, Perkin Warbeck) .

MD 5   *Richard Brinsley Sheridan* edited with an Introduction by Louis Krónenberger (The Rivals, St. Patrick's Day, The Duenna, A Trip to Scarborough, The School for Scandal, The Critic)

MD 6   *Camille and Other Plays* edited, with an Introduction to the well-made play by Stephen S. Stanton (Scribe: A Peculiar Position, and The Glass of Water; Sardou: A Scrap of Paper; Dumas, *fils*: Camille; Augier: Olympe's Marriage)

MD 7   *John Dryden* edited, and with an Introduction by George Saintsbury (The Conquest of Granada, Parts I & II, Marriage à la Mode, Aureng-Zebe)

MD 8   *Ben Jonson* Volume I edited, with an Introduction and Notes, by Brinsley Nicholson and C. H. Herford (Volpone, Epicoene, The Alchemist)

MD 9   *Oliver Goldsmith* edited by George Pierce Baker with an Introduction by Austin Dobson (The Good Natur'd Man, She Stoops to Conquer, An Essay on the Theatre, A Register of Scotch Marriages)

MD 10   *Jean Anouilh* Volume 1 (Antigone, Eurydice, The Rehearsal, Romeo and Jeannette, The Ermine)

MD 11   *Let's Get a Divorce! and Other Plays,* edited, and with an Introduction on The Psychology of Farce by Eric Bentley (Labiche: A Trip Abroad, and Célimare; Sardou: Let's Get a Divorce!; Courtline, These Cornfields; Feydeau: Keep an Eye on Amélie; Prévert: A United Family; Achard: essay on Feydeau)

MD 12   *Jean Giraudoux* adapted and with an Introduction by Maurice Valency (Ondine, The Enchanted, The Madwoman of Chaillot, The Apollo of Bellac)

MD 13   *Jean Anouilh* Volume 2 (Restless Heart, Time Remembered, Ardèle, Mademoiselle Colombe, The Lark)

MD 14   *Henrik Ibsen: The Last Plays* Introduction and translation by William Archer (Little Eyolf, John Gabriel Borkman, When We Dead Awaken)

MD 15   *Ivan Turgenev* translated by Constance Garnett (A Month in the Country, A Provincial Lady, A Poor Gentleman)

MD 16   *George Farquhar* edited, with an Introduction and Notes, by William Archer (The Constant Couple, The Twin-Rivals, The Recruiting Officer, The Beaux' Stratagem)

MD 17   *Jean Racine: Five Plays* Introduction and translation by Kenneth Muir (Andromache, Britannicus, Berenice, Phaedra, Athaliah)

MD 18   *The Storm and Other Russian Plays* Introduction and translation by David Magarshack (The Storm, The Government Inspector, The Power of Darkness, Uncle Vanya, The Lower Depths)

MD 19   *Michel de Ghelderode* Introduction by George Hauger (The Ostend Interviews, Chronicles of Hell, Barabbas, The Women at the Tomb, Pantagleize, The Blind Men, Three Players and a Play, Lord Halewyn)

MD 20   *Lope de Vega: Five Plays* edited, with an Introduction by R. D. F. Pring-Mill (Peribáñez, Fuenteovejuna, The Dog in the Manger, The Knight from Olmeda, Justice without Revenge)

MD 21   *Calderón: Four Plays* Introduction and translation by Edwin Honig (Secret Vengeance for Secret Insult, De-

votlon to the Cross, The Mayor of Zalamea, The Phantom
Lady)
MD 22 *Jean Cocteau: Five Plays* (Orphée, Antigone, Intimate Re-
lations, The Holy Terrors, The Eagle with Two Heads)
MD 23 *Ben Jonson* Volume II (Every Man in His Humour,
Sejanus, Bartholomew Fair)
SD 1 *The Last Days of Lincoln* by Mark Van Doren
SD 2 *Oh, Dad, Poor Dad, Mamma's Hung You in the Closet and
I'm Feelin' So Sad* by Arthur L. Kopit
SD 3 *The Chinese Wall* by Max Frisch. Introduction by Harold
Clurman

CRITICISM

D 1 *Shakespeare and the Elizabethans* by Henri Fluchère. Fore-
word by T. S. Eliot
D 2 *On Dramatic Method* by Harley Granville-Barker
D 3 *George Bernard Shaw* by G. K. Chesterton
D 4 *The Paradox of Acting* by Denis Diderot and *Masks or
Faces?* by William Archer. Introduction by Lee Strasberg
D 5 *The Scenic Art* by Henry James. Edited with an Introduction
and Notes by Allan Wade
D 6 *Preface to Hamlet* by Harley Granville-Barker
D 7 *Hazlitt on Theatre* edited by William Archer and Robert
Lowe. Introduction by William Archer
D 8 *The Fervent Years* by Harold Clurman
D 9 *The Quintessence of Ibsenism* by Bernard Shaw
D 10 *Papers on Playmaking* edited by Brander Matthews
D 11 *Papers on Acting* edited by Brander Matthews
D 12 *The Theatre* by Stark Young
D 13 *Immortal Shadows* by Stark Young
D 14 *Shakespeare: A Survey* by E. K. Chambers
D 15 *The English Dramatic Critics* edited by James Agate
D 16 *Japanese Theatre* by Faubion Bowers
D 17 *Shaw's Dramatic Criticism* (1895-98) edited by John F.
Matthews
D 18 *Shaw on Theatre* edited by E. J. West
D 19 *The Book of Job as a Greek Tragedy* by Horace Meyer Kallen
D 20 *Molière: The Man Seen Through the Plays* by Ramon
Fernandez. Translation by Wilson Follett
D 21 *Greek Tragedy* by Gilbert Norwood
D 22 *Samuel Johnson on Shakespeare* edited with an Introduction
by W. K. Wimsatt, Jr.
D 23 *The Poet in the Theatre* by Ronald Peacock
D 24 *Chekhov the Dramatist* by David Magarshack
D 25 *Theory and Technique of Playwriting* by John Howard
Lawson
D 26 *The Art of the Theatre* by Henri Ghéon. Introduction by
Michel Saint-Denis
D 27 *Aristotle's Poetics* with an Introduction by Francis Fergusson
D 28 *The Origin of the Theater* by Benjamin Hunninger
D 29 *Playwrights on Playwriting* by Toby Cole